A Host of Tongues

DATE DUE			

A HOST OF TONGUES

Language Communities in the United States

Nancy Faires Conklin
Margaret A. Lourie

THE FREE PRESS
A Division of Macmillan, Inc.
NEW YORK

Collier Macmillan Publishers
LONDON

The Free Press
A Division of Macmillan, Inc.
866 Third Avenue, New York, N.Y. 10022

Collier Macmillan Canada, Inc.

Library of Congress Catalog Card Number: 82-48389

Printed in the United States of America

printing number

1 2 3 4 5 6 7 8 9 10

Library of Congress Cataloging in Publication Data
Conklin, Nancy Faires.
    A host of tongues.

    Bibliography: p.
    Includes index.
    1. United States—Languages.   2. English language—
United States.   3. Languages in contact—United States.
4. Language policy—United States.   I. Lourie,
Margaret A.   II. Title.
P377.C66   1983   409′.73   82-48389
ISBN 0-02-906390-6
ISBN 0-02-906500-3 (pbk.)

Contents

List of Tables

List of Figures

Preface

LANGUAGE VARIATION in the United States has evolved out of a long history of cultural diversity. Before Europeans began to colonize this country, native peoples spoke hundreds of different languages. Colonists brought with them Spanish, French, English, Dutch, and German, as well as slaves who spoke a number of distinct West African languages. In the nineteenth and twentieth centuries massive immigration has continued to replenish our linguistic resources with a host of tongues from virtually every other nation in the world. Some of these languages have disappeared with hardly a trace, but a surprising number have either continued to be spoken in the United States or have left their mark on American English.

Americans may be a polyglot people, speaking many languages and many varieties of English. But for the most part we have conducted our public life as if we were all monolingual English speakers. Only in the last two decades have we begun—often reluctantly—to respect linguistic diversity and minority rights enough to validate nonstandard dialects, offer bilingual education, or make public information available in non-English languages. Since the late 1970s our non-English-speaking population has been swollen by increased immigration, a large influx of illegal aliens, and refugees from Indochina, the Soviet Union, and Latin America. Consequently, the question of how to treat our non-English speakers is more pressing now than it has been at any time since World War I.

In the next decade the United States will confront a complex set of issues that focus on minority languages and their speakers. We will have to decide whether to keep admitting more non-English speakers into our society. We will need to plan for the education and integration of those who are already here. We will have to evaluate bilingual education programs begun in the late 1960s and determine whether their results warrant continued public funding. And, in general, we will need to ask ourselves whether we wish to encourage or discourage the continued use of minority languages. *A Host of Tongues* seeks to promote informed deliberation by all those concerned with these vital issues: teachers and prospective teachers of English, English as a second language, bilingual education, foreign languages, language arts, or any subject in a multicultural community; teachers and students of linguistics or American ethnic history and culture; community leaders and organizers; educational and public policy makers.

In order to account for our current language situation, the book first explores the origins of language diversity in the United States. Part I sketches the history of our many language communities, stressing the social, economic, and political pressures that led some communities to maintain their ethnic tongues and others to abandon theirs. Part II traces the historical causes for the ascendancy of English over other U.S. languages and explains how regional dialects and an American standard emerged. While Parts I and II bring to bear the insights of social history on our present linguistic pluralism, Parts III and IV apply the key concepts of sociolinguistics. Part III describes how situational and demographic factors influence language use and ensure variation among English speakers. Part IV demonstrates how non-English languages change through interaction with English and illustrates these processes with six case studies of American language communities. Building on the historical and linguistic analyses presented in Parts I–IV, Part V discusses the consequences of linguistic pluralism for public policy, education, and everyday interaction. Each part concludes with a list of background readings for those who wish to pursue particular topics in greater depth and suggested activities for individual or class projects. An Appendix of language samples offers further data for analyzing language variation.

No previous background in linguistics should be necessary to read this book. New linguistic terms are introduced in boldface and are defined where they first appear. In addition to these, readers should become familiar with—and may wish to refer back to—the brief explanation of phonology and grammar in the paragraphs below.

Because the fundamental medium of language is speech, **phonology,** or the study of sound systems, is the first step in the study of language structure. Within phonology, **phonetics** is the study of that continuous stream of sounds and pauses which comprise any speech event. Technically, this stream of sounds is infinitely various. Any two utterances of the same sentence never sound exactly alike even when the speaker is the same. To impose order on this infinite variety, speakers of a language unconsciously agree to consider certain sound differences nonsignificant and have a hard time distinguishing the differences among these sounds even when they are demonstrated. For example, most speakers of English do not notice that the *t* sound in *top* (accompanied by a slight puff of air) is not the same as the *t* sound in *stop* (no puff of air). In English this difference between the two *t*'s is nonsignificant. Similarly, differences between the *r* and *l* sounds in Japanese or *v* and *w* sounds in German are nonsignificant and difficult for speakers of those languages to distinguish in English. There are, of course, other sound differences that speakers of a language agree to consider significant. These are sounds which, like the initial sounds in English *park* and *bark,* differentiate units of meaning. Linguists call these significant units of sound **phonemes** (conventionally represented between slant lines, i.e. /t/).

The number of phonemes in any language is never overwhelming; English has thirty-five by most counts. What differentiates these sounds from one another is the place and manner of articulation along the human vocal tract. A knowledge of where and how the sounds of English are articulated can explain why certain sounds merge with or replace other similar sounds in some varieties of English discussed later in this book. (See the sketch of the human vocal apparatus in Figure A.) Consonants are formed by stopping or obstructing the airflow along the vocal tract as it is exhaled from the lungs. The obstruction may be created by the lips, the walls of the glottis, or, most frequently, the tongue. Consonants can be classified 1) according to their **point of articulation,** 2) according to whether they are **voiced** (vocal cords vibrating) or **voiceless** (vocal cords relaxed), and 3) according to their **manner of articulation;** that is, whether they are **stops,** which shut off the airflow completely; **fricatives,** which narrow the vocal passage at some point; **affricates,** which are stops followed by fricatives; **nasals,** which shut off the airflow in the mouth but allow it to be released through the nose; **liquids,** which divert the air around the sides (/l/) or over the top (/r/) of the tongue; or **semivowels,** which glide to or from the articulation point of related vowels. Table A uses these classifications to group English consonants. Vowels, which are transitional sounds intervening between consonants or consonant clusters to make words pronounceable, shape rather than obstruct the airflow along the vocal passage. Since the tongue, the most movable part of the vocal apparatus, is crucial in shaping the air for vowels, they can be classified according to tongue position, as shown in Table B. Pronouncing aloud each of these consonant and vowel sounds should clarify their classifications and the relationships among the various sounds of English.

Phonemes build into sequences which speakers recognize as minimal units of meaning, or **morphemes.** The study of these meaning units and the way they combine into words is **morphology.** Morphemes are classed as **free** when they can stand independently as words (e.g. *swim, girl*) and as **bound** when they must be accompanied by other morphemes to stand as words (*dis-, -ment, kniv-, -ed*).

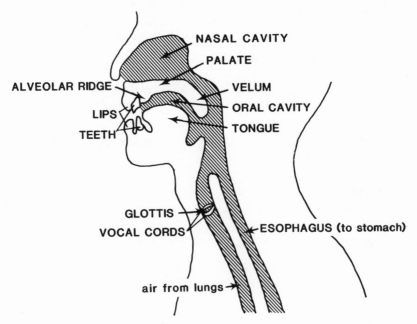

FIGURE A. Human Vocal Apparatus

TABLE A. Consonants

POINT OF ARTICULATION

MANNER OF ARTICULATION	BILABIAL (both lips)	LABIODENTAL (lower lip, upper teeth)	INTERDENTAL (tongue be-tween teeth)	ALVEOLAR (tongue on alveolar ridge)	PALATAL (tongue on palate)	VELAR (tongue on velum)	GLOTTAL (glottis constricted)
Stops:							
Voiceless	p			t		k	
Voiced	b			d		g	
Fricatives:							
Voiceless		f	θ (thin)	s	š (ash)		h
Voiced		v	ð (then)	z	ž (rouge)		
Affricates:							
Voiceless					č /t + š/ (cheap)		
Voiced					ǰ /d + ž/ (jeep)		
Nasals, voiced	m			n		ŋ (sing)	
Liquids, voiced				l, r			
Semivowels, voiced	w				y		

TABLE B.   Vowels

	Tongue front	Tongue center	Tongue back
Monophthongs (one sound)			
Tongue high	i (beat) ɪ (bit)		u (boot) ʊ (put)
Tongue mid	e (bait) ɛ (bet)	ə (but)	o (boat)
Tongue low	æ (bat)	a (pot)	ɔ (bought)
Diphthongs (two sounds combined)		ai (bite) au (bout)	ɔi (Boyd)

NOTE: Pronunciation guide words are not valid for all varieties of American English. Some varieties collapse contrasts shown here.

Bound morphemes, in turn, fall into two main categories: **derivational** and **inflectional.** Derivational morphemes are affixes, which can be attached to either the beginning (e.g. *undo, repay*) or the end (e.g. *slowly, handful*) of another morpheme. The other major class of bound morphemes is the inflectional morpheme, which indicates grammatical relationship and in English is usually a suffix, including the plural, the past tense, the possessive.

The rules by which morphemes chain together into sentences constitute **syntax,** which is considerably more complicated than either phonology or morphology. One reason for the complexity is that syntax actually consists of several hierarchical levels: words combine into phrases (e.g. *in the morning, the first green bed quilt, carried away*), phrases into clauses (e.g. *to come back in the morning, after she had laboriously stitched the first green bed quilt, carried away by their own enthusiasm*), and clauses into sentences. To cite just one syntactic rule at the level of phrase formation, English requires that modifiers in noun phrases occur in a certain order: determiners (*the, some, this,* etc.), then ordinators, which place items in the context of other related items (*three, first, best,* etc.), then adjectives (*interesting, old, yellow,* etc.), then nouns acting as modifiers (as in *bus* station). *The best local woman announcer* is thus a well-formed English noun phrase, while any other word order would not be. There are scores of other rules for assembling clauses out of phrases and sentences out of clauses. The **grammar** of a language consists of its morphology and syntax together.

Several people have graciously read all or part of this manuscript while it was in preparation. For their insightful criticism, kind encouragement, and generous sharing of information, the authors wish to thank: Maryse Brouwers, the late Ralph E. Cooley, Jed Dannenbaum, Nora Faires, Janis Butler Holm, Donald M. Lance, Maria Makris-Gouvas, Linda K. Pritchard, Sandra Silberstein, and Patricia A. Tamarin of the University of Alabama's Cartographic Lab. Any remaining errors or infelicities are, of course, our own.

PART I

A Historical Demography of American Languages

This generation, of which I am a part, never had to face the problem of pulling away from Polonia. We had never properly belonged to it. To us it was a slowly decaying world of aged folks living largely in a dream. One day it would pass and there would remain only Americans whose forebears had once been Poles.

—a Polish American

CHAPTER 1

Indigenous and Colonial Languages

Most Americans take it for granted that English is the language of the United States and even imagine that every American speaks it fluently. According to the 1980 U.S. Census, however, 11 percent of Americans come from non-English-speaking homes, and over 1 percent of the U. S. population speaks English not well or not at all. No indicators suggest that these percentages will soon decrease.

Non-English speakers live in all fifty states of the union. Figure 1 displays their relative population densities. In two states—Hawaii with its large proportion of Asian Americans and New Mexico with its many Spanish speakers and American Indians—over 25 percent of the population is non-English-speaking. In California, Arizona, Texas, Louisiana, New Jersey, Connecticut, Rhode Island, Massachusetts, New York, and North Dakota, between 16 and 25 percent of the population claims a non-English-speaking background. In twenty-three states the non-English language minority comprises 10 percent or more of the total population. Clearly, then, non-English languages can be heard today in every region of the country. A comparable language situation has characterized all of American history.

Before Europeans landed in North America, the entire continent was inhabited by native peoples who spoke several hundred distinct

3

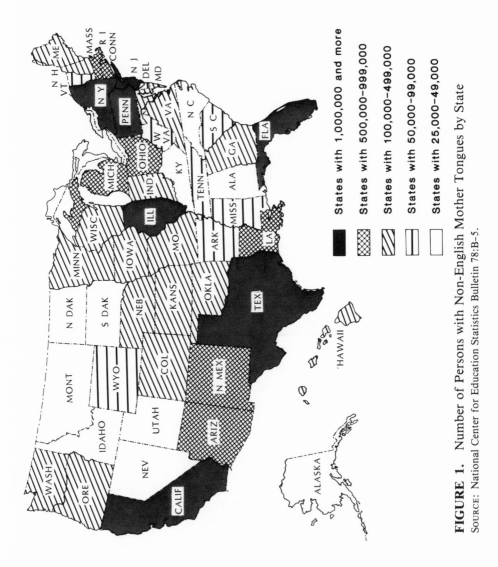

FIGURE 1. Number of Persons with Non-English Mother Tongues by State

Source: National Center for Education Statistics Bulletin 78:B-5.

languages. Often misperceived as incomplete or inferior communication systems, these indigenous languages were purposefully eradicated in many parts of the country by European settlers. The same destructive attitude toward native American tongues still pervades much of the public policy determining Indian education today.

Even among the European colonists, English was not without serious rivals during the colonial era. Spanish in Florida and the Southwest, French in Louisiana, German in Pennsylvania, and Dutch and, briefly, Swedish in the New York-Delaware area all served as official languages before English became predominant. As a result of their early primacy, these colonial languages have continued to be perceived as more acceptably American than the speech of later immigrants.

This favorable predisposition has helped speakers of colonial languages to retain their native tongues over many generations, especially in the areas of their original settlement. Those who had been forced to immigrate because of religious or cultural persecution maintained particularly cohesive language communities. German Pietists and Acadian French, for example, have continued to speak their mother tongues for more than two centuries. In regions with large concentrations of non-English colonists, mother-tongue schools and churches were established, often without English rivals. Many European colonists were literate and set up presses to publish news, information, religious tracts, and legal documents in their native languages. These mother-tongue institutions helped colonists retain a sense of unique cultural identity, including a desire to pass on their language. During the Revolutionary period, however, many non-English speakers living in the thirteen British colonies adopted the cause of national independence and assimilated culturally and linguistically to the dominant English-speaking population.

The West Africans imported by European slave traders brought with them a wide variety of native tongues. But the conditions of servitude made it impossible for them to maintain homogeneous language communities. At the same time, their social isolation made it equally impossible for them to assimilate completely to European speech. As a result, they evolved an African-influenced variety of English, traces of which still survive in the speech of many black Americans. Like native American languages, Afro-American speech has persisted not because of prestige or institutional support but because of social and economic ghettoization.

This chapter briefly recounts the histories of the major American language communities present during the colonial era. Circumstances influencing language retention or assimilation are emphasized. Accounts of immigration and change subsequent to the Revolution bring the history of each community up to the present day. Insofar as possible, these communities are discussed in the order in which they first appeared on the American continent.

INDIGENOUS LANGUAGES

The diversity of languages already spoken on the North American continent when European exploration began equaled that of all the language groups that subsequently settled here. The native peoples spoke perhaps a thousand distinct languages or dialects, stemming from language families as different from each other as the languages of Europe are from those of Africa or Asia.

When European contact began, no area of the continent except the extreme northern glacial cap was devoid of inhabitants. Although estimates vary, it seems safe to assume that at least one million natives lived in the area north of Mexico in the seventeenth century. Figure 2 demonstrates the geographic distribution of the largest language families.

After Europeans arrived, native peoples were reduced drastically by wars, by diseases contracted from the white colonists, and by the radical transformation that settlers brought to their environment. Both those tribes that resisted European encroachment and those that sought peaceful coexistence were exterminated or pushed aside onto reservations in undesirable, unsettled areas, often far from their traditional homelands.

Once they had expropriated precious metals and gems, Spanish armies marching north from Mexico largely ignored the native peoples. Exploration parties in the American Southwest and along the Pacific Coast established only a string of outposts, often with missions servicing the Indians. The northern European explorations on the East Coast, however, had a more far-reaching impact. Finding no fabulous wealth to expropriate or take in trade, the English embarked on an extensive program of settlement, creating villages, clearing forests for farmland, and, naturally, falling into competition with the native residents over territory and land use. The coastal peoples were pushed back onto lands occupied by other, often hostile tribes or enslaved by the Europeans or sold to tribes farther west. Enslavement was es-

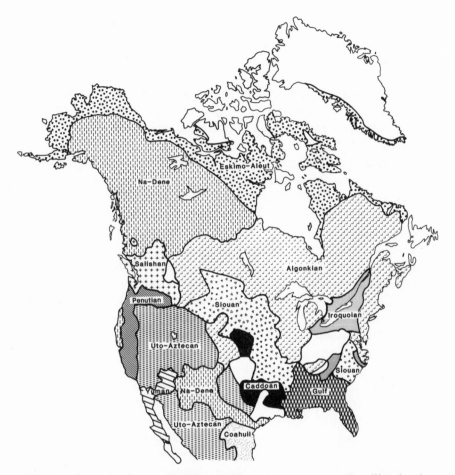

FIGURE 2. Locations of Major Indigenous Language Families in the Continental United States at the Time of European Contact

pecially practiced in the southern colonies; in 1708 a third of Carolina's 4,300 slaves were Indians.

Increasing immigration from Europe meant continuing repression of the native peoples. Revolutionary War soldiers were paid in land grants—in former Indian territories. Attempts to assimilate the native peoples, to teach them white values and skills, were at best partially successful. Indians were pleased to learn useful skills but did not come to value acquisition of goods and property—the basis of European social structure. Rather, they repudiated the idea of individual ownership and individual achievement, maintaining instead their traditional communal and cooperative attitudes.

By 1829 the demand for lands brought Andrew Jackson, famed as an Indian fighter and advocate of extermination of the natives, to the Presidency. His Indian Removal Act decreed expulsion of all remaining major tribes to areas west of the Mississippi River. Many thousands died on the march; tribes that resisted were massacred wholesale. Those who survived the forced march were resettled in Indian Territory, now the state of Oklahoma. Remnants of most Northeast, Southeast, and North-Central language communities can be found in Oklahoma today.

In the second half of the nineteenth century destruction of native societies continued unabated in the West Coast, Mountain, and Great Plains regions. In 1840 approximately 175,000 Indians inhabited the California mountains and valleys, coexisting peacefully with the coastal Spanish settlements. A mere forty years later, after the Gold Rush and the land rush from the Eastern states, only 20,000 of these people remained alive. Confrontation between Plains peoples and Europeans became inevitable with the construction of the transcontinental railroad. Whites began to attack the buffalo herds, basis of the nomadic hunting economy. Between 1872 and 1874 alone— while Indians killed only 150,000 buffalo to provide themselves with food, clothing, and shelter—whites wantonly destroyed 3,500,000. White settlements followed railroad routes, driving the Indians back from their traditional lands and lives onto small reservations or into Oklahoma. In 1900 there were just 200,000 natives on the reservations of the entire United States.

Figure 3 shows the location of Indian lands today. The 1970 U.S. Census reports 790,000 native Americans in the contiguous states, only half of whom live on reservation lands. Indians can be found in any urban center, especially those close to reservations, but the largest urban Indian community is the Los Angeles area, with over 60,000 representing tribes throughout the Southwest.

During our own century government policy continued to undermine native culture and language. Indian children have been forcibly removed from their tribes to attend white-run schools where all instruction takes place in English, and use of native tongues is a serious offense. In the last decade native Americans have reasserted their right to their own cultures and languages. Reservation-based, Indian-oriented curricula have raised the percentage of high school graduates from 20 percent in 1965 to 33 percent in 1978. Still, these figures compare unfavorably with those for Hispanics, blacks, and whites.

Some tribes have turned to intensive study and practice of their native languages. Though many are spoken only by a handful of el-

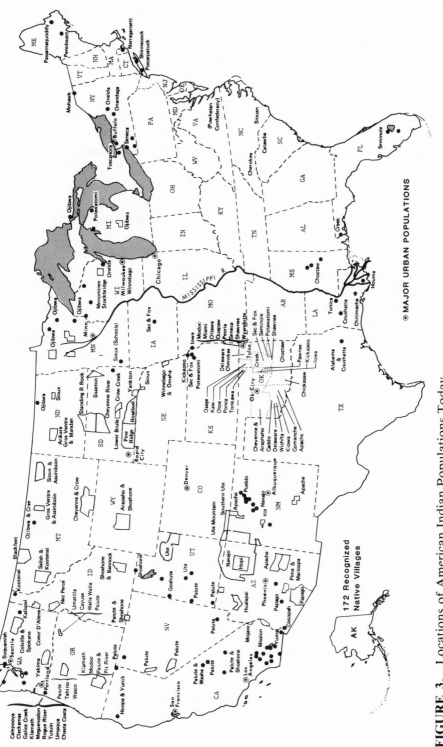

FIGURE 3. Locations of American Indian Populations Today

9

derly people, others are in use as primary community languages. The largest speech community is the Navajo tribe, with over 89,000 speakers. Some viable native language communities continue today; over 200 languages are still spoken or studied. Yet tribal languages are not likely to reemerge as the medium of day-to-day communication among groups currently speaking English or Spanish. This is especially true for the growing urban Indian population, which must find a common tongue. Still, one-third of all native Americans—over 270,000—reported use of the tribal tongue in the 1970 U.S. Census. Table 1 lists the numbers and locations of native mother-tongue claimants. Languages within each family are listed in descending order of the number of speakers.

Table 1 also includes mother-tongue claimants for Hawaiian, the indigenous language of the Hawaiian Islands. The Hawaiians migrated to the islands from the western Pacific before A.D. 1000. They set up a monarchy which remained autonomous until 1893 when it was overthrown by white plantation owners and allied interests. By the time the territory was annexed to the United States, European and Asian immigration had made Hawaiians a minority in the islands. Although Hawaiian is still spoken today, many ethnic Hawaiians speak English as well or a mixed language called Hawaiian Creole.

SPANISH

When native peoples first encountered European explorers on what was to become United States soil, the language they heard was not English but Spanish. And not only is Spain the oldest colonial power in this country, but Hispanics today constitute our nation's largest non-English-speaking minority. Consequently, the situation of Spanish speakers in the United States is both historically and sociologically complex.

In 1513 Juan Ponce de León discovered Florida while searching for Bimini, the legendary Fountain of Eternal Youth. But native American resistance, tropical storms, and food shortages prevented this and several later attempts at settlement. Only in 1565, afraid of losing Florida to the French Huguenots who had settled at present-day Jacksonville, did the Spanish finally establish a permanent colony in St. Augustine. Thus began an uninterrupted two hundred year history of Spanish language and culture in eastern Florida. Political events in the late eighteenth century, however, weakened this Spanish heritage:

TABLE 1. Indigenous Languages Spoken in the United States

Language Family and Mother-Tongue Claimants (1970 U.S. Census)	Major Language Communities	Original Territory	Present Location
Continental United States:			
Algonkian 25,000	Ojibwa (Chippewa)	Lake Superior area	N Midwest
	Blackfoot	N Great Plains	Montana
	Cheyenne	NW Great Plains	Montana, Oklahoma
	Arapaho	NW Great Plains	Wyoming, Oklahoma
	Fox	Wisconsin	Kansas, Oklahoma
Caddoan 700	Pawnee	Central Great Plains	Oklahoma
	Caddo	Arkansas-Texas area	Oklahoma
Eskimo-Aleut 30,000	Inupik and Yapik (Eskimo)	N and W Alaska	N and W Alaska
	Aleut	Aleutian Islands	Aleutian Islands
Gulf, Muskogean branch 18,000	Creek	Georgia	S Alabama, Oklahoma
	Choctaw	Mississippi	Mississippi, Oklahoma
	Chicasaw	Mississippi, Tennessee	Oklahoma
	Seminole	S Florida	S Florida, Oklahoma
	Cherokee	S Appalachia, Piedmont	North Carolina, Oklahoma
Iroquois 20,000	Seneca	NW New York	SW New York, Oklahoma
	Mohawk	NE New York	N New York
	Oneida	NE New York	Central New York

(cont.)

11

TABLE 1. Indigenous Languages Spoken in the United States (*Continued*)

LANGUAGE FAMILY AND MOTHER–TONGUE CLAIMANTS (1970 U.S. CENSUS)	MAJOR LANGUAGE COMMUNITIES	ORIGINAL TERRITORY	PRESENT LOCATION
Na-Dene 120,000 Athapaskan branch	Navajo	Arizona, New Mexico, S Utah	Arizona, New Mexico, S Utah
	Apache	SW Great Plains	Arizona, New Mexico, Oklahoma
	Tanaina, Tanana, Kutchin, Koyu-kon	Inland Alaska	Inland Alaska
Coastal branch	Haida, Tlingit	Alaska Panhandle	Alaska Panhandle
Pueblo group 13,000	Zuni	New Mexico	New Mexico
	Keresan	New Mexico	New Mexico
	Tanoan	Arizona, New Mexico	New Mexico
Salishan 1,500	Flathead	Montana	Montana
	Coeur D'Alene	Montana, Idaho	Idaho
Penutian group 1,400	Shahaptian (Nez Perce)	Idaho	Idaho
	Yakima	Oregon, Washington	Washington
	Klamath	Oregon	Oregon

Siouan 25,000	Lakota (Sioux)	Great Plains	N Plains
	Crow	Wyoming, Montana	Montana
	Omaha	Central Great Plains	Nebraska
	Winnebago	Wisconsin	Wisconsin, Nebraska
	Assiniboin	N Montana and Dakota	Montana
Uto-Aztecan 20,000	Papago	S Arizona	S Arizona
	Shoshoni	Nevada, Rockies	Nevada, Southwest
	Pima	Arizona	Arizona
	Hopi	Arizona	Arizona
	Ute	Utah, Colorado	Utah
	Paiute	Rockies, Great Basin	Nevada, Utah, E California
	Kiowa	Kansas, Colorado	Oklahoma
	Commanche	W Texas	Oklahoma
	Yuman	S California, SW Arizona	SW Arizona
Yuma 2,500	Mojave	SW California	SW California
Hawaii:			
Polynesian 7,500	Hawaiian	Hawaiian Islands	Hawaiian Islands

Florida was ceded to the British in 1763, returned to the Spanish in 1783, and permanently annexed to the United States in 1821. Under these circumstances, most Florida Hispanics either fled or assimilated to the Anglo culture. The only significant exception was a group of 1,200 from Minorca, a Mediterranean island off the coast of Spain. These people had originally been brought by the British in 1768 to work on plantations near New Smyrna but eventually settled in St. Augustine, preserving their unique Spanish dialect and culture well into the twentieth century.

At about the time that Ponce de León had tried in vain to colonize Florida, Hernán Cortés had met with much better success in Spain's major North American incursion, the conquest of the Aztec Empire in Mexico. By 1540 Francisco Vázquez de Coronado had explored northward from Mexico into what are now Arizona, Texas, Colorado, and New Mexico. Yet, as in Florida, Spain with its extensive New World commitments could only spare the resources for settling its territories north of Mexico when threatened by other colonial powers. Thus, fearing that the British Sir Francis Drake had discovered the Northwest Passage, Spain sent Juan de Oñate into its northern territories where in 1598 he founded Gabriel de los Españoles (today called Chamita), the oldest continuous Spanish settlement in the Southwest. Santa Fe was established in 1609, and other settlements in present-day New Mexico, southern Colorado, Arizona, and western Texas soon followed. As not only the oldest but the most tenacious of Spanish areas in the southwest United States, New Mexico even today preserves features of the archaic Castilian dialect spoken by its original Hispanic settlers, as well as remnants of the stratified social structure in which *criollos* (of Spanish ancestry) form a small elite while *mestizos* (of mixed Spanish and native American heritage) and native Americans work as peons. Since 95 percent of all Mexicans are at least part native American, it is not surprising that New Mexican Hispanics also preserve many of the customs and even some of the vocabulary of the Pueblo Indians with whom they intermarried.

More than a century passed before the Spanish decided to settle central and eastern Texas in order to ward off the French expansion from Louisiana. Founding San Antonio in 1722, they imported Canary Islanders and established penal colonies to populate this unpopular region where Indians were unfriendly and agriculture difficult.

Later in the eighteenth century, the Spanish settled California in response to Russian and English activity on the Pacific Coast. Between 1769 and 1823 the Franciscan Father Junípero Serra founded twenty-one missions along the California coast from present-day San Diego in the south to San Francisco in the north. California became both the most prosperous and the most isolated from Mexico among the three northern provinces of New Spain.

Since New Mexico, Texas, and California were settled at different periods, attracted different members of the Hispanic population, and developed different economies, they represented three distinct Hispanic subcultures, each with its own dialect of Spanish. In the nineteenth century frequent incursions into Texas by neighboring Anglos and the discovery of gold in California significantly reduced the dominance of these two later Spanish subcultures.

In addition to settling in Florida and moving north from Mexico, the Spanish also held the Louisiana Territory between 1763 and 1800. Although Louisiana remained primarily French in language and culture during this period, settlers from Málaga in southern Spain founded New Iberia, and a group of Canary Islanders settled along lower Bayou Lafourche and north of Lake Mauripas, bringing with them their *isleño* dialect of Spanish. A few thousand *isleño* speakers still live in this area today.

After Spain had yielded Louisiana in 1800 and Florida in 1821, Mexico finally lost her holdings in the present-day southwestern United States through the independence of Texas in 1836 and the Mexican Cession of 1848. Thus ended over three hundred years of Spanish and Mexican colonialism in this country. Yet it would be a serious mistake to underestimate the linguistic and cultural influence of America's oldest colonial power—a power which at various times had controlled almost all of the United States west of the Mississippi and Florida in the East (see Figure 4). Spain's decline as a world power and racial mixing in the Western Hemisphere have lowered the prestige of the Spanish language in the last two centuries. But at least two factors have ensured the persistence of the Hispanic influence in early settlement regions: 1) as the oldest European culture in these areas, Hispanics were more resistant to Anglo assimilation than were members of other cultures who arrived later; and 2) the proximity of the southwestern United States to Mexico and of the southeastern United States to the Spanish-speaking Caribbean islands has reinforced the Spanish language and culture in the South. But, even more

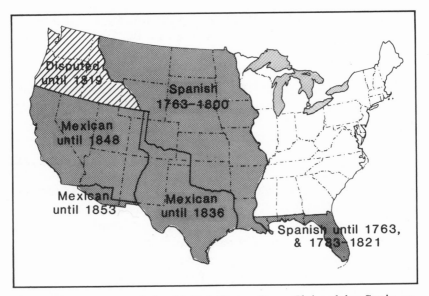

FIGURE 4.   Areas of the United States Once Claimed by Spain or Mexico

importantly, the persistence of Hispanic culture has been virtually guaranteed by massive immigration from Mexico, Puerto Rico, and Cuba in this century.

Between 1909, when the Mexican Revolution broke out, and 1930, when the Depression cut off employment possibilities, approximately 15 percent of the entire population of Mexico emigrated to the United States to supply the shortage of farm, mine, and railway workers in the Southwest. After 1924, when national origin quotas depleted the supply of European and Asian factory workers, Mexicans, who were exempt from the quota system, also moved in large numbers to work in the steel foundries of Illinois, Ohio, and Pennsylvania and the automobile plants of Michigan. One million Hispanics now live in Chicago alone and constitute 20 percent of that city's population. During World War II when the agricultural labor shortage recurred, the Mexican and U.S. governments set up the *bracero* program, which allowed Mexican nationals to work for short periods and low wages on U.S. farms. This program, which lasted until 1964, probably indirectly fostered the enormous number of illegal immigrants who came even though they had not been selected for the *bracero* program. These illegal aliens (*mojados* or wetbacks) suffered under the constant threat of deportation and worked for even less pay than the *braceros*. Nor has the flood of illegal Hispanic aliens diminished in recent years. To-day an estimated eight to twelve million of them, about 90 percent Mexican, join the twelve million legal Hispanic residents of this country.

Because of the high visibility of the United Farm Workers, the contemporary Mexican American, or *Chicano,* has been stereotyped as a farm laborer or migrant worker. In reality, however, 80 to 85 percent are urban, and fully one-third of these are concentrated in the Los Angeles, San Antonio, San Francisco, and El Paso *barrios,* where Spanish language and culture predominate. In fact, nearly a third of the population of Los Angeles and closer to half of its kindergartners are Chicano, making Los Angeles the second largest Hispanic population center in North America—second only to Mexico City. And in spite of a growing Chicano middle class, most are poor. In Los Angeles 19 percent of Chicano families live below the poverty line.

Besides the 7.2 million legally resident Chicanos, two other groups of Hispanics have recently migrated in great numbers to the continental United States—Puerto Ricans and Cubans. These islanders are both ethnically and linguistically different from the Chicanos. Unlike Chicanos, who tend to have Spanish and native American ancestors, many Caribbean Hispanics inherit a mixture of Spanish and African blood. Because of these ethnic differences—as well as their earlier colonization—Caribbean Hispanics also differ from Chicanos in their spoken dialect, called Antillean Spanish.

Moreover, Puerto Ricans differ significantly from Cubans as well. An American territory since 1898, Puerto Rico has experienced eighty years of strong Anglo influence, and Puerto Ricans have been U.S. citizens since 1917. It was not until after World War II, however, that Puerto Ricans responded to poverty and overpopulation at home by moving in large numbers to the continent, about 80 percent of these 1.8 million migrants settling in the New York City area, where they sought the same low-paying service and industry jobs for which blacks were also competing. The poorest of all United States Hispanics, Puerto Ricans in New York are economically more depressed than their black neighbors: in 1978, 48 percent of them earned less than $7,000 a year, as compared with 42 percent among blacks, and 34 percent of Puerto Ricans were on welfare that year. Partly as a result of these poverty conditions, Puerto Ricans no longer come to the mainland in great numbers.

Cubans, on the other hand, have arrived more recently and fared much better economically than Puerto Ricans. Although about six thousand Cuban cigar makers lived in Miami and Key West in the late nineteenth century, the chief influx of Cubans—totalling about 800,000—occurred shortly after 1959 when the Castro regime began. About 5 percent of Cuba's entire population—mostly the wealthy and educated—emigrated to the United States. More than half of these people settled in or near Miami, and they now comprise the majority of the city's population. Because they have prospered as businessmen and professionals, this first wave of Cuban immigrants has significantly affected the economy of the Miami area—establishing 230 Latino restaurants, 30 furniture factories, 20 garment plants, 30 cigar factories, and a shoe factory. Cubans also make up 60 percent of the construction work force and control fourteen of the sixty-seven local commercial banks. Since 1980 the "Freedom Flotilla" has brought an additional 125,000 Cubans to U.S. shores. Unlike their predecessors, they have come with few possessions and little education and thus face significant obstacles to successful assimilation.

Overall, the recent influx of Chicanos, Puerto Ricans, and Cubans (in addition to 2.4 million other Hispanics from Latin America or Spain) brings the estimated total Hispanic population of this country to at least 20 million, or 9 percent of the U.S. population. Demographers predict that they may soon overtake blacks as our nation's largest minority. Particularly since U.S. Hispanics have for centuries remained resistant to both linguistic and cultural assimilation, they, more than any other non-English-speaking minority, provide the ultimate test of this country's definition of cultural pluralism.

FRENCH

Like Spain, France had begun to populate North America before the English disembarked at Jamestown. Samuel de Champlain settled the Atlantic coast of Acadia (now Nova Scotia) in 1604 and founded Quebec in 1608. By the mid-seventeenth century, the French had also laid claim to the Caribbean islands of St. Christopher, Martinique, Guadeloupe, Dominica, and present-day Haiti in Hispaniola.

From these New World beginnings, French language and culture gradually gained a foothold in the United States. French fur traders from Canada established outposts in the Great Lakes region, then proceeded down the Ohio and Mississippi Rivers, claiming Louisiana in 1682. Along the way important French trading posts sprang up in what would become Detroit, St. Louis, Memphis, Natchez, and New

Orleans. Close military and economic ties with native Americans led these explorers and traders to incorporate numerous native American vocabulary items into their French.

Besides these small French colonies in the West, Eastern cities underwent some French influence when in the 1680s Huguenots, fleeing religious persecution, settled in New England and Charleston. Many of these well-educated Protestants quickly adapted to the British language and culture of the East Coast. Their descendants, including Paul Revere, often rose to political and commercial prominence, especially as slave traders and tobacco and cotton agents.

With the closing of the French and Indian War in 1763, French political influence in the East Coast colonies came to an end. But many French settlers along the Mississippi moved to St. Louis and other communities along the west bank, where their influence and even some use of archaic French have persisted into the twentieth century. The French language and culture also left a lasting imprint on the Delta region. By 1800 Louisiana could claim three different French-speaking populations, each using a distinct variety of French. The white descendants of the original French settlers, who had founded Mobile, Biloxi, and New Orleans, spoke what is now called Louisiana Standard French. Between five and ten thousand Acadians, expelled from their Canadian homeland in 1755, relocated in Louisiana, bringing to southwestern Louisiana and eastern Texas their own brand of French, which is often called Cajun. Finally, the West Africans, imported to work on plantations, spoke a combination of French and West African languages called Louisiana French Creole. Although the Louisiana Purchase in 1803 brought rapid Anglicization, the French influence in Louisiana remains strong today: in 1976, 524,000 Louisianans regularly spoke some form of French, and in remote areas many monolingual English speakers have French accents. Out of respect for its numerous French speakers, Louisiana in 1968 became officially bilingual.

One force that promotes French language retention in Louisiana and elsewhere is the continuing prestige of French as a world language. Its high status increased during the 1790s when as many as 40,000 French aristocrats sought refuge in American cities from the French Revolution and slave uprisings on Santo Domingo. For several years the future King Louis Philippe even held court in Philadelphia, bringing French dress, cuisine, manners, and language into public prominence.

In the nineteenth century immigrants from France, as from other western European countries, helped settle the American West. During the Gold Rush years, for instance, seven thousand French speakers took up residence in San Francisco, where their pride in French language and culture prompted them to resist assimilation.

But by far the greatest nineteenth- and twentieth-century influx of French speakers consisted of French Canadians, also called Franco-Americans, who migrated to New England to work in textile mills and shoe factories. Three factors combine to foster the preservation of the French language among the half million Franco-Americans who now live in New England: 1) continuing poverty and strong ethnic identification, which have slowed assimilation to the English-speaking population; 2) the establishment of French language churches, schools, presses, and radio broadcasts to preserve their heritage in hopes of returning to Canada; 3) proximity to French-speaking Canada, which helps Franco-Americans retain the language and traditions of their homeland.

During the twentieth century, Haitians have joined the ranks of French speakers in the United States. Like their Puerto Rican neighbors, most Haitians have arrived since World War II in search of economic opportunities, and 200,000 of them have settled in New York City. Since the late 1970s, many thousands of Haitian refugees have landed on the Florida coast and taken up residence, often illegally, in the Miami area. West African by descent but enslaved by French plantation owners until 1801, Haitians speak a language called Haitian French Creole which, like Louisiana French Creole, combines features of West African languages and French.

As the fourth largest language community in this country, French speakers currently number about two million, 78 percent of whom are native-born Americans. With its long colonial history, its high status among world languages, and its dominance in nearby Quebec, French seems unlikely to disappear from the American scene in the near future.

ENGLISH

In the rush to emulate Spain's New World empire, England's Queen Elizabeth sponsored a series of exploratory voyages to as-yet-unclaimed territories along the Atlantic seaboard—north from Spain's Florida all the way to Newfoundland. In 1605 a company was chartered to establish a colony in the Virginia territory; it founded

Jamestown in 1607 and then a string of farming and tobacco-producing settlements in the Tidewater area. By the 1630s a cluster of towns, begun as a haven for dissenters from the Church of England, was flourishing far up the coast in New England. Both the New Englanders and the Virginia colonists relied initially on a labor pool of indentured servants—largely displaced farmers from the south and east of England, who brought their nonstandard East Anglian dialect with them. The Southern planters soon shifted to black slave labor, so that until the Civil War the region's white population was still predominantly descended from the old English colonial stock.

The English gradually exerted control over the American coast, but the English-speaking areas were not united as a continuous territory until late in the century. After 1681 William Penn and his Quaker followers began settling in the Delaware River Valley. Although their movement had arisen first in the northern Midlands, its adherents stemmed from all parts of England and, with Penn's active and open promotion policies, Pennsylvania soon attracted settlers from Scotland and Ulster as well.

Scotch-Irish Ulsterites constituted the largest non-English immigrant group throughout the eighteenth century. By the time of the Revolution they made up 7 to 10 percent of the white population, numbering over four million. Arriving nearly penniless, they passed through settled areas of Pennsylvania toward the free land just to the west, going north into western New England and upper New York and south along the Appalachian Mountains as far as North Carolina. After the Revolutionary War opened up western Pennsylvania and Ohio to settlement, the Scotch-Irish moved rapidly westward, continuing to follow the frontier throughout the nineteenth century (see Figure 14). The Scotch-Irish who settled in the remote mountain valleys of central Appalachia remained highly resistant to outside influences. They developed a unique dialect of English that has influenced the speech of the entire region. During World War II thousands of Appalachian English speakers came north to work in factories, especially in Michigan. There, too, they have established their own communities and maintain their own way of speaking.

When massive immigration resumed after the disruptions of the American Revolution and the Napoleonic Wars, the preponderance of English-speaking newcomers no longer came from England, Scotland, and Ulster but rather from Ireland. Between 1819 and 1840, 45 percent of all immigrants were Irish; only 14 percent were from the rest of the British Isles. Crop failures in Ireland drove additional hundreds of thousands of Irish poor to choose emigration in the decades prior to the Civil War.

Although they had the advantage of sharing the English tongue, the Irish were not so readily assimilated as previous English-speaking immigrants. At the beginning of the American Revolution, the colonies consisted of an assortment of British and northern European cultures. But by 1820, when large numbers of Irish began arriving, shared experience and the forty-year hiatus in immigration had created among whites a culture that was more homogeneously Anglo-Saxon than any before or since. Newcomers were perceived as foreign, the Irish particularly so, for their religion and cultural values were at odds with the established society. Because they arrived destitute, the Irish could not push on to the frontier to establish their communities. They congregated instead in the ports of entry, especially New York, Philadelphia, and Boston, which was the most frequent American port of call for ships from the east of England bound for Canada. Major urban areas in the Northeast and, in the latter half of the century, in the Upper Midwest absorbed 90 percent of the Irish who came to the United States. In 1860 two-thirds of the 1.6 million Irish lived in New York, New Jersey, Pennsylvania, and New England.

Irish immigration resumed following the Civil War, though it was eventually exceeded by immigration from other parts of Europe. As construction workers, the Irish moved west along canals and railroad routes and constituted the first large English-speaking group in San Francisco. A significant number, especially middle-class Irish, immigrated to New Orleans, where they were more readily received into the predominantly Catholic society.

The Irish maintained strong ethnic identity and a distinct variety of English well into the twentieth century. In 1972 Ireland was still the fourth largest source of U.S. immigrants. Irish Americans often served as linguistic models for their non-English-speaking ghetto neighbors, affecting particularly the speech of working-class Bostonians. In the late twentieth century the Irish have become fully a part of the Anglo-American cultural and linguistic majority.

Throughout the nineteenth century immigrants continued to arrive from the rest of the British Isles as well—many of them skilled workers and artisans. English and Welsh miners were prized laborers in the Pennsylvania coal fields and the hard-rock mines of the American West. Between 1860 and 1880 severe economic depression drove between one-fourth and one-third of all Cornish workers to the United States. Growing competition from German and American industry brought hard times to English and Scottish workers at the end of the century, and the number of emigrants to the United States rose dramatically. As white English-speaking Protestants, immigrants from these areas were quickly accepted as "American" by the native population.

When severe national origin restrictions were placed on immigration in 1924, the British and even the Irish were favored with disproportionately large quotas. Preference for English speakers was encoded into immigration law and remained in force until the mid-1960s. The numbers of ethnically English Americans were further swelled by a large influx of Anglo-Canadians, who settled in the Great Lakes area and on the West Coast in the first third of this century.

Despite these large numbers of immigrants from the British Isles, less than 30 percent of today's Americans can trace a significant portion of their ancestry to England. Though politically independent for over two hundred years and inhabited predominantly by peoples from other nations, the United States continues to be dominated by the myth of a common, British cultural and linguistic heritage.

WEST AFRICAN LANGUAGES

Black Americans, who now constitute our nation's largest minority group, look back to a linguistic and cultural history unique in this country. Their West African ancestors began arriving in Virginia just twelve years after the British. Yet, whereas their European predecessors came voluntarily and looked forward to new opportunities in America, West Africans came under compulsion and could expect only slavery. European colonists dictated not only the arrival of West Africans in the United States but also where and how they lived. The institutions of slavery and racism made it impossible for blacks to assimilate to the dominant culture as European colonists could or to maintain their culture under circumstances of their own choosing. As a result of all these conditions, black American speech developed differently from any other American language variety.

Between 1619 and 1808, slaves were imported to the American South from the West African coast—first mainly from Senegal, Guinea, the Slave Coast (parts of present-day Ghana, Togo, Benin, Nigeria) and later from farther south in Nigeria, the Congo, and Angola (see Figure 27). These West Africans originally spoke a variety of tribal languages (Mende, Ewe, Ibo, and Wolof, to name a few), primarily from the Niger-Congo language family. Yet these African native languages seldom survived intact for even a single generation in the New World. Africans could not use their native tongues to communicate with each other since slave traders punished use of native languages and often separated members of the same language community to prevent conspiracy. And slaves had to learn quickly how to communicate with the whites who controlled their fate. Thus they developed a creole language which combined elements of West African languages with English or, in the case of Louisiana slaves, with French.

The first blacks who came to Virginia and Maryland worked on tobacco and rice plantations. So vigorous was the early slave trade that by 1750 blacks comprised 21 percent of the entire U.S. population. In the next half century plantation agriculture, which began to include cotton, moved south to the Carolinas and Georgia, then west to Alabama, Mississippi, Louisiana, and Tennessee. Along with the plantation system went the black slaves.

When the slave trade from Africa declined in the early nineteenth century, slave owners in the older plantation states of Virginia and Maryland began to breed slaves for the newer plantation states to the south and west. By 1850 three states had slave majorities: South Carolina (59 percent black) and Mississippi and Louisiana (each 51 percent black). Actually, blacks predominated in a considerable portion of the entire plantation region (see Figure 5).

The plantation system had other linguistic implications besides the rapid development of a creole. Slaves who worked in the house and a few skilled laborers approximated the English of their masters while field workers had little contact with whites and continued to speak a creole English with a number of African features. Some blacks could shift from a more creolized to a more standard English depending on the situation. In addition, the entire black population was slowly assimilating to standard speech. In short, a continuum evolved from creole to standard English, and an individual black speaker might fall anywhere along this continuum depending upon social status, speech situation, and point in history.

Moreover, the English of the dominant culture has apparently been affected more by the speech of black Americans than by any other minority language. In part, this influence may simply reflect the very large percentage of blacks in the overall Southern population. But it can also be traced to the uniqueness of the master-slave relation-

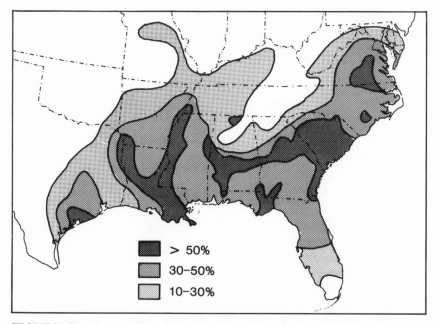

FIGURE 5. Proportion of the Southeast Population Black in 1850

SOURCE: Richard L. Morrill and O. Fred Donaldson, "Geographical Perspectives on the History of Black America," *Economic Geography* 48 (1972):19. Used by permission.

ship, whereby young masters often grew up with black nurses and played only with black children. Predictably, these wealthy white children, who would set the standard for cultured speech in their region, learned to speak the language of their black intimates, and some black language features remained even in their prestigious adult varieties of Southern American English.

Ironically, the Civil War, which legally freed the slaves, had the practical effect of segregating blacks from whites more than had been the case in the pre-War South. In the late nineteenth century Jim Crow laws disenfranchised black voters, segregated all public facilities, and established segregated neighborhoods in much of the South and in some Northern states as well. Obviously, such policies precluded cultural assimilation for blacks, including the many who moved to Southern cities after the War, and undoubtedly retarded linguistic assimilation too.

As for Northern blacks, their numbers remained small until the twentieth century. A few escaped slavery by making their way to Pittsburgh in the eighteenth century, later to Cleveland, and eventually to

Baltimore, Cincinnati, New York, Chicago, Rochester, Philadelphia, and Boston. But by 1910 only 5 percent of the Northern population was black, and only 11 percent of the black population lived in the North.

Between 1910 and 1920, however, half a million Southern blacks, suffering under the injustices of the sharecropping system and a decline in cotton prices, came to Northern cities for the industrial jobs opened up by World War I. By 1940, fully 10 to 15 percent of the total black population had left the rural South for the urban North, and sizable black ghettos developed in Chicago, Detroit, Philadelphia, and New York. Between 1940 and 1960, a million blacks moved to California. As a result of these massive population shifts, by 1970 New York, California, and Illinois had the highest black populations in the country (see Figure 6).

Even in crowded Northern cities, the social distance between blacks and whites has impeded both linguistic and cultural assimilation. In general, Northern blacks speak a more standard version of English than Southern blacks, but any city dweller can testify that differences between black and white speech patterns persist. Segregation, poverty, and, in a different way, black separatism have all operated to keep black Americans a relatively cohesive speech community. Only since the Civil Rights movement of the 1960s has a substantial black middle class developed and fully assumed the language and values of the mainstream culture. Many Northern blacks either now belong or aspire to belong to this growing bourgeoisie, and for them capability in standard English is increasingly essential.

DUTCH

For forty years, from 1624 until 1664, when the English forcibly took control, the New Netherland colony flourished along the Hudson River Valley. During the century of English rule and increasing English immigration, the Dutch maintained their linguistic community, importing teachers and ministers from Holland and even establishing their own college, now Rutgers University, in 1766. When the colonies joined forces against England, many Dutch were drawn into close contact with the dominant language group, and, by the end of the Revolutionary period, the majority of the Dutch, especially those in the New York City area, had fully assimilated to the emerging

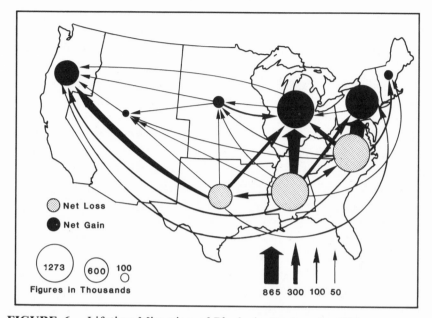

FIGURE 6. Lifetime Migration of Blacks by Region, to 1960

SOURCE: Richard L. Morrill and O. Fred Donaldson, "Geographical Perspectives on the History of Black America," *Economic Geography* 48 (1972): 19. Used by permission.

Anglo-American culture. In rural areas, however, the Dutch language continued in use into the nineteenth century, often as a second language for Dutch/English bilinguals. In remote areas of New Jersey a dialect mixing Dutch and English and influenced by the Delaware Indian language was spoken by a few farming people up to 1900.

More immigrants from Holland came to the United States in the first half of the nineteenth century. Some settled in the traditional Dutch areas, but most established new farms in the Upper Midwest. Dutch-speaking communities arose in Michigan, Wisconsin, Illinois, and Iowa. At the close of the century most of these pre-War immigrants spoke English but faithfully preserved their Dutch culture and religion.

Dutch and Flemish—Dutch-speaking Belgians—have continued to immigrate to the United States in this century. They are particularly prominent on the West Coast as owners of farms and dairies. Their linguistic and cultural similarity to English-speaking Americans has led to quick assimilation into mainstream American society. Although the 1970 U.S. Census reports 350,000 Dutch mother-tongue claimants, many of these speak English in their everyday lives.

GERMAN

In the middle colonies in the pre-Revolutionary period and again in the Midwest in the nineteenth century, German attained a prominence unparalleled by any other non-English tongue and equaled only by the use of Spanish in the Southwest today. Germans arrived in North America in numbers second only to the combined number of English speakers from the British Isles; they are the largest single ethnic group among all U.S. immigrants.

From a peak of nine million in 1910, the number of active German speakers had fallen to less than a million in 1970, although 2.75 million Americans still live in German-speaking households. German speakers constitute the fifth largest language community in the United States today. At times confronted by fierce anti-foreign and anti-German sentiment and in some cases steadfastly rejecting any intercourse with the dominant society, German speakers have nevertheless been assimilated more rapidly and more completely than any other non-English-speaking group because of their close physical, cultural, and linguistic resemblance to Anglo-Americans.

Although lacking a unified political structure to make territorial claims in the name of the German people, eighteenth-century German speakers, like other western Europeans, made their way to America. Germans belonged to exploration parties of all the European nations and were present from earliest days in Spain's California settlements, in French Louisiana, in New Netherland, New Sweden, and the English colonies south of New England. The wave of religious repression that led New England Puritans and Penn's Quakers to seek sanctuary outside England also swept German areas. German religious dissenters, their ranks swelled by refugees from ongoing wars and agricultural failures, began arriving in Pennsylvania in 1683 and soon established themselves as the majority in the southeast Pennsylvania farmlands. These Pennsylvania Germans—also called "Pennsylvania Dutch"—spread out to central Pennsylvania, adjacent Maryland, and Virginia's Shenandoah Valley and constituted a third of the population of Pennsylvania by the time of the Revolution.

The Germans preferred to remain aloof from their English and Scotch-Irish neighbors, but the American independence movement forced them into contact with the English-speaking population. Though at first opposed to the war with England, the Germans eventually joined the Revolutionaries, persuading at least five thousand Hessian mercenaries to defect from the British side and join the

German-speaking community. After the War, Germans moved west to the newly opened farmlands in western Pennsylvania, Ohio, and, later, Indiana and Illinois.

Pennsylvania was a bilingual state immediately after the Revolution, and German language newspapers were being printed in New York, Philadelphia, and Boston, but by 1815 the vast majority of colonial Germans had merged, linguistically and culturally, into Anglo-American society. Only members of strict, traditionalist religious sects such as the Amish and Old Order Mennonites have continued to use the old language in their self-imposed isolation.

It is this minority which has maintained Pennsylvania German as a distinct dialect for over two hundred years. Pennsylvania German is an archaic dialect, based on the variety spoken in the settlers' home Rhineland province, with considerable influence from English. It is not the language spoken by nineteenth- and twentieth-century German immigrants. In the late nineteenth century Pennsylvania German may have been spoken by as many as 750,000 people; today some knowledge of the language is reported by over 300,000 people, two-thirds of them in southeast Pennsylvania.

German immigration resumed after 1815 and continued throughout the nineteenth century. Crop failures, overpopulation, war, and political and ethnic oppression all contributed to swell the tide. Between 1819 and 1840 only Irish immigrants were more numerous than the German speakers from the German states, the Austro-Hungarian Empire, Luxembourg, Switzerland, Poland, and Russia. Unsuccessful republican revolts in 1830 and 1848 brought large numbers of intellectuals and professionals eager to set up German culture in the New World. In the face of anti-foreigner feelings in the 1830s and 1840s, Germans withdrew further into their own language community; German press and education flourished. Throughout the decades after the Civil War Germans far outnumbered all other immigrant groups, making up no less than 25 percent of all newcomers and reaching a high of 41 percent of the total in the decade of the 1860s.

By the end of the nineteenth century, large German language islands existed in rural areas of the Midwest from Michigan and Minnesota to Texas. German-speaking districts had arisen in major cities all across the country and were particularly large in St. Louis, Baltimore, New York, Chicago, Milwaukee, Philadelphia, and Cincinnati (see Figure 7). Although they spoke a plethora of dialects, the Germans adhered to a common literary language; of eight hundred or

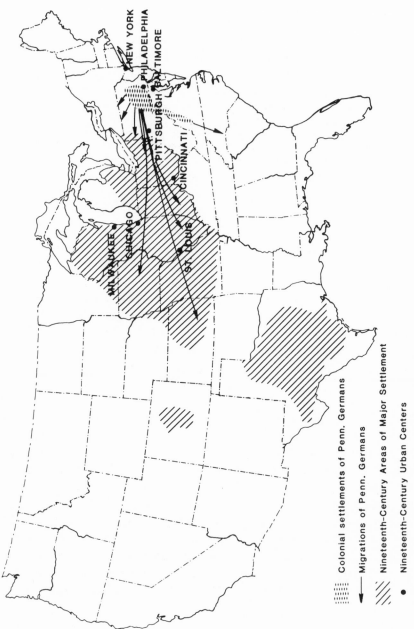

FIGURE 7. German-American Settlements to 1900

Colonial settlements of Penn. Germans

Migrations of Penn. Germans

Nineteenth-Century Areas of Major Settlement

Nineteenth-Century Urban Centers

so German language periodicals, several newspapers enjoyed nation-wide circulation. A resurgence of anti-immigration sentiment put pressure on private as well as public schools to use English as the language of instruction, but education in German continued up to World War I. German-only and bilingual public schools could be found in all the Midwestern states, in Oregon, Colorado, and else-where. In 1900 German speakers were the largest foreign-born population in eight of the ten largest American cities and in twenty-six of the forty-five states. In spite of religious and political differences which still hampered unification of the German states in Europe, German speakers in the United States had come to think of themselves as a distinct nationality.

In the years preceding World War I German Americans drew to-gether as a political bloc, lobbying to keep the United States neutral. With U.S. entrance into the War, anti-German backlash swept the country, directed not only against ethnic political figures but against ethnic maintenance itself. Scores of restrictive language laws were passed, eliminating German in public and even private schools and severely damaging the foreign language press.

While much of this legislation was eventually declared unconstitu-tional, the anti-German fervor had done its work. German Americans opted for assimilation rather than ostracism. During the Great Depression, economic hardship accelerated assimilation by making separate institutions too costly. German schools, churches, and children were Anglicized and eventually fully Americanized. The 1940 U.S. Census testifies to the speed with which German Americans reversed their attitudes about language maintenance. While 1.6 million foreign-born and 2.4 million second-generation Americans gave German as their mother tongue, only 900,000 third- and later-generation Americans claimed German as the language of their childhood.

German speakers who arrived in the United States as refugees from Nazism in the 1930s and 1940s had little reason to want to main-tain the German language or culture. In the twentieth century German-speaking immigrants have been primarily urban rather than rural. Many are professionals and assimilate readily. Chicago has at-tracted the greatest numbers; in 1960, 10 percent of Chicagoans spoke German.

Significant German-speaking communities still do survive in both rural and urban America. In addition to the Pennsylvania German speakers, enclaves of descendants of nineteenth-century immigrants continue some use of their mother tongue in Texas, Minnesota, Wisconsin, Kansas, and in lesser numbers throughout the Midwest. Most of these people are bilingual in English. German can be heard in almost any major urban area, both from recent immigrants and from remnants of the earlier German-speaking communities. In 1961 German language publications were printed in forty-four states.

Besides the British, the Germans are the only ethnic group to be represented in substantial numbers in all fifty states of the union. German has had some impact on spoken English, especially in Pennsylvania, where German words and translations from German have found widespread use.

CHAPTER 2

Immigrant Languages

IN THE MID-NINETEENTH CENTURY, speakers of colonial languages continued to immigrate, especially from Ireland and Germany. These western Europeans were joined by considerable numbers of Scandinavians. After 1880, however, southern and eastern Europe began to experience the industrialization and overpopulation that had displaced so many northern and western Europeans the generation before. Thus between 1880 and 1920 the greatest numbers of new Americans came from southern and eastern Europe. In general, these turn-of-the-century immigrants were illiterate peasants whose village societies and religious beliefs departed notably from those of the northern and western Europeans who preceded them to the United States. Also during this period immigration itself became an industry with headquarters in New York City, which thus served as the port of entry for nearly all the new immigrants. Many remained either there or in other Northern cities, where the greatest economic opportunities now lay. The new immigrants, then, faced an urban life without previous urban experience in an adopted country which espoused alien values. Quite naturally, many of them met this situation by maintaining close-knit ethnic neighborhoods in which their Old World language persisted for several generations. Southern and eastern Europeans were considered more foreign than and culturally inferior to their western European predecessors. Similarly, their languages were regarded as unfit for use by American citizens. Among the new European immigrants this attitude caused a profound ambivalence toward the home language.

Beginning at mid-century, Chinese men—and later Japanese and Filipinos—were imported as contract laborers. Anti-foreigner sentiment was stronger against these Asians than against Europeans. Perceived as unassimilable, resident Asians were denied U.S. citizenship and isolated in ghettos where they continued their own languages and cultures. Further immigration from Asia was prohibited by a series of racially motivated restrictions beginning in 1882 with the Chinese Exclusion Act.

Nativist attitudes toward Asians grew to encompass immigrants in general. As a result of burgeoning immigration after 1880, 15 percent of the total U.S. population in 1910 was foreign-born. Alarmed by this population boom and fearing the pollution of their language and values, native-born Americans radically restricted all immigration in the 1920s. Quotas based on national origin wholly excluded Asians and favored northwestern Europeans, who by then were immigrating in fewer numbers anyway. In fact, 65 percent of the total allotment was reserved for the British, Irish, and Germans. Since immigration from the Western Hemisphere remained unrestricted, new sources of labor were found in Mexico and the Caribbean.

The restrictive legislation drastically curtailed immigration by non-English speakers after 1920. During the 1920s and 1930s language maintenance efforts suffered gravely both from lack of reinforcement by new immigrants and from the nativist political climate. Except for special acts of Congress which admitted displaced persons and political refugees, this situation remained unchanged until 1965. Current legislation still limits total numbers of immigrants but without respect to national origin.

The history of immigrant language communities in the United States has been shaped by immigration trends and regulations in addition to social and economic factors affecting language maintenance. In many cities, sizable minority language communities have maintained themselves since the nineteenth century, particularly where they have been replenished by ongoing immigration. Large numbers, close-knit neighborhoods, strong ties to the homeland, and low social mobility all tend to favor retention of the ethnic tongue. These language communities are introduced below in the order of their major immigration.

SCANDINAVIAN LANGUAGES

The extreme overpopulation that drove thousands of Germans and Irish to American shores in the latter part of the nineteenth century precipitated massive emigration from Scandinavia as well. Though far smaller numerically than the German immigrant community, at times Scandinavian emigration was proportionately as large, reaching the rate of over 1 percent of the total population per annum at its peak. For Scandinavian immigrants the lure of land ownership was particularly strong, and they moved quickly through the Eastern states to the frontier land grant areas, creating whole communities in the familiar cold climate of the Upper Midwest.

Swedes and Norwegians clustered first in northern Illinois, then settled northern and western Wisconsin and Minnesota, and finally the Dakota territory, establishing farms in Iowa and Nebraska as well. Approximately 90 percent of all Scandinavian immigrants were Swedes and Norwegians, the former twice as numerous as the latter. The Danes also settled largely in the Upper Midwest but were not so rurally oriented and assimilated very rapidly to the English-speaking environment. The Finns followed yet a different pattern. Many settled in northern Michigan and Minnesota, but Finnish-speaking communities grew up in western Massachusetts and other parts of New England as well. Finns found jobs in industry, especially mining, in addition to agriculture.

By 1890, 900,000 Scandinavians resided in the United States, the vast majority in the Upper Mississippi Valley. One-fifth of them lived in Minnesota alone, where they constituted 15 percent of the state population.

In small numbers Scandinavians had played a role in American history since European contact began. Norse-speaking Vikings voyaging from Iceland were the first Europeans to visit the continent. The short-lived colony New Sweden attracted perhaps five hundred Swedish and a handful of Finnish farmers to the lower Delaware Valley in the eighteenth century. This tiny speech community managed to maintain the Swedish language for over one hundred years. A Swedish-English pidgin facilitated the transition to full Anglicization; by 1800 the colonial Scandinavians were no longer an identifiable ethnic group.

Swedish speakers in the United States did not reach their maximum numbers until 1930, when over 1.5 million Americans reported Swedish as their language. Although the major areas of Swedish settlement were established by 1890, new waves of immigrants arrived right up to World War I and again immediately thereafter. In 1910 Swedes constituted 1.5 percent of the U.S. population. Twentieth-century immigrants from Sweden often took up residence in urban areas, particularly those within traditionally Swedish districts such as Chicago. Swedish Americans were highly language retentive until the 1930s, when the number of speakers declined rapidly. The 1940 U.S. Census found only 831,000 Swedish speakers, 28 percent of whom were Minnesotans. In a study of a heavily Swedish township carried out in the late 1960s, over half of the Swedish Americans over fifty years of age spoke the language fluently while none under thirty could speak more than a few words.

Norwegian immigration peaked in the 1880s, when 3 percent of Norway's population emigrated to the United States, and again in the 1900s. A total of 750,000 came to America. Norwegian Americans remained overwhelmingly rural, pioneering the prairies and later the valleys of the Pacific Northwest. The first European settlers in the northern Rocky Mountains came from the mountain provinces of Norway. Twentieth-century Norwegians also established a community in Brooklyn. Like the Swedes, the Norwegians set up parochial schools taught in the native tongue. Their attempts at language maintenance were not quite as successful institutionally, although the language flourished into the twentieth century. By 1917, 83 percent of the instruction in Norwegian schools took place in English. Only a handful of Norwegian language church services were heard after 1930.

Finnish Americans are the most language retentive of the Scandinavians. Perhaps because they speak a language unrelated to other Scandinavian languages or to European languages in general, Finns assimilated at a slower rate, despite their smaller numbers. Finnish is spoken today in northern Michigan, Wisconsin, and Minnesota.

Like other Scandinavians, Finns were attracted by recruiters from American land and transport companies, who blanketed northern Europe with descriptions of the fine farm and forest land available in the United States. Many, too, followed relatives and friends whose letters home reported glowingly on life in the new land. The high literacy rate in Scandinavia and especially in Finland not only encouraged immigration but enabled newcomers to locate their friends and settle near them in compact communities. Thus for all Scandinavian groups regional dialects were maintained until the languages were supplanted by English.

Since 1890 approximately 2.5 million Scandinavians have settled in the United States. Today at least 660,000 Americans come from Scandinavian-speaking homes. In heavily Scandinavian areas even English speakers retain the hallmarks of their linguistic heritage in vocabulary and often in accent and intonation.

CHINESE

The experience of the first immigrants from Asia contrasts starkly with that of the highly-sought-after northern Europeans. Radically different from the emerging Anglicized majority in culture, language, and physical appearance, Chinese laborers were employed where needed but were forbidden to participate fully in American life.

Recruitment teams organized in part by established Chinese merchants brought 300,000 Chinese workers to California in the boom years following the discovery of gold in 1848. They came almost exclusively from war- and famine-ridden Kwangtung (Canton) province in the south of China. Like so many colonial immigrants from Europe, they were indentured—committed to a number of years' labor as return payment for their passage. Only rarely were women permitted to accompany their husbands; individual workmen supported entire extended families who remained in China. They found jobs where European men were loathe to work—kitchen and laundry service, scorned as women's work, and the grueling hand labor in agriculture and road- and rail-building. Though most Chinese lived in California, Chinatowns sprang up along the construction lines all over the West.

By the 1870s boom was turning to bust on the West Coast, and the tide of opinion began to turn against the Chinese. California nativists promoted anti-Chinese riots through the 1870s, and they spread wherever Chinese had settled. Further hatred was fomented against indentured Chinese when they were shipped all over the country to serve as strikebreakers. Most Western states passed racist legislation barring Chinese from certain occupations, from land ownership, and from bringing their wives and families to the United States. Although it was found unconstitutional by the Supreme Court, Congress solved the "Chinese Problem" in 1882 with the Chinese Exclusion Act. Renewed and kept in force into the twentieth century, the Act prohibited new immigration from China as well as immigration of the families of resident Chinese. A subsequent act forbade reentry of Chinese Americans who went abroad to visit their families. The 150,000 Chinese men still in the United States were compelled to choose between a life of exile and loneliness and return to starvation conditions in China. Well into the twentieth century the ratio of Chinese American men to women was over one thousand to one. Chinatowns were filled with aging Chinese workmen. By 1920 their population was reduced to 61,000.

The national origin quotas in the 1924 immigration law maintained the ban on Chinese immigration. As a "reward" for serving as our allies against Japan in World War II, a token 106 immigrants per year were permitted starting in 1943, and the ban on Chinese wives was lifted. The 1965 reform of the immigration law eliminated racist restrictions and opened the way for the recent influx of Chinese. In 1970 alone, 10,000 Chinese speakers immigrated to the United States. Over half of these chose to reside in the established Chinese communities of California.

The Chinese have proved among the most language retentive of all Americans. Ostracism, strong emphasis on family ties, and the extreme distance between Asian language and culture and Anglo-American norms have hindered assimilation. The majority of Chinese Americans come from southern China and speak Cantonese. Since 1965, however, many Hong Kong and Taiwan Chinese have entered the United States. These people speak Mandarin, the literary language of China, and have little in common with the Cantonese. They are often professionals rather than unskilled laborers and rarely choose to live in Chinatowns. In Boston, for instance, only 25 percent of Chinese lived in Chinatown in 1970, down from 80 percent in 1950. Still, three-fourths of Boston's Chinese were reported to speak little or no English.

BASQUE AND PORTUGUESE

Two groups of southwestern Europeans joined the Chinese in helping to settle the American West. In the 1850s Basques, whose homeland lies on the border between Spain and France and who speak a language unrelated to any other, responded to the Gold Rush. After the Civil War, nearly all 15,000 of them went as sheep herders to Idaho, Oregon, and Nevada, where they remain today. Strong ties to their homeland have aided the Basques in maintaining their language.

More numerous were the Portuguese, who began to appear in the San Francisco Bay area in the 1850s. From there they spread out into the San Joacquin and San Leandro Valleys, where they prospered as fruit and dairy farmers, or to San Diego, where they took up tuna fishing. In 1944 most Portuguese Americans in California, according to one report, still spoke Portuguese. A colony of Portuguese in Hawaii entered manufacturing and cattle ranching.

At the beginning of the nineteenth century, Portuguese speakers from the Azores had begun arriving in the whaling towns of Massachusetts and Rhode Island, especially New Bedford. When the whaling industry faltered later in the century, they worked in farming, fishing, and textile manufacturing. Cape Verdeans, of mixed African and Portuguese language and descent, often had to resort to the despised occupation of harvesting cranberries. The low education and literacy levels of many New England Portuguese Americans, in addition to continued immigration from Portugal and the Azores, have helped maintain a sizable community of Portuguese speakers. As of 1976, 489,000 U.S. residents claimed a Portuguese language background, and about half of these were native-born Americans.

ITALIAN

Among the southern and eastern European immigrants who began arriving after 1880, the greatest number, as many as four million, came from Italy. The few northern Italians who settled in the United States mainly arrived before 1890 with the groups of immigrants from northwestern Europe. By the turn of the century many of them were assimilated and prospering in their new country.

But after 1890 the great majority of Italian immigrants had been born in the farming villages of southern Italy. During the peak years of Italian emigration just before 1914, most southern provinces lost 2 to 3 percent of their population each year. Poverty, overpopulation, cholera epidemics, and poor markets for Italian wine and citrus caused this mass exodus. A few of these southern Italian peasants found agricultural work in the American South, where they were seriously mistreated, but most looked for jobs in Northern cities. Hence, 75 percent of them settled in the urban areas of New York, New Jersey, Pennsylvania, and New England, although some others moved to Detroit, Chicago, New Orleans, Denver, and San Francisco.

Italian Americans clustered in occupations which promoted group cohesion and language maintenance: construction, heavy industry, railroads, and mining. Some owned small businesses and restaurants; others established virtual monopolies of the produce business in such cities as New York and New Orleans. Those who went west sometimes became truck farmers. Most successful were those who owned California vineyards or fruit orchards. Many Italian American women worked at home, where they had no need to learn English.

Several other circumstances slowed the linguistic and cultural assimilation of southern Italians. First, more than a million Italians—almost all male—stayed in the United States only long enough to accumulate savings before returning to Italy. These temporary residents had little reason to learn American ways. Second, strong village and family loyalties, combined with fervent anti-Italian sentiment among Anglo-Americans, kept those who remained in this country in ethnic enclaves. Sometimes a whole village would resettle in the same neighborhood of an American city, preserving its distinct Calabrian, Abruzzian, or Sicilian dialect. Particularly among first- and second-generation Italian Americans, Italian continued to be spoken at home. Finally, the large size of the Italian American community and continued immigration from Italy have reinforced use of the native tongue. In 1976 about three million Americans claimed an Italian language background, making it our nation's third largest language community.

Still, most second- and third-generation Italian Americans did learn English, partly because so many of them attended English-oriented public schools, partly because the English-speaking Irish dominated the Catholic Church hierarchy. Seeking social mobility more often through property and business ownership than through formal education and the professions, Italian Americans maintained close contact with their ethnic community. The English they learned was most often identified with the working class, to which the majority belonged. In such cities as New York and Boston, Italian Americans apparently also influenced the pronunciation of working-class speech.

YIDDISH

Next to the Italians, eastern European Jews from White Russia, the Ukraine, Lithuania, Poland, Galicia in Austria-Hungary, and Romania comprised the second largest population to reach America during the massive late nineteenth-century immigration. Three-quarters of these two million Jews came from the czarist regions of Russia and Poland to escape the harsh anti-Semitism of the pogroms. Like southern Italians, the Jews settled in the big cities of the Northeast but, unlike their Italian neighbors, they often rose rapidly out of their initial poverty. Their upward mobility within the dominant culture resulted from the urban and commercial experience that many brought with them to the United States and from the traditional Jewish emphasis on education. Immigrant Jews worked in the garment, toy, cigar, or printing industries and functioned as peddlers or shopkeepers; but 75 percent of their children typically gained middle-class status as retailers, accountants, or professionals.

Although easily the largest group, eastern European Jews who arrived after 1880 were by no means the first Jewish Americans. As early as the seventeenth century a few Sephardic Jews, who spoke Judeo-Spanish (also called Dzhudezmo or Ladino) and came originally from Spain and Portugal, established themselves in New York, Philadelphia, Charleston, and Savannah as wealthy merchants and shippers. By 1750, however, this small group of Sephardim was outnumbered by German Jews, who also began settling as shopkeepers in Eastern cities. In the mid-nineteenth century some of these German Jews started the ready-to-wear garment industry. Others participated in the move westward, acting as traveling merchants or opening shops in Western towns. Perhaps the most famous of these frontier Jews was Levi Strauss, who invented the denims that still bear his name.

Another sizable group of Jews entered the United States as refugees after World War II. About 72,000 German and eastern European Jews who survived the Holocaust found sanctuary in this country under the refugee legislation enacted in 1948.

The language shared by most of the German and eastern European Jews—although not by the Sephardim—is Yiddish, originally a dialect of middle High German spoken by Ashkenazic Jews who settled in the Rhine basin during the eleventh century. From the thirteenth century onward the Ashkenazim moved east through present-day Germany, Austria, Czechoslovakia, and Hungary to Poland, Romania, and the Soviet Union. The Yiddish of the Ashkenazim developed at least four regional dialects but in general combined approximately 70 percent German with 20 percent Hebrew and Aramaic and 10 percent Slavic vocabulary. Many eastern European Jewish peasants spoke only Yiddish; those who interacted more with the dominant culture often spoke both Yiddish and the dominant language. A few wealthy Ashkenazim spoke only the language of their adopted country, particularly in Russia. Thus eastern European Jewish immigrants to the United States were overwhelmingly Yiddish-speaking, but some spoke other eastern European languages as well.

Between 1880 and 1920 Yiddish flourished in this country through a strong Yiddish press, Yiddish theatre, and the teaching of Yiddish in some secular schools. But since then several factors have militated against the maintenance of a large Yiddish-speaking community in the United States. In the first place, few Jews who settled in the United States had any intention of returning to Europe and so had little incentive to retain a European language. Even more important, their rapid entry into English-dominated professions required them to learn English quickly. Moreover, because their religion and traditions linked them to their ethnicity, many Jews felt no need to retain Yiddish as an additional sign of ethnic solidarity. Also, the stature of Yiddish suffered when Israel adopted Hebrew as its national language. Today most Jewish immigrants speak Hebrew or an eastern European language rather than Yiddish, leaving the American Yiddish-speaking community unreplenished.

Consequently, between 1940 and 1960 the number of Yiddish speakers in the United States declined by 45 percent, although Yiddish can still be heard in a few areas like the Hasidic section of Brooklyn. According to one estimate, about one-quarter of today's six million Jewish Americans can understand some Yiddish, but only about 13 percent claim a Yiddish language background.

Yet, even if Yiddish is destined to disappear from the inventory of American languages, it has left a distinct mark on American English. The pronunciation, inflections, and word order of the speech of New York City and other large metropolitan areas have been influenced by Yiddish. And, probably because of the high visibility of Jews in the media, many Yiddish words have come into our general vocabulary.

SLAVIC AND OTHER EASTERN EUROPEAN LANGUAGES

During the same years that eastern European Jews were emigrating, at least three million Gentiles from eastern Europe also sought a new life in the United States. By far the greatest number of them were Polish. But their ranks included Bulgarians; Czechs and Slovaks from present-day Czechoslovakia; Russians and Ukrainians from what would become the Soviet Union; and Serbs, Croatians, Slovenians, Macedonians, and Montenegrins from what is now Yugoslavia. Table 2 reveals where the major Slavic groups settled and how many mother-tongue claimants each group had in 1970.

Joining in this emigration were non-Slavic eastern Europeans: Romanians, who use a Romance language descended from Latin; Hungarians, who brought their language to Europe from Siberia in the ninth century; Estonians, whose language is related to Finnish; Latvians and Lithuanians, who speak Baltic languages; and Romanies (or gypsies), whose language traces its roots to northern India.

Like others who immigrated between 1880 and 1920, these eastern Europeans tended to settle in the cities of the industrial North, stretching in an arc from Connecticut to Minnesota. Even less likely than southern Italians to arrive as professionals or skilled workers, the vast majority found jobs in heavy industry, where some knowledge of English was mandatory for both communication and safety reasons. Some industrialists, most notably Henry Ford, set up English language programs for their immigrant employees. Thus first-generation men from eastern Europe often acquired at least a rudimentary command of English.

A few Polish American families had been in the United States since the colonial era. But most arrived at the turn of the century. Similar in several ways to the southern Italians, these Poles came from a Catholic peasant society and had little formal education. Although a few eventually farmed onions and tobacco in Massachusetts, many more gravitated to meat packing, mining, steel mills, and automobile factories. And more than half of this overwhelmingly male group returned to their homeland once they had saved enough money to buy a small plot of land there. Again like the Italians, Poles established large ethnic enclaves in big cities such as Chicago and Detroit. Social mobility tended to occur within the ethnic community—through real estate ownership, for instance—rather than through English-dominated channels, and the home language could therefore be preserved for several generations. Until lately, Polish Americans were slightly more language retentive than Italian Americans, partly because they established parochial schools and the Polish National Church, which both support the maintenance of the Polish language. By 1976, however, Polish language retention had plummeted due to the dramatic rise in Polish American upward mobility and the virtual absence of ongoing immigration.

Most other eastern Europeans came from similar societies and in-

T A B L E 2. Major Slavic Groups in the United States

Group	Main Settlement Regions	Language	Mother-Tongue Claimants (1970 U.S. Census)
Poles	Chicago, New York City, Detroit, Milwaukee, Pittsburgh, Buffalo, Cleveland	Polish	2,437,000
Czechoslovakians			
Slovaks	Pittsburgh area, Illinois, New York, Ohio, New Jersey	Slovak	510,366
Czechs	Chicago, Cleveland, New York City	Czech	452,812
Russians	New York, Pennsylvania, Alaska	Russian	334,615*
Ukrainians	Pennsylvania, New England, Chicago	Ukrainian	249,000
Yugoslavs			
Croatians	Chicago, Pittsburgh, Milwaukee, New York City after 1945		
Serbs	Chicago, Detroit, Pennsylvania, Ohio, Milwaukee	Serbo-Croatian	239,000
Slovenes	Cleveland, Milwaukee, Chicago, Joliet (Ill.), Pennsylvania	Slovenian	82,000

*95% of Russian-speaking emigrants represented ethnic minority elements of the Russian population, primarily Jews.

itially displayed the same settlement and employment profile as the Poles. As the largest language communities, however, Poles and Slovaks tended to preserve their native tongues longer than other eastern European groups, which more often sought mobility within the mainstream culture.

Czechs departed somewhat from the typical patterns of immigration and assimilation for Slavic peoples. They began arriving in this country earlier—about 1860—and by 1910 almost one-third of them had gone into agriculture on land grants in the Mississippi Valley, Nebraska, and Texas. Moreover, in the decade before 1910, 25 percent of Czechs came as professionals or skilled workers, as compared with 3 to 9 percent for other Slavic peoples. Czech free thinkers established secular schools which helped preserve the Czech language.

Among some eastern European groups, the major influx of immigrants between 1880 and 1920 has been augmented by the arrival of refugees from the same language community since World War II. After 1948, the United States offered asylum to over 160,000 Polish displaced persons. And in the decade following 1948 at least 80,000 Ukrainian refugees swelled the ranks of Ukrainian Americans who had arrived before World War I. Unlike their predecessors, however, these Slavic refugees tended to be urban, nationalistic, well-educated, and professional or semi-professional. The Ukrainian newcomers set up secular schools and organizations in which the literary language, rather than the folk language spoken by the earlier immigrants, was transmitted. Yet their arrival infused new life into the language maintenance efforts of Ukrainian Orthodox churches. In fact, these post-World War II immigrants now take most of the responsibility for language retention in the Ukrainian American community. Lithuanian refugees and, even more recently, Soviet Jews and political dissidents and 500,000 Romanian Christians have similarly enhanced the Lithuanian, Russian, and Romanian language communities.

Hungarian Americans have also been reinforced by post-War refugees from their homeland. The United States welcomed 16,000 Hungarian displaced persons from 1948 to 1952 and 42,000 Hungarian freedom fighters in 1956. Like the Ukrainian refugees, these recent Hungarian immigrants were mainly urban and well-educated. But unlike the Ukrainians, many of them have wished to assimilate as quickly as possible to American culture and have therefore done little to stimulate Hungarian language maintenance, which has been declining since the 1920s. Even in Cleveland—the center of Hungarian culture in this country—language maintenance efforts are dwindling.

And the Catholic Church presently does almost nothing to preserve the home language of 447,000 Hungarian Americans.

GREEK

In large part, the Greek experience paralleled that of other turn-of-the-century immigrants from southern and eastern Europe. Mostly peasants, they left their farms because of overpopulation, a shrinking overseas currant market during the 1890s, and a crop failure during 1907. Although Greek immigration reached significant proportions after 1880, the greatest numbers arrived between 1905 and 1915, somewhat later than the Italians and eastern Europeans. By World War II an estimated 500,000 had settled in this country.

Like other immigrants during this period, many Greeks were channeled into the employment market by *padroni,* private labor agents who recruited workmen in the old country and delivered them to American employers. In the case of the Greeks, this system served to disperse the newcomers throughout the United States. They took industrial jobs in New England, Chicago, Detroit, and San Francisco. They worked on the railroads, ranches, mines, and mills of Colorado, Wyoming, Montana, Idaho, and California. In almost every major city they worked as street vendors, shoeblacks, and hat cleaners.

Their drive for independence, however, soon turned Greek Americans to the ownership of small businesses. As early as the 1920s they operated 2000 restaurants, 150 grocery stores, and numerous flower and candy shops in our nation's cities. These small businesses often functioned as important social centers where Greek language and culture were preserved. Many third-generation Greek Americans have gone into the professions.

Intense nationalism and respect for education led immigrant Greeks to set up day schools and afternoon classes so that their children could learn Greek. The Greek Orthodox Church also proved instrumental in early language maintenance efforts. But the pressures of assimilation and American nativism prompted most second- and third-generation Greek Americans to abandon the Greek language. A 1972 survey of Chicago area Greek Americans showed that in spite of significant recent immigration, only 16 percent used mainly Greek as their home language.

Yet, like Ukrainian, the Greek language in America has recently been revitalized by the arrival of 56,000 refugees from 1946 to 1960 and thousands more since then. In 1976, 542,000 Americans claimed a Greek language background. Since more than half of these were born in the United States, a large number of Greek speakers must be transmitting their language to their children.

NEAR EASTERN LANGUAGES

During the 1890s the Muslim Turks threatened to exterminate Near Eastern Christians, driving hundreds of thousands of Armenians, Syrians, and Lebanese away from their homelands. Between 1895, when the Turks began the "Armenian Massacre," and 1930, about 100,000 Armenians settled in New England, New York, Pennsylvania, Milwaukee, Detroit, Chicago, and California, where they initially took jobs in textile mills, shoe factories, foundries, packing houses, canneries, cement works, and on farms. Like eastern European Jews, many Armenians came with peasant backgrounds, but a significant number, again like the Jews, had commercial experience and soon owned small businesses. Oriented toward education and success, most Armenian Americans have assimilated rapidly to the dominant culture. Usually this has meant loss of the Armenian language by the second generation in spite of a very high level of language maintenance by the Armenian Orthodox Church. Today there are about 250,000 Armenian Americans.

Besides the Armenians, about 450,000 Syrians and Lebanese reached American shores beginning in the 1890s. These Arabic-speaking Christians, like the Greeks, were often recruited by *padroni* to peddle notions and dry goods, but many preferred factory and railroad work. Eventually, they became owners of wholesale and retail businesses and large trucking, clothing, amusement, and food enterprises. Today sizable Syrian and Lebanese communities thrive in New England, New York, Pennsylvania, Michigan, and Ohio and in smaller numbers in cities throughout the country.

JAPANESE, PHILIPPINE, AND OTHER ASIAN LANGUAGES

When the United States annexed the Hawaiian Islands in 1898, the number of Asians in U.S. territory increased by over 50 percent. American businessmen had begun importing indentured laborers from East Asia at mid-century, making the ethnic Hawaiians a minority in 1900.

As on the mainland, peasant workmen from southern China were the first to be recruited. But by 1880 Japanese began to supply the core of the Hawaiian labor force. Unlike other Asian governments, Japan encouraged emigration, hoping to extend Japanese culture as well as establish overseas markets for Japanese goods. Thus the Japanese, unlike other Asians, brought their wives and families with them, expecting to establish permanent residence.

After 1882, when Chinese immigration was outlawed on the mainland, Japanese began to replace Chinese workers on the West Coast as well, especially in agriculture. In the five years after the United States annexed Hawaii, 60,000 Japanese moved from the islands to the mainland for better working opportunities. Centered particularly in the Los Angeles area, many Japanese families eventually were able to purchase land and businesses, handling a large share of California fruit and vegetable production and distribution. As their numbers increased, so did animosity from the Euro-American population. Anti-Asian agitation culminated once again in immigration restrictions. A 1906 treaty forced on Japan precluded immigration except for certain highly skilled workers and wives of Japanese Americans.

When World War II began, ethnic Japanese made up only 2 percent of the West Coast population, yet anti-Japanese hysteria was quickly rekindled. Presumed guilty of treasonous tendencies solely because of their ethnicity, 110,000 Japanese Americans were forcibly removed from their homes and lands and placed in internment camps in the interior. Even after enduring loss of freedom and property, most Japanese chose to remain in America after the War. Though many returned to California, significant numbers established themselves in Chicago, Minneapolis, Philadelphia, Denver, and Cleveland. Displaced from agriculture, Japanese Americans were compelled to seek new occupations. By tradition oriented toward education, they are now highly represented in professions and skilled trades. Wives of U.S. servicemen returning from the War were the first immigrants from Japan in forty years. Since immigration law reform in 1965, the Japanese American community has received moderate increases from abroad.

Unlike other Asian American groups, the Japanese American community consists overwhelmingly of second- and third-generation U.S. citizens. Thus Japanese language maintenance should be compared with that of turn-of-the-century immigrants from southern and eastern Europe rather than with Chinese, Koreans, or Filipinos. As of 1976, Japanese were apparently retaining their home language significantly more tenaciously than either Italians or Poles, even though they are a far smaller community. Almost half a million Americans reported a Japanese language background. Factors accounting for the high retention rate include racism and World War II-era incarceration, family-oriented culture and values, and the extreme dissimilarity between Japanese and English. The international importance of Japanese as a medium of communication in business, science, and technology contributes to language retention as well as to language study by young people no longer fluent in Japanese.

Just as Japanese laborers were sought as replacements for the excluded Chinese, Filipinos replaced Japanese as a cheap labor pool after Japanese immigration was restricted in 1906. The United States acquired the Philippine Islands in 1898 as part of the settlement following the Spanish-American War. Within ten years Filipino peasants made up a significant portion of the Hawaiian plantation labor force, and in the 1920s they found places in agriculture and service jobs all along the West Coast and in canning in the Northwest and Alaska. As U.S. nationals, Filipinos were the only non-Western Hemisphere residents not restricted under the 1924 national origin quotas (see Table 3). Although Filipinos were not permitted to bring their families to the United States, and few intended permanent settlement, anti-Asian sentiment once more emerged as their community

T A B L E 3. Primary Asian Immigrant Groups Prior to 1975

		NUMBERS OF IMMIGRANTS		
ORIGIN	LANGUAGES	*1924–34*	*1960*	*1974*
China, Taiwan, Hong Kong	Cantonese; recently also Mandarin Chinese	Excluded	4,156	22,684
Japan	Japanese	Excluded	5,471	4,860
Philippines	Early immigrants: Ilocano, Bisaya, Cebuano; recently: Tagalog	45,000	2,954	32,857
Korea	Korean	Excluded	1,507	28,028
India, Pakistan, Bangladesh, Sri Lanka	Early immigrants: Gujarati, Punjabi, Bengali; recently: Hindi-Urdu, some bilingual in English	Excluded	391	12,779

grew. In 1934 the United States restricted immigration to the mainland, though leaving Hawaiian growers free to import Filipino labor.

After World War II the character of Philippine immigration changed. In 1946 the United States granted independence to the Philippine Islands, and only a small number of Filipinos—mostly wives of U.S. servicemen—could continue to qualify for entrance under the national origin quotas. When the Immigration and Naturalization Service dropped its ethnic discriminations in 1965, Filipinos began arriving in renewed numbers. Now, however, most are professional people seeking greater opportunities in the United States. Filipinos are particularly visible in the health professions, and significant Filipino communities can be found in Chicago, Detroit, Philadelphia, and New York in addition to the West Coast.

While pre-War immigrants primarily spoke regional languages such as Ilocano and Bisaya, Filipinos arriving since 1965 are overwhelmingly speakers of Tagalog (Filipino), the national language of the Philippines and the regional language of the Manila area. Many also come with considerable command of English. In 1976, of the estimated 522,000 speakers of Philippine languages in the United States, only 30 percent were native-born Americans. It remains to be seen how many Philippine Americans will pass their languages on to their American-born offspring.

After 1900 a small community of Korean workers and their families was established in Hawaii. But immigration from Korea ceased in 1910 when it was annexed by Japan and fell under the restrictions on Japanese immigration. Korean immigration to the mainland United States did not begin on a major scale until the late 1960s. Since then large numbers of South Koreans, especially educated and professional people dissatisfied with the policies and opportunities in their homeland, have applied for admittance. By 1974 South Korea ranked third behind Mexico and the Philippines in number of immigrants to America (see Table 3). About 20 percent of all Korean immigrants settle in California, especially Los Angeles. A 1973 survey of the Los Angeles Korean community estimated that 40 percent knew no English, while 10 percent were fully fluent.

Far fewer in number but sharing a similar immigration history are Americans from South Asia—the area now India, Pakistan, Bangladesh, and Sri Lanka. Between 1900 and 1917 perhaps five thousand East Indian workmen were imported to the West Coast, most for lumbering and canning. They too faced racist attacks, and the U.S.

government again responded to nativist pressures by excluding them. By 1930 the East Indian population in the United States had dwindled to 2500. Recently, immigration from South Asia has begun again. The number arriving in 1974 alone (see Table 3) nearly equaled the 13,000 total U.S. population of East Indian ancestry found in the 1970 Census. The largest South Asian center in the United States is now New York City.

A large number of languages belonging to several unrelated language families are spoken on the South Asian subcontinent. Many early immigrants to the United States spoke varieties of Gujarati, Bengali, and Punjabi. Recent immigrants speak the languages of the major urban centers—especially Hindi or Urdu, the mutually intelligible national languages of India and Pakistan, respectively. Many of the newer East Indian immigrants are highly educated people, schooled in English as well as their native tongues.

Since World War II, when the United States added a number of Pacific islands to its list of territories, Malayo-Polynesian peoples have joined the Hawaiian Asian population. Samoans are the most numerous. Many of them speak their own version of Pidgin English, using Samoan forms where other ethnicities use Japanese, Ilocano, Cantonese, or another Asian language in a structured mix with English.

NEW LANGUAGE COMMUNITIES

In spite of restrictive immigration policies, the United States in the late twentieth century remains a highly multi-ethnic nation. As the United States assumed political and economic leadership as a world power, it began—often reluctantly—to assume the responsibilities as well. Open immigration from Western Hemisphere countries was permitted under the 1924 statutes, providing a new source of cheap labor from Mexico and the Caribbean. Northwestern Europeans, favored under the national origin quotas, continued to join those ethnic communities already well established in the United States. Though three-quarters of a million refugees were admitted in the post-World War II period, racially discriminatory policies were maintained until 1965.

Under current legislation priority is still given to persons with close relatives in the United States. On the one hand, this policy encourages immigration by nationalities which have traditionally supplied large numbers of American immigrants. Ireland, for example, was still the fourth largest source of new residents in 1973. On the other hand, it benefits the large numbers of Asian Americans long denied the right to bring their families to the United States. As a result of American political involvement in East Asia, the number of Asian immigrants swelled so dramatically that they constituted a third of all newcomers in the mid-1970s. And, for the first time in American history, over half of all immigrants were female.

Economic and political upheavals continue to be the primary factors precipitating emigration. Turmoil in the Near East has encouraged two million Arabs to seek residence in the United States. Chaldean Christians—Arabic speakers from Iran and Turkey—have established communities in Detroit, Jacksonville (Florida), and Washington, D.C. They appear to be assimilating quickly: 70 percent are bilingual in English; 80 percent occupy professional and managerial positions. Even more recent are Muslim Arabs: Lebanese, Syrians, Yemenis, and displaced Palestinians. Detroit's established Arabic-speaking community attracts the largest number, even though many are forced to take low-paying or temporary employment. Some have established their families in the United States, but the number who have learned English remains small.

For the thousands of refugees from Southeast Asia, return to the homeland is an impossibility. The first of these immigrants were ethnic Vietnamese—many educated and some already bilingual in English—who chose to follow the Americans out of Vietnam in 1975. Others did not leave voluntarily. Vietnam began expelling residents of Chinese ancestry in 1977. The Chinese had lived in Indochina for centuries, often owning small shops. Many of them were the "boat people" who arrived at refugee camps both ill and destitute. Rural villagers, too, joined the flood of exiles. Among these were a significant number of Hmong and Mien, who are culturally and ethnically distinct from the ruling Vietnamese. Speaking their own languages rather than the better-known national languages, often illiterate in any, and entirely unfamiliar with urban life, these rural minorities have little in common with the major Southeast Asian national groups and find American life totally alien. Other refugees include Cambodians, Laotians, and minority peoples from those countries—all ethnically unique and frequently encountering Western culture for the first time.

In the seven years following the Vietnam War, the United States accepted over 600,000 Southeast Asians. Though California is the locus of their largest communities, Southeast Asians have been settled in all parts of the country. Except for the Chinese among them, these peoples are the first of their ethnicities to enter the United States and thus lack the bridge that settled fellow countrymen provided for other twentieth-century immigrants. Southeast Asians must therefore depend largely on the public schools for instruction and acculturation and must directly confront the English-speaking world.

CURRENT STATUS OF MINORITY LANGUAGES

For the first time in over half a century, the United States in the 1980s is once again experiencing massive immigration. In addition to the 290,000 immigrants annually permitted by current legislation, the United States pledged to absorb 200,000 Indochinese refugees in 1980 alone. In 1979, 555,000 new residents, overwhelmingly non-English speakers, settled in this country—the highest number since the peak immigration years of the early twentieth century.

Table 4 summarizes the status of the largest American minority language communities as of 1976. The table displays the breakdown for the more than 15 million Americans over the age of four who report active use of a non-English language. It also shows how many of these persons usually speak their ethnic tongue rather than English and how many employ the ethnic tongue only as a secondary language. The column labeled "Difficulty with English" indicates what percentage of those who usually use the ethnic language speak English not well or not at all. Predictably, the three long-established, northern European communities—Germans, French, and Poles—are most likely to use their ethnic tongue only as a secondary language and least likely to report any difficulty with English. By contrast, most Korean speakers have come to the United States in the last twenty years. Over half of them report using English as a secondary language, and almost three-quarters of these report limited English proficiency. Half of all Americans reporting non-English language use are Spanish speakers. Although almost three-quarters of Spanish speakers were born in the United States, half retain Spanish as their primary language.

Preliminary reports from the 1980 U.S. Census indicate that these trends continue. Of all respondents reporting a non-English home language, 49 percent speak Spanish. However, a larger proportion of

T A B L E 4. Status of Minority Languages, 1976

Language Spoken	Total Non-English Speakers 4 and Over*	Non-English Language Usual Number	Non-English Language Usual Difficulty with English	Non-English Language Secondary
All non-English languages	15,354,000	6,389,000	42.1%	8,965,000
Spanish	7,755,000	3,848,000	46.3%	3,906,000
Italian	1,196,000	374,000	43.6%	822,000
French	874,000	229,000	23.1%	645,000
German	844,000	150,000	10.7%	694,000
Polish	544,000	135,000	34.1%	408,000
Chinese	432,000	245,000	45.7%	187,000
Greek	343,000	139,000	38.1%	204,000
Filipino	315,000	129,000	17.8%	186,000
Portuguese	307,000	157,000	53.5%	150,000
Japanese	233,000	89,000	62.9%	145,000
Korean	127,000	73,000	72.6%	54,000
Other	2,384,000	821,000	30.7%	1,564,000

* As distinct from the larger figures for those who report a non-English language background but may no longer actively use their other language.

Source: U.S. Department of Health, Education, and Welfare Survey of Income and Education 1976.

the Spanish speakers are school-aged children. Of the adult non-English speakers, 44 percent report Spanish while 65 percent of non-English speakers in the five to seventeen age range are Hispanics.

Today's minority language communities must be located both by region of the country and by neighborhood in major urban areas. Figure 8 shows the distribution of non-English communities in the five regions of the United States. The Northeast and Southwest, approximately equal in numbers of residents with non-English native tongues, demonstrate the contrasts resulting from historical developments most clearly. In the Southwest, which is the region with the largest proportion of non-English speakers in its population, almost two-thirds are Spanish-speaking. In the Northeast, the major waves of European immigration are still reflected in language distribution, accounting for 60 percent of the total non-English-speaking population. In the Southeast and North Central regions, European immigrant languages likewise make up half or more of the total. As settlement history would predict, French looms large among the major immigrant tongues in the Southeast, and German predominates in the North Central states. The two Western regions have substantial Asian language communities. In all regions Spanish speakers constitute a significant portion of the non-English-speaking population, nowhere falling below 15 percent. German is the second most widely distributed language, reaching 5 percent even in the Southwest.

Within regions minority language communities are by no means evenly distributed. In urban areas the newest immigrants, who still use the native tongue, often cluster in compact inner city neighborhoods and have minimal contact with outside language groups. Older immigrant groups, especially those that have assimilated linguistically, may be dispersed throughout the city and its suburbs. Detroit, a major industrial center in the North Central region, illustrates community maintenance. Figure 9 locates neighborhoods consisting of 50 percent or more of the designated ethnicity or set of ethnicities in Detroit and its inner suburbs. Undesignated areas may be mixed ethnicity or non-residential. Detroit attracted thousands of central, southern, and eastern European immigrants as the automobile industry developed early in this century. Though many no longer live in identifiably ethnic neighborhoods, those remaining in established working-class areas have maintained strong cultural identity and, often, their native tongue. This is especially true of Detroit's large Polish population. Some suburban areas, such as the large Jewish neighborhoods north of Detroit, remain ethnically cohesive but tend to be more assimilated

FIGURE 8. Percent of Major Non-English Native Tongues by Region, 1976

SOURCE: National Center for Education Statistics Bulletin 1978.

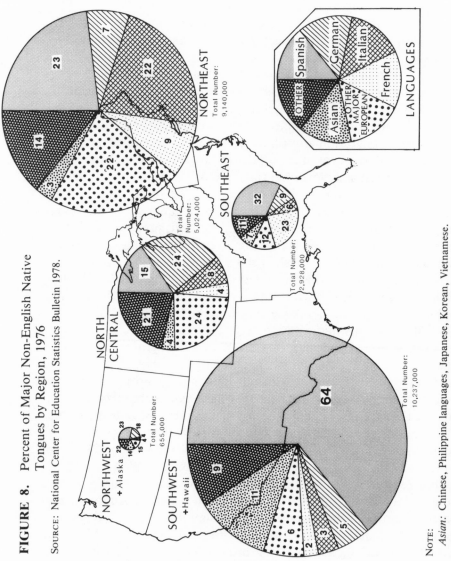

NOTE:

Asian: Chinese, Philippine languages, Japanese, Korean, Vietnamese.
Other major European: Greek, Polish, Russian, Scandinavian languages, Yiddish.
Other languages: smaller European and Asian language communities, American Indian languages, African languages, Near Eastern languages.

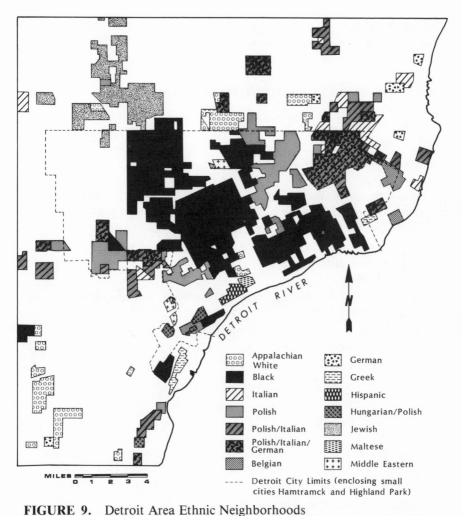

FIGURE 9. Detroit Area Ethnic Neighborhoods
Source: Bryan Thompson, Detroit Area Ethnic Groups 1971, Department of Geography, Wayne State University.

linguistically. Industrial expansion in the World War II era brought a large influx of workers from the American South. Both blacks and Appalachian whites brought their native varieties of English with them and continue to use them today, though they may employ standard English as well. Newcomers, such as Spanish speakers from Mexico and the American Southwest and Christian and Muslim Arabic speakers from the Middle East, congregate in inner city areas abandoned by older immigrants. With its patchwork of Anglicized and ethnic neighborhoods and its complex of languages and varieties, Detroit typifies what is most exciting and at the same time most problematic about the American linguistic scene.

FURTHER STUDY IN HISTORICAL DEMOGRAPHY

READINGS

General Ethnic Histories

DINNERSTEIN, LEONARD, ROGER L. NICHOLS, and DAVID M. REIMERS. *Natives and Strangers: Ethnic Groups and the Building of America.* New York: Oxford University Press, 1979.

GREELEY, ANDREW M., and WILLIAM C. MCCREADY. *Ethnicity in the United States: A Preliminary Reconnaissance.* New York: John Wiley and Sons, 1974.

JONES, MALDWYN ALLEN. *American Immigration.* Chicago: University of Chicago Press, 1960.

SELLER, MAXINE. *To Seek America: A History of Ethnic Life in the United States.* New York: Jerome S. Ozer, 1977.

TAYLOR, PHILIP. *The Distant Magnet: European Emigration to the U.S.A.* London: Eyre and Spottiswoode, 1971.

Specific Ethnic Groups

DRIVER, HAROLD E., and WILLIAM C. MASSEY. *Comparative Studies of North American Indians. Transactions of the American Philosophical Society,* n.s. 47 (1957), Part 2.

ECCLES, W. J. *France in America.* New York: Harper and Row, 1972.

FERNANDEZ-FLOREZ, DARIO. *The Spanish Heritage in the United States.* 3rd ed. Madrid: Publicaciones Españolas, 1971.

HASSELMO, NILS. *Amerikasvenska: En bok om språkutvecklingen i Svensk-Amerika.* Stockholm: Esselte Studium, 1974.
On Swedish speakers in America.

IORIZZO, LUCIANO J., and SALVATORE MONDELLO. *The Italian-Americans.* New York: Twayne Publishers, 1971.

"It's Your Turn in the Sun." *Time* (16 October 1978), 48–61.
On United States Hispanics.

LEARSI, RUFUS. *The Jews in America: A History.* New ed. New York: KTAV Publishing House, 1972.

LOPATA, HELENA ZNANIECKI. *Polish Americans: Status Competition in an Ethnic Community.* Englewood Cliffs, N.J.: Prentice-Hall, 1976.

LYMAN, STANFORD M. *Chinese Americans.* New York: Random House, 1974.

MEIER, MATT S., and FELICIANO RIVERA. *The Chicanos: A History of Mexican Americans.* New York: Hill and Wang, 1972.

MELENDY, H. BRETT. *Asians in America: Filipinos, Koreans, and East Indians.* Boston: Twayne Publishers, 1977.

SALOUTOS, THEODORE. *The Greeks in the United States.* Cambridge, Mass.: Harvard University Press, 1964.

SMITH-THIBODEAUX, JOHN. *Les Francophones de Louisiane.* Paris: Editions Entente, 1977.
On speakers of the several varieties of French in Louisiana.

WOLFORTH, SANDRA. *The Portuguese in America.* San Francisco: R & E Research Associates, 1978.

Language Data

FISHMAN, JOSHUA A., et al. *Language Loyalty in the United States: The Maintenance and Perpetuation of Non-English Mother Tongues by American Ethnic and Religious Groups.* The Hague: Mouton, 1966.

WAGGONER, DOROTHY. "Non-English Language Background Persons: Three U.S. Surveys." *TESOL Quarterly* 12 (1978): 247–62.

ACTIVITIES

1. Investigate language retention in your region. There may be valuable information on settlement history in your local library or historical society collection. You can also interview older residents about their experience of population change and language shift.

2. Try to determine the linguistic history of your area by studying regional maps for the ethnic derivation of place names, street names, and geographical features. Geographical features are most likely to be named in the language of the original residents. Pay particular attention to name changes, as these may indicate successive waves of settlement and community leadership.

3. Study language retention in your own family by interviewing family members about their language use and that of their parents and grandparents. Try to find out not only what languages they used but when they used them and how they felt about them. Family letters, diaries, and official documents may shed light on these questions.

PART II

The Rise of a Standard Language

As our countrymen are spreading westward across the continent, and are brought into contact with other races, and adopt new modes of thought, there is some danger that, in the use of their liberty, they may break loose from the laws of the English language. . . .

—William Fowler, *English Grammar,* 1887

CHAPTER 3

The Ascendancy of English

Such a variety of languages weaves through our history that the United States might plausibly have evolved into a strongly bilingual or multilingual society. In other countries with a history of linguistic diversity, more than one language has often gained widespread popular use and sometimes official acceptance. Switzerland, Paraguay, the Soviet Union, China, and Canada are prominent cases in point. The Soviet Union, for example, provides a political umbrella for over a hundred different ethnic homelands, each with its own language and culture. Although Russian serves as the official medium of communication, it is the first language of less than 60 percent of the Soviet population. A number of Soviet Republics conduct all their local activities in their non-Russian home languages. To cope with this complex language situation, the Soviet government supports education and literacy in its many regional languages while encouraging the use of Russian in national and international affairs.

Canada, where the national languages were brought by European settlers, appears to parallel the United States more closely than does the Soviet Union, where minority languages have been rooted in their home regions for centuries. Yet, unlike the United States, Canada is officially bilingual; that is, Canadians use both French and English in media, business, and government. Public education occurs in both languages, and bilingualism is required for a number of public service positions.

The United States, despite its complex linguistic heritage, little resembles the Soviet Union or Canada with respect to language use. Instead of adopting two or more languages in public life, this country is overwhelmingly monolingual. English is the language in which business and government are conducted; it is the major medium of instruction at every educational level; it is the vehicle for high culture and for technology. All three national television networks program in English. Lyrics of popular songs, film scripts, signs, labels, major newspapers and magazines all attest to the prevalence of English in every aspect of national life.

The situations of the Soviet Union and Canada demonstrate that political union does not necessarily produce the linguistic unity that characterizes the United States. Other social, political, and ideological factors must have contributed to the rise of English as the predominant language in the United States, whose citizens originally spoke such a variety of languages.

The chief social force explaining the persistent preeminence of the English language in the United States has to do simply with numbers of speakers. From the beginnings of European settlement in North America in the seventeenth century, England alone showed a decided interest in populating the New World. The French, Dutch, and Spanish governments valued the Western Hemisphere largely for its natural resources—furs and precious metals, in particular. Thus they tended to establish skeletal settlements with just enough colonists to facilitate the export of raw materials. England, on the other hand, actually wished to populate North America, partly to solve the problem of primogeniture—a system of inheritance in which first sons received all the family land, leaving other sons without property unless they emigrated. The British also saw that sizable American colonies would provide new markets for English trade and a labor force for cash crops. Unlike the other colonial powers, then, England actively encouraged its population to emigrate in significant numbers.

As a result of England's unique attitude toward settling the New World, the United States during the colonial and early national periods always had more English-speaking settlers than it had speakers of any other European language. As early as 1660, the North American population consisted of 70,000 in the English colonies, as compared with 5,000 Dutch in New Netherland, 3,000 French in

Canada, and an even smaller number of Spanish. By 1700 the English and African population of North America had grown to 250,000, while French and Spanish speakers totalled only 7,500. In 1790 the new nation could claim a white population that was 76 percent English-speaking. Even as late as 1860, 53 percent of the foreign-born in the United States came from the British Isles. In short, the early history of this country was that of a predominantly English-speaking people. The later massive immigration by non-English speakers could never seriously encroach on the English language tradition, which, by the mid-nineteenth century, had been long and firmly established.

ENGLISH AND OTHER COLONIAL LANGUAGES

Non-English colonial languages had the best chance of competing with English when they were spoken by large, cohesive populations that settled particular areas and established their own institutions before or simultaneously with the British. Such was the case with the Germans who began settling Pennsylvania in the late seventeenth century, at the same time as the English. Initially, the Pennsylvania Germans set up German language presses, schools, churches, and municipal authorities. British settlers courted the allegiance of the Germans before and during the Revolution by publishing government documents in German. So substantial was the German presence in Pennsylvania that German schools received public funding well into the nineteenth century.

Yet, even though so firmly established, the German population of Pennsylvania (except in isolated "Pennsylvania Dutch" pockets) had largely adopted English by 1815. Once again, the numerical dominance of English speakers partially explains the assimilation of the Germans, who never exceeded a third of the Pennsylvania population. Even more important, however, was the resulting political strength of the British settlers, who controlled the Pennsylvania Assembly. First in the French and Indian War, then in the War for Independence, Germans came to realize that their own welfare depended upon allying themselves with the dominant English-speaking population. Thereafter, leaders of the German community cast their lot with the English-speaking majority, promoting higher education in English and encouraging Germans to participate fully in mainstream American life.

The same major factors—greater numbers and political dominance—explain the ascendancy of English when, in the nineteenth century, English-speaking Americans moving west encountered another large and long-established concentration of non-English speakers. White English-speaking Americans (called Anglos whether or not of British descent) were not the first Europeans in the region. Hispanics had preceded them into the Southwest by more than a century, establishing small Spanish language communities and missions in the territory just north of present-day Mexico and up the Pacific Coast as far as San Francisco. The process whereby English overtook Spanish in these areas can be illustrated by contrasting the Anglicizing of California with that of New Mexico.

When California was ceded to the United States in 1848, its established Hispanic population numbered about 7,500. The Gold Rush attracted the same number of Mexican newcomers, for a total of 15,000 Spanish speakers. Yet the concurrent influx of 80,000 Anglos reduced the Hispanic population to a minority of less than 20 percent by 1850 when California became a state. Taking advantage of their greater numbers and political power and manifesting racist inclinations, Anglos soon began ignoring the property, language, and cultural rights guaranteed to the Mexicans by the Treaty of Guadalupe Hidalgo. The California state constitution stipulated bilingual legislation, but this article was consistently evaded. Instead, Anglo squatters wrested land from Mexican rancheros, who could not defend themselves in a foreign legal system administered in English. Anglo miners imposed an excessive Foreign Miners' Tax even on the native-born Californios, effectively driving Mexican competition out of the gold fields. So rapid was the rise of English in California that by 1855 the California Bureau of Public Instruction had mandated English as the only medium of public education. English had become the language of government, education, and dominant economic concerns. Spanish speakers had the choice of learning English or remaining a despised minority outside mainstream society. Spanish would never again rival English as the language of the California power structure.

The relationship between Spanish and English evolved somewhat differently in New Mexico. Spaniards had settled in northern New Mexico before 1600, two centuries prior to the arrival of the Anglos. By the early nineteenth century, this self-contained Spanish community, a province of Mexico after 1821, claimed a population of over 20,000. Ceded to the United States in 1848, New Mexico experienced no early wave of Anglo migrants. English speakers remained a minority until after 1900, and, consequently, Spanish speakers shared political and economic power with the Anglo newcomers. The Spanish version of the bilingual territorial laws generally took precedence over the English in disputed cases. Spanish continued in use, along with English, in the territorial legislature, courts, and administrative offices, and in legal notices until the twentieth century. Among the public schools, 69 percent in 1874 and 30 percent in 1889 were administered entirely in Spanish.

While these conditions may seem to have afforded Spanish a nearly equal status with English in New Mexico, one significant political lever ensured the eventual ascendancy of English: the U.S. government refused to grant statehood and the attendant self-governance until 1912, when Anglos finally outnumbered Hispanics. In 1902 a special Congressional committee had actually recommended that statehood be postponed until domestic in-migration sufficiently "Americanized" the New Mexico territory. Thereafter, the Spanish language declined precipitously in public use; reportedly, by 1911 Spanish was neglected completely in the schools, and by 1935 it had ceased being an official language in the legislature. The example of New Mexico demonstrates that, in the rare instances when English speakers did not overwhelm non-English speakers by sheer force of numbers, political coercion could tip the scales in favor of the language of Anglo-America.

ENGLISH AND IMMIGRANT LANGUAGES

If non-English colonists who settled before or along with the English could not seriously challenge the dominant language, it should hardly seem surprising that later immigrants made even fewer linguistic inroads. In spite of the arrival of huge numbers of non-English speakers in the late nineteenth and early twentieth centuries, the preeminence of English was maintained and even augmented. Numbers and political dominance, of course, continued to favor English speakers and still do today. For instance, Spanish, currently our largest language minority, is the mother tongue of about 9 percent of the U.S. population, while 28 percent of Canadians claim French as their first language—a difference of proportion that helps explain why French is the second official language of Canada while the United States remains monolingual. But other conditions also militated against the deep rooting of later immigrant languages in American soil.

Some of these conditions grew out of conscious public policy about the Americanization of immigrants. In 1818, at the opening of the period of significant non-British immigration, Congress legislated that no nationality could establish a new homeland within the borders of the United States. This law did not prevent large populations of one ethnicity from settling in the same region. But it did mean that no section of the country would be reserved exclusively for a single group and that no ethnic enclave could become autonomous or self-governing. This policy effectively preserved English as the common language at the local as well as the national level—in sharp contrast to the Soviet Union, where particular regions may be dominated by a single non-Russian language community and local affairs may be conducted in the ethnic tongue. Similarly, the strength of the French language in Canada stems partly from the regional dominance of French speakers, who comprise 81 percent of the Quebec population. No such regional power has been allowed to accrue to any non-English language in the United States.

The federal government has adopted other measures which promote English even more directly. Since 1906 naturalization laws have required that new citizens be able to speak English, and since 1950 literacy in English has been required too. These rules do not affect the substantial number of native-born non-English speakers or immigrants who choose not to apply for citizenship. But it does stress to would-be citizens that English is considered a necessary tool of American life.

Nowhere did public policy contribute to Anglicizing immigrants more than in the sphere of education. By 1870 every state in the union had committed itself to compulsory education. Consequently, the great wave of immigration that began around 1880 placed thousands of non-English-speaking children in the public charge. School systems, particularly in large cities, responded to this challenge by determining to Americanize their foreign-born students. Some educators set out to eradicate all traces of immigrant culture; others tried to nurture selected ethnic traits. But all agreed that every new American needed to learn English. So immigrant children studied English at school during the day while their parents were encouraged to attend one of the numerous evening English classes sponsored by public schools and sometimes by employers. The YMCA and settlement houses, such as Jane Addams' famous Hull House in Chicago, tried to ease the transition to American culture by promoting immigrant traditions, but they also offered English classes to those anxious to assimilate. Largely because of these initiatives, the percentage of foreign-born unable to speak English plunged from a peak of 31 percent in 1910 to 15 percent in 1920 and 8.5 percent in 1930. The massive educational effort, probably more than any other single factor, guaranteed the continued primacy of English even in an era when unprecedented numbers of non-English speakers were crowding into American cities.

ENGLISH AND AMERICAN NATIONALISM

In addition to these conscious policy decisions, Americans developed a particular ideology that emphasized both the positive aspects of assimilation and the negative effects of remaining culturally or linguistically different. On the positive side lay that cluster of beliefs that undergird the American dream. According to this philosophy, anyone—at least anyone white—could become a fully acculturated American by simply adhering to a certain attractive set of abstractions: liberty, democracy, equality, free enterprise. Unlike the foundations of various European nationalisms, these American ideals apparently attach to no particular ethnicity. That is, they can appeal to people of diverse ethnic backgrounds without seeming to threaten a loss of ethnic identity. Furthermore, these ideals promise the economic and social rewards of upward mobility to anyone willing to adopt them. And, since most immigrants to the United States arrive hoping and expecting to conform to them, assimilation to American values has been regarded as both relatively easy and highly beneficial. Learning English has naturally been fundamental to the assimilation process.

The negative aspects of cultural difference are implied in American nationalism and in its obverse, American nativism; both have often addressed the fears rather than the hopes of newcomers. Even before American independence, British colonists felt superior to their non-British neighbors. In 1751 Benjamin Franklin (quoted in Weaver 1970:57) queried,

> Why should the *Palatine Boors* [Germans] be suffered to swarm into our Settlements and, by herding together, establish their Language and Manners, to the Exclusion of ours? Why should *Pennsylvania,* founded by the *English,* become a Colony of *Aliens,* who will shortly be so numerous as to Germanize us instead of our Anglifying them?

Such denunciations of non-Anglos, which echo throughout American history, trace their origins to the doctrine of Anglo-Saxon superiority—an ideology that developed in England during the period of American colonization and later shaped American nationalism and nativism. In its nationalist aspect this doctrine asserts that the virtues of individual liberty and self-government belong uniquely to the Anglo-Saxons (or English) and by extension to the American "race." American nationalists elaborated this concept, insisting not only on their special genius for freedom and democracy but also on their ability to assimilate the best features of other white races without losing their basic Anglo-Saxon character. Americans and British alike considered it their moral duty to impose these Anglo-American virtues—and the institutions that sustain them—on as many of the world's other cultures as possible. For them, the English language symbolized their superiority, and the adoption of English by other peoples demonstrated conversion to the Anglo-American ideal. Those who could not or chose not to convert—especially Catholics, Jews, non-whites, or radicals—became the targets of American nativism, which sometimes led to violence and repressive measures against aliens.

This complex of American nationalism/nativism could cut two ways for immigrants. On the one hand, nationalism encouraged newly arrived Europeans to think that they could participate fully in American life by adopting Anglo-Saxon virtues, including the English language. This notion provided a positive incentive to assimilate. On the other hand, nativism threatened dire consequences for anyone who failed to conform to the Anglo-American norm and confronted newcomers with a powerful negative incentive to assimilate.

Nativist fervor operated most blatantly during the first twenty years of this century when immigration was burgeoning. World War I consolidated this tendency by aligning all Americans against German Americans and, by extension, against foreign elements in general. Unassimilated or unnaturalized immigrants experienced mounting pressure to demonstrate their American patriotism. Educators, as already mentioned, were determined to teach them English. In Iowa—with its large German population—the chairman of the Council of Defense promised, "We are going to love every foreigner who really becomes an American, and all others we are going to ship back home" (quoted in Higham 1955:221). In 1918 Iowa Governor W. S. Harding banned the use of any non-English language in schools and church services as well as in public and telephone conversations. Idaho and Utah required non-English-speaking aliens to attend Americanization classes. By 1919 fifteen states had mandated that only English be used in schools, whether public or private. Under such severe nativist constraints, it seems likely that those who had not already learned English voluntarily did so finally out of fear.

In sum, English is not now nor has it ever been the only language of the United States. Yet is has always prevailed in the public arena—a situation currently reinforced by the status of English as the primary language of international communication. The above discussion has illustrated the processes by which English took precedence over every other U.S. language. It is important to understand that these processes are not consensual or logical: Americans have not agreed to use English simply because they need a common language and imagine that English has some sort of intrinsic merit. Rather, these processes are political and sociological, reflecting the dominance first of British settlers, then of an Anglo-American system of government, and finally of an Anglo-Saxon ideal. So solidly are these traditions established that no amount of present or future immigration is likely to challenge the public preeminence of English in American life.

CHAPTER 4

Regional Dialects of American English

T HE RISE OF ENGLISH to a position of undisputed priority over other U.S. languages scarcely begins to explain the complexity of the American language situation, for the English that has become so pervasive in this country exists in many different varieties. Anyone who has traveled between North and South or East and Midwest can readily testify that New Yorkers speak differently from Virginians and that Bostonians are easily distinguished from Chicagoans. What causes these geographical differences, known as **regional dialects**?

One fundamental concept underlies every type of language variation discussed in this book: all spoken languages change constantly. Some linguistic changes reflect new experiences, ideas, or technological advances in the lives of language users. For instance, *gasohol, cuisinart, videodisc, funkadelic,* and *Reaganomics* have all recently entered the vocabulary of American English, while words like *tricorn* ("a three-cornered hat"), *cuirass* ("armor to protect the breast and back"), or *phaeton* ("a light four-wheeled horse-drawn vehicle") have virtually disappeared.

Other linguistic innovations grow out of processes inherent in language history. Modern-day English has gradually evolved out of earlier forms of the language. Although it is the ancestor of modern

English, Old English (spoken in England from the eighth to the twelfth centuries) differs so radically from its descendant in grammar, vocabulary, and pronunciation that it is a foreign language to twentieth-century English speakers. To cite a typical grammatical difference, Old English verbs had three distinct present tense endings for first, second, and third person singular and a fourth ending for the plural. Modern English, however, has come to have only two present tense forms: an *s* for third-person singular (as in *she writes*) and no ending elsewhere (as in *I, you, we, they write*).

Some Old English vocabulary items lost ground to words brought by conquering peoples. The Viking invasions in the ninth and eleventh centuries introduced such words as the Old Norse *sky*, which replaced the Old English *wolcen*. As a result of the Norman Conquest in 1066, many Old English words gave way to French; the Old English *ceaster* and *æthele,* for instance, yielded respectively to the French-derived *city* and *noble*.

Systematic sound changes since the Old English period have produced new ways of pronouncing English words. Some older pronunciations are preserved in modern spellings that no longer correspond to current usage: the *k* in *knife*, the *g* in *gnaw*, the *b* in *lamb* were at one time pronounced, as were the *k* and the *gh* in *knight*. Vowel sounds have been transformed even more dramatically than consonants. During the fifteenth century, English speakers began to pronounce long vowels higher in the mouth. Before that time *feet* would have sounded like present-day *fate, bite* like present-day *beat, root* like present-day *rote*.

Sound changes, particularly in the vowel system, are still in progress today. For instance, many Americans pronounce words like *cot* and *caught* with two distinct vowel sounds—/a/ and /ɔ/, respectively. But in the system of American English vowels, this distinction is being gradually and, to the average listener, imperceptibly lost, just as vowel sounds at earlier stages of the language underwent change. Thus for most West Coast speakers and for many speakers in New England, western Pennsylvania, and the Midwest, *cot* and *caught* are pronounced identically. This innovation seems to be spreading southward and may eventually constitute the American norm.

Once it is understood that no living language remains static, the branching of a common ancestor language into divergent varieties can be seen as a natural process. As groups of speakers migrate away from a common language center, they lose touch with other members of their original language community. Particularly before the advent of modern travel and communication, these outward movements caused migrants to communicate almost exclusively with others in their new region, creating their own community of speakers. Inevitably, their language changed in response to both cultural and purely linguistic innovation. But the changes were specific to the group of speakers in their community. Other changes affected other communities, and eventually distinct dialects of the same original language emerged. This is the process that accounts for the regional dialects of English that arose first in England, then in the United States.

RELATIONS AMONG BRITISH AND AMERICAN DIALECTS

Since England already had regional dialects when American colonization began, it makes sense to ask whether regional differences in this country reflect prior differences in seventeenth-century British English. In fact, British settlers at both Jamestown in Virginia and Massachusetts Bay came from various parts of England, though in both cases the majority originated in the London area and presumably spoke a southeastern British dialect. The Mid-Atlantic states, especially Pennsylvania, were settled by Quakers from the north and west of England and by Scotch-Irish, who also spoke a northern variety of British English.

The major dialect areas of the eastern United States coincide roughly with the regions of England from which their original settlers came. Dialect geographers have studied the distribution of various vocabulary and pronunciation features and conclude that the eastern United States divides into Northern, North Midland, South Midland, and Southern dialect areas. (See Figure 10. Regional features are detailed in Tables 5 and 6 and explained on pages 83–91.) It is certainly worth noticing that settlers from around London came to the Northern and Southern U.S. dialect areas while colonists from northern Britain gravitated to the Midland regions.

In spite of their links with particular areas of England, however, American regional dialects have not replicated British regional varieties: no single feature from one of the U.S. dialect areas can be convincingly traced to a specific region of England. It seems instead that settlers of any one region brought with them many varieties of British English, which mixed into a new dialect after they arrived. The various results of this mixing process (called **dialect leveling**) may par-

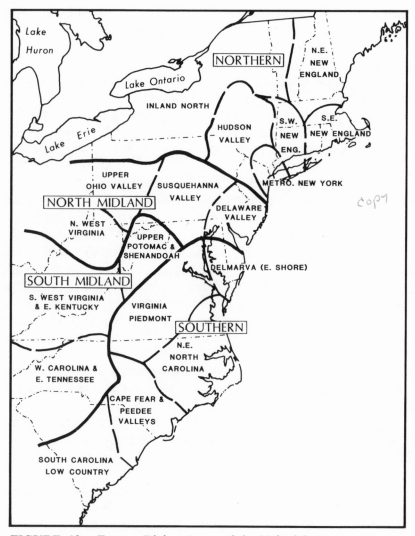

FIGURE 10. Eastern Dialect Areas of the United States

SOURCE: Hans Kurath, *A Word Geography of the Eastern United States* (Ann Arbor: University of Michigan Press, 1949), Figure 3. Copyright 1949, 1970. Adapted by permission.

tially account for the similarities and differences among American regional dialects.

Besides developing its own regional dialects, American English as a whole began to diverge from British English. American colonists added new words to their vocabulary to describe their experiences in the New World. Many of these they adapted from native American words: *catalpa, hickory, pecan, squash, tamarack, hominy, succotash, chipmunk, moose, muskrat, opossum, raccoon, skunk, woodchuck.* Other words arose from their contact with French, Spanish, West African, Dutch, or German neighbors.

In addition, American colonists were too isolated from England to keep up with all the changes in British English. In fact, all colonial languages are more conservative than the language of the homeland. That is, certain features continue to be used in colonial languages after they have disappeared or changed in the old country. This generalization holds for American English as well as for Mexican Spanish, Pennsylvania German, and Canadian French. At the level of vocabulary, American colonists brought with them, for example, the word *druggist*, which came into use in England during the early seventeenth century. But about 1750 the British began to substitute *chemist* for *druggist* while the older form has persisted in the United States to the present time. Similarly, in mid-seventeenth-century England, *apartment* meant "a suite of rooms," just as it does today in the United States. But in British English *apartment* came to designate only one room by the early eighteenth century, and *flat* was introduced to function in the older sense. *Fall* began to mean "autumn" in British English in the mid-seventeenth-century. While Americans continue to use *fall* in this sense, the British now consider it archaic. At the level of pronunciation, the British once had the same vowel sound in *derby, clerk,* and *Berkeley* that Americans still have. But the British have now systematically converted this vowel sound to the one that most Americans use in *dark*. This conservative tendency in European languages brought to the New World is captured in the term **colonial lag**.

Yet American English by no means developed in complete isolation from British English. The high-prestige dialect of London— called **British standard**—continued to serve as a model for Americans even after they were long settled in their new land. One Eastern U.S. pronunciation feature in particular shows the continued influence of British standard on American English: the loss of **postvocalic r** (that is, *r* after vowels) in such words as *sister, park, far*. During the period of initial colonization in America, most speakers of British standard sounded postvocalic *r*, just as most Americans do today. Thus the first American leaders brought with them an *r*-pronouncing norm. Not until the eighteenth century did loss of postvocalic *r* become fashionable in British standard.

Commercial and cultural connections between England and the American elite remained strong until and, to some extent, even after the Revolution, particularly in Boston and in the plantation areas of the South, which centered in Richmond and Charleston. It is true that Boston differed in its religious beliefs from England and therefore could not send its sons to Oxford or Cambridge, which accepted only Anglicans. But, as cultural arbiter for New England, Boston still considered London the hub of the English-speaking world. Even in the mid-nineteenth century, such an astute observer as Henry Adams judged Boston a colonial society, which continued to bow to English standards. The Southern plantation owners had even closer ties to upper-class England. Since they were wealthy Anglicans, they were received as equals in London society and normally educated their sons at British universities.

Not surprisingly, then, wealthy East Coast Americans imported clothes, furniture, literature, opinions—and language habits—from London. Consequently, in the eighteenth and early nineteenth centuries the newly prestigious London *r*-lessness made its way to British-oriented Boston, Richmond, and Charleston. It then expanded outward to a radius of about 150 miles from each of these centers of culture and commerce. (Such centers of linguistic diffusion are called **focal areas**.) New York City looked to Boston as its model for cultivated speech and so imitated New England *r*-less pronunciations, although New York City *r*-lessness never extended very far beyond the confines of the city. In the South, plantation owners around Charleston and Richmond adopted *r*-lessness, and, since they set the local standard, *r*-lessness came to be identified with cultivated speech wherever the plantation system and its cultural influence spread: from Virginia and South Carolina to North Carolina, Georgia, Alabama, Mississippi, Tennessee, Kentucky, Louisiana, and eastern Texas. The resulting distribution of *r*-lessness in the Eastern states is displayed in Figure 11. The Midland regions—dominated by Quakers, Germans, and Scotch-Irish with no interest in emulating London—continued to pronounce postvocalic *r*. Thus the importation of *r*-lessness helps explain the major dialect boundaries already presented in Figure 10.

Another well-known pronunciation feature of Boston and, to a lesser extent, eastern Virginia, also originated in England: the "broad *a*" (/a/ as in *father*) of *half, bath, pasture, aunt*. Up until the late eighteenth century, British standard and American English both had the "flat *a*" (/æ/ as in *cat*) pronunciation which still characterizes

  Primary areas of r-lessness

Diffusion of r-lessness with the plantation system

FIGURE 11. Regions Lacking Postvocalic *r*

most of the United States today. Sometime after 1775 both British standard and the British-influenced Boston and Richmond dialects introduced the "broad *a*" in certain words.

NON-ENGLISH LANGUAGES AND AMERICAN DIALECTS

The British influence cannot entirely explain the complexities of American dialect regions and subregions, even in the eastern United States. Another factor that must be considered is the impact of non-English languages. This factor is likely to prove important only when speakers of English came into contact with large non-English communities and is most significant when the contact began early in American history.

The West African-influenced language of black slaves probably exerted a greater impact than any other non-British variety on American regional dialects. The West African creole spoken by American slaves so deeply affected Southern regional speech partly because blacks were brought to America early (beginning in 1619) and represented a large portion of the Southern population (see Chapter 1). Even more important was their close contact with wealthy plantation owners, who acquired a number of creolized features in early childhood and who later, as standard setters for their region, passed these features along to the general Southern population. Some of these features still persist in the casual speech of the upper classes and in nonstandard Southern varieties generally.

Almost every distinctive feature of black speech has also been attested—though often at different levels of frequency—in the English of white Southerners. Although some researchers conclude that these overlapping features only show the influence of Southern white English on black English, it seems more probable that the influence moved in the other direction as well. Certainly, whites borrowed a number of West African vocabulary items: *cola, yam, okra, banana* and, especially in the South, *goober, tote* ("carry"), and *buckra* ("white man"). Even such basic Americanisms as *okay, uh-uh,* and *uh-huh* may have West African origins. Joel Chandler Harris' famous *Uncle Remus Stories*, based on African folk tales, further demonstrate the power of black language and culture to penetrate the dominant white society.

Among the many pronunciation and grammatical features shared by blacks and some Southern whites (these include all the items in Table 21), two grammatical features stand out as most probably black in origin. The West African creoles from which black English derives mark the perfect tense (representing recently completed action) with *done*, where standard English calls for *have/has*, as in *I done lost my hat* for *I have lost my hat*. Even though *done* quite clearly originates in creoles, many white Southerners have adopted it in nonstandard speech. Similarly, West African creoles have *it* for standard English *there*, as in *It's a girl in my class named Helen* instead of *There's a girl in my class named Helen*. This "existential *it*" has passed from black English into some nonstandard white Southern dialects. Even the ubiquitous Southern *you-all* may have creole origins. Since at least these Southern regional features seem to have descended from creoles, it is worth noting that West African creoles also lack *r* after vowels—which must certainly reinforce the *r*-less pattern discussed above even if Southern *r*-lessness cannot be wholly attributed to a creole source. Thus both the Southern and the South Midland dialect regions in Figure 10 are defined in part by features common to blacks and whites, some of which are traceable to the West African-derived English of black Southerners.

Pennsylvania Germans offer a second interesting instance of non-English influences on regional dialects. The long presence of so many people with German language background actually accounts for much of what is distinctive about the Susquehanna dialect subregion in Figure 10. The vocabulary of Pennsylvania English shows two kinds of effects from contact with German. One is the translation of German expressions (called **loan translations**) to replace native English words. *Rainworm*, from the German *Regenwurm*, occurs instead of *earthworm*; *sawbuck,* from *Sägebock*, takes the place of *sawhorse. A little piece*, for "a short distance," derives from *ein kurzes Stück*, and *fatcakes,* for *doughnuts*, from *Fettkuchen*. The other effect is the adoption of German words in English: *snits* for "slices (of food)," *toot* for "paper bag," and *peep* for "baby chick."

Even the pronunciation of Pennsylvania English has been somewhat affected by German. In the southeastern part of the state, final /g/ can sound like /k/ (*dog* can become *dok*), just as final consonants in German always lose voicing. German also contributes to the boundary between the Northern pronunciation of the verb *grease* and the Midland and Southern *greaze*, illustrated in Figure 12. For the most part, this line conforms to the Northern/North Midland regional boundary in Figure 10, but it dips noticeably in southeastern Pennsylvania, where a high concentration of "Pennsylvania Dutch" resides. At least for this area, the *s* in *grease* is traceable to German, which has no *z* sound at the end of words. In general, it is worth remembering that the pronunciation of the verb *grease* is a simple and reliable way to distinguish Northern from Midland or Southern speakers anywhere east of the Mississippi.

Similarly, the unique characteristics of Metropolitan New York speech in Figure 10 owe something to the numerous immigrant groups that settled there, particularly Jews and Italians. Because New York serves as the nation's advertising and media center, many of its ethnic vocabulary items now have wide currency throughout the United States. Italian words such as *antipasto, minestrone, spaghetti, pizza* testify to the visibility of Italians in the restaurant business. National contributions from Yiddish include *kibitzer* ("one who offers un-

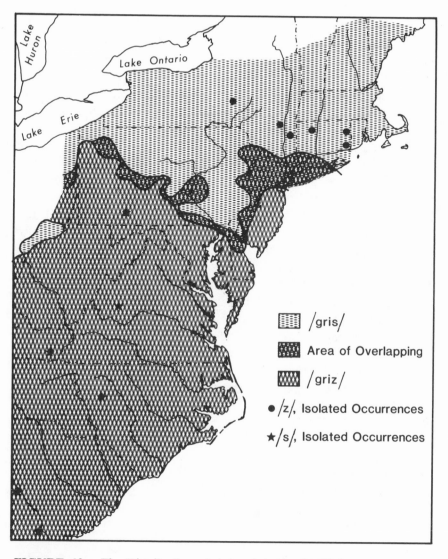

FIGURE 12. The Distribution of /s/ and /z/ in the Verb *grease*

SOURCE: Atwood 1950:260.

NOTE: Northern Maine and Eastern Georgia (not shown on the map) show the same usage as the adjoining areas. At the time of this study, no field records were available for Northern New York.

solicited advice''), *nosh* ("snack"), *schmaltz* ("excessive sentimentality"), *schlock* ("inferior merchandise"), *schlemiel* ("habitual bungler''); the New York City area has many more. A number of Yiddish expressions are commonly translated into New York City English: *I should live so long, if you'll excuse the expression, I should worry.*

Italian- and Yiddish-speaking immigrants have also affected the pronunciation of New York City English. Since non-English languages rarely contain the *th* sound, New Yorkers who say *dese and dose* for *these and those* are probably showing the influence of a non-English language environment, even if English is their first language. In New York, Italian Americans exhibit an especially high incidence of this pronunciation feature.

Another influence from Italian and Yiddish sounds has a more complicated explanation. Many New Yorkers, regardless of ethnicity, pronounce the /æ/ sound of *bad* so that it resembles a lengthened version of the /ɛ/ sound of *bed* and sometimes even the /e/ sound of *bade*. Because of where these sounds are produced in the vocal tract, this phenomenon is called **raising** and can be diagramed as in Figure 13. Since Yiddish has no /æ/ sound, the English of first-generation New York Jews tends to substitute /ɛ/ for /æ/ so that *bad* sounds like *bed*. Immigrant Jews thus participate in the general raising process. Italian also has no /æ/ sound, but the English of first-generation New York Italians substitutes /a/ for /æ/, so that *cat* might sound like *cot*. This tendency reverses the ongoing raising process that characterizes New York City English. Second-generation Italian Americans, however, stigmatize their parents' accented speech and perhaps also wish to emulate the speech of the more assimilated Jewish community. They thus overcompensate for their parents' lowered /æ/ by raising this sound, often even farther than Jews do. Second- and third-generation Italian Americans, then, are the group most likely to pronounce *bad* something like *bed* or even *bade*. By this process of overcompensation (or "hypercorrection," as it will be called in Chapter 6), Italian Americans have accelerated the rate of /æ/ raising in New York City English (Labov 1972b:297–98).

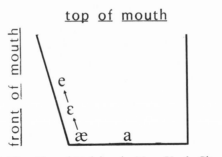

FIGURE 13.   Vowel Raising in New York City

OTHER INFLUENCES ON REGIONAL DIALECTS

Obviously, the four major dialect areas and eighteen subregions in Figure 10 cannot be entirely explained by mixtures of British English and contact with later British standard or by influences from African creoles, German, and later immigrant languages. Other aspects of settlement history account for some other dialect subregions. The Southwestern New England subregion, for instance, was settled in the 1630s by Thomas Hooker and others who left the Massachusetts Bay colony (in the Southeastern New England subregion) in search of economic opportunity and religious freedom; these dissenters did not subsequently maintain the strong commercial and cultural ties with England that Boston area colonists had and were thus not *r*-less. The Hudson Valley subregion represents the Dutch-influenced New Netherland area. The Delaware Valley subregion was originally dominated by Quakers and reflects their northern British dialect, which was never modified by the importation of southern British *r*-lessness.

T A B L E 5. Regional Pronunciation

FEATURE	EXAMPLE	REGION
Consonants:		
Contrasts		
/s/ vs. /z/, especially between vowels	grea*s*y vs. grea*z*y	Northern vs. Midland, Southern
/ð/ vs. /θ/, especially in *without*	/wɪð/ vs. /wɪθ/	Northern vs. Midland
Merger		
/hw/ → /w/ in *wh* words	*wh*ether = *w*eather	New York City, North Midland, spreading
Deletions		
/h/ before /yu/	*h*uman, *H*ugh	Eastern United States, especially New York City
/l/ before /p/, /b/, /f/	he*l*p, bu*l*b, wo*l*f	Southern
/r/ after vowels	pa*r*k, ca*r*, siste*r*	Eastern New England, New York City, plantation-influenced South

(cont.)

T A B L E 5. Regional Pronunciation (*Continued*)

FEATURE	EXAMPLE	REGION
Vowels:		
Contrasts		
/e/ vs. /ɛ/ before /g/	/eg/ vs. /ɛg/	Eastern New England, Southern vs. elsewhere
/a/ vs. /æ/	/ant/ vs. /ænt/	Boston, Richmond vs. elsewhere
/ʊ/ vs. /u/	/rʊf/ vs. /ruf/	Northern vs. elsewhere
/yu/ vs. /u/	/dyu/ vs. /du/	Southern, South Midland vs. elsewhere
Mergers		
/a/ = /ɔ/	cot = caught	Eastern New England, western Pennsylvania, Midwest, Rocky Mountains, West Coast, spreading south
/ɪ/ = /ɛ/ before /m/, /n/, /ŋ/	pin = pen	Southern, spreading to Midwest and West Coast
/ai/ = /au/ before voiced consonants	find = found	Southern, South Midland
/oi/ or /ɔi/ = /ɔ/, especially before /l/	boil = bawl	Southern, South Midland
Vowels Before /r/:		
Contrasts		
/a/ vs. /o/	/farən/ vs. /forən/	Eastern New England, New York City, Southern vs. elsewhere
/ʊ/ vs. /u/	/šʊr/ vs. /šur/	Northern vs. elsewhere
Mergers		
/æ/ = /e/ = /ɛ/	marry = Mary = merry	Northern, North Midland, West
/æ/ = /ɛ/	marry = merry	Southern, South Midland
/e/ = /ɛ/	Mary = merry	New England
/i/ = /e/	beer = bear	Southern, South Midland
/u/ = /o/	poor = pour	Southern, Midland
/ɔ/ = /o/	horse = hoarse	Everywhere but eastern New England, coastal South

Barriers to settlement also affected dialect boundaries. The Northern/North Midland boundary through Pennsylvania shows the northern limits of original settlement. Above this line the powerful Six Nations of the Iroquois impeded settlement throughout the colonial period. The South Midland/Southern boundary separates the coastal low country from the Appalachian Mountains, which retarded movement westward. Even a river could effectively define different spheres of influence: the Connecticut River divides the Southeastern and Southwestern New England subregions.

The oldest settlements in this country display the most distinctive regional dialects because limited travel and communications in the early days restricted outside influences and allowed cohesive language communities to emerge. That is why dialect regions and even small subregions can be reliably defined for the eastern United States. The most salient pronunciation features that distinguish Eastern regions are summarized in Table 5, with some of their westward extensions also specified. The Checklist of Regional Expressions in Table 6 shows regional differences in vocabulary for some items.

TABLE 6. Checklist of Regional Expressions *copy*

For some of the checklist items below, distribution among major regional dialect areas is given in parentheses (N = Northern, M = Midland, NM = North Midland, SM = South Midland, S = Southern). Others are left for individual fieldworkers to discover.

1. Container used for milk or water: pail (N, NM), bucket (S, M)
2. Devices at edges of roof to carry off rain: eave spout (N), gutter (M), guttering (M), eaves trough (N), water trough (N, S), spouts (M), spouting (M), eave troft (N), rain gutter
3. Playground item that consists of a board balanced across a sawhorse: teeter board (N), teeter totter (N, M), seesaw (S, M), ridy-horse (S), hickey horse (S)
4. Worm used for fish bait: night crawler (N), fishing worm (M), fish worm (M), redworm (SM), bait worm (S, M), angleworm (N), earthworm, rainworm
5. A carbonated drink: cold drink (S), tonic (Boston area), soda, pop, soda pop, soft drink, coke, soda water
6. A stream of water not big enough to be a river: creek (M), crick (N, NM), brook (N), branch (S, SM), run (NM), draw, resaca
7. Paper container for groceries, etc.: bag (N), sack (M, S), poke (M), toot (Pennsylvania German)
8. Device found on outside of house or in yard or garden: faucet (N), spicket (S, M), spigot (S, M), hydrant (S, M), tap

(cont.)

T A B L E 6.   **Checklist of Regional Expressions** (*Continued*)

9. Window covering on rollers: blinds (M), curtains, roller shades, shades, window blinds, window shades

10. People related by blood: my family, my folks, my parents, my people, my relatives, my relations, my kin, my kinfolks, my kind

11. Of children: brought up, fetched up, raised, reared

12. New limited-access road: turnpike, toll road, freeway, parkway, pay road, tollway, thruway, expressway, interstate

13. Grass strip in the center of a divided road: median, center strip, separator, divider, barrier, grass strip, boulevard, island

14. Animal with strong odor: skunk (N, M), polecat (S), woodspussy (M), woodpussy (M)

15. Insect that glows at night: fire bug (M), firefly (urban N, NM), lightning bug (S, M, rural N), candle bug, glow worm, june bug

16. Large winged insect seen around water: darning needle (N), devil's darning needle (N), mosquito hawk (S), snake doctor (S, M), snake feeder (S, M), sewing bug (N), dragonfly, ear-sewer, sewing needle

17. A spreadable luncheon meat made of liver: liver sausage, liverwurst, braunschweiger

18. A glass containing ice cream and root beer: float, root beer float, black cow, Boston cooler

19. Corn served on cob: corn-on-the-cob (N, M), roasting ears (S, M), green corn (N), mutton corn, sugar corn, sweet corn, garden corn

20. Large sandwich designed to be a meal: hero (New York), hoagy (Philadelphia), grinder (Boston), poor-boy (S), submarine

21. Children's cry at Halloween time: trick or treat! tricks or treats! beggar's night! help the poor! Halloween! give or receive!

22. Call to players to return because a new player wants to join: allie-allie-in-free, allie-allie-oxen-free, allie-allie-ocean-free, bee-bee bumble bee, everybody in free, newcomer-newcomer

23. To hit the water flat when diving: belly-flop, belly-flopper, belly-bust, belly-buster, belly-smacker

24. To be absent from school: bag school, bolt, cook jack, lay out, lie out, play hookey, play truant, run out of school, skip class, skip school, skip off from school, ditch, flick, flake school, blow school

25. Holds small objects together: rubber band, rubber binder, elastic binder, gum band, elastic band

26. A time of day: quarter of seven (N), quarter till seven (S, M), quarter to seven (N, S), 6:45, quarter before seven

27. Become ill with a cold: catch a cold (N), take a cold (S, M), catch cold, get a cold, take cold, come down with a cold

28. Nauseated: sick in one's stomach (M), sick on one's stomach (M), sick to one's stomach (N), sick of one's stomach, sick with one's stomach, sick at one's stomach

29. Grass strip between sidewalk and street: berm, boulevard, boulevard strip, parking strip, parkway, parking, sidewalk plot, tree lawn, neutral ground, devil strip, tree bank, city strip, yard extension

30. Of peas: to hull (M), to shuck (S), to pod, to shell

REGIONAL DIALECTS AND WESTWARD EXPANSION

As Americans moved west across the continent, they took their Eastern dialects with them. So, particularly for the region east of the Mississippi, dialect boundaries mainly follow early migration routes—whether through mountain passes, along the few roads, or over waterways. West of the Mississippi, settlers came together from so many Eastern areas that their dialects tended to blend, obscuring clear regional patterns.

The most influential of the early westward migrants were the Presbyterian Scotch-Irish, who began landing in religiously tolerant Philadelphia before 1720. Lacking the financial resources to buy land in the East, they soon began to move west through Pennsylvania to the Alleghenies, where French strongholds made further westward progress impossible. They then turned south into mountain passes, wending through the Shenandoah Valley into Virginia. From there some continued south into the western parts of the Carolinas and Georgia. Others proceeded northwest through West Virginia to the Ohio River. Figure 14 traces this Scotch-Irish migration pattern.

Because the Scotch-Irish spoke English and were often the first to settle a new region, they deeply influenced the speech of every area that they reached, especially during the colonial period. Their *r*-ful English (i.e. pronouncing postvocalic *r*), for instance, dominated in the South Midland region of Figure 10. The linguistic effects of this early migration still operate today: the eastern region of South Midland in Figure 15 roughly coincides with the pre-Revolutionary progress of the Scotch-Irish. Subsequent southward and westward movements by the same group eventually introduced their South Midland dialect into the Gulf Southern region in Figure 15, where it mixed with the Southern that had already spread there (from the Southern region shown in Figure 10) along with the plantation system. The western South Midland region in the Ozarks resembles the eastern South Midland area in that the originally Scotch-Irish dialect encountered little competition from Southern. Both South Midland regions were too mountainous for plantation agriculture and too isolated to feel the effects of plantation culture. Later settlement, dialect mixing from the North Midland and South Midland areas, and the influence of Spanish produced Plains Southern.

Gradually, then, the migration begun by the Scotch-Irish dispersed South Midland dialect features, sometimes mixed with Southern features, throughout the South Midland, Gulf Southern,

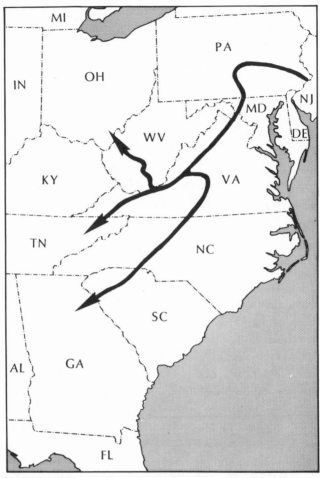

FIGURE 14.   Eighteenth-Century Scotch-Irish Migration

and Plains Southern areas in Figure 15. The northern boundary of this region—beginning in Virginia in the East, traveling north of the Ohio River, through central Missouri, north of the Oklahoma border, and dipping down to the Mexican border in eastern New Mexico—constitutes one of the most significant dialect demarcations west of the original eastern settlement area. One feature that distinguishes Americans who live south of that line from those who live north is the pronunciation of the first vowel sound in *Mary, merry,* and *marry.* For Northerners, except those living in the *r*-less areas of eastern New England and New York City, all three of these words have the same vowel. Southerners, on the other hand, have at least two different vowels in these words. In *r*-less regions on the East Coast all three are

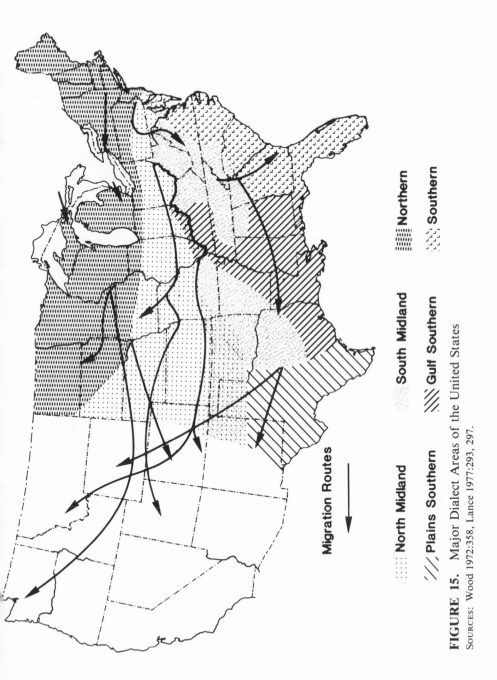

FIGURE 15. Major Dialect Areas of the United States

SOURCES: Wood 1972:358, Lance 1977:293, 297.

Migration Routes

::::: North Midland   ::::: South Midland   ::::: Northern

//// Plains Southern   ///// Gulf Southern   ::::: Southern

likely to have distinct vowels. This important dialect boundary also divides *you* to the north from *you-all* to the south.

The North Midland strip in Figure 15 represents the post-Revolutionary westward movement of Quakers, Germans, and Scotch-Irish from Pennsylvania—along with a few New Englanders and Virginians. After 1811 many used the National Road, which connected Wheeling, West Virginia, with Vandalia, Illinois. Because they moved later than the South Midland Scotch-Irish and were ethnically more heterogeneous, these settlers developed somewhat distinct dialect features, although the prominence of the Scotch-Irish among them meant that their dialect shared many common features with South Midland. North Midland terms—particularly common among older, less educated residents—include *snake feeder* ("dragonfly"), *spouting* ("gutter" or "eaves trough"), *nicker* ("whinny"), and *bellybuster* ("riding face down on a sled").

One facet of settlement history in the North Midland region had particularly interesting consequences for the student of regional dialects. After the Revolutionary War, the federal government parceled out Western lands to land companies and Eastern states to pay its war debts. This policy encouraged cohesive groups from one Eastern dialect region to settle a particular area of what was then the Northwest Territory, sometimes creating an island of one dialect in a sea of another. In 1788, for instance, the Ohio Company sent people from western Massachusetts to colonize Marietta, Ohio, in the midst of the North Midland dialect region. Many of the Northern dialect features that these settlers brought with them still persist around Marietta today. Such an area is called a **speech island**.

As for the Northern region in Figure 15, western New Englanders first moved to upstate New York, then went along the Mohawk Valley (and after 1830 the Erie Canal), following the Great Lakes to Michigan, Wisconsin, Minnesota, northern Iowa, and the Dakotas. Distinctive Northern terms include *dragonfly* (vs. Midland *snake feeder*), *cherry pit* (vs. *cherry seed*), *sick to one's stomach* (vs. *sick at*), *pail* (vs. *bucket*). Northern pronunciations include the /ʊ/ of *put* in *roof* (vs. the /u/ of *pool*) and *greasy* (vs. *greazy*).

As Figure 15 also illustrates, the western United States does not fall neatly into regional dialect areas. Instead, these more recently settled territories show dialect leveling, which results from the complicated migration patterns made possible by modern transportation. In general, Southern and Midland terms occur in the rural West. The Rocky Mountain states have a mixture of Northern and North

Midland features, with the Midland items apparently gaining ground. In the Pacific Northwest, Northern items predominate in Idaho, Midland terms in Oregon, while Washington has a mixture. The original settlers of the navigable waterways in Washington, Oregon, and northern California—Puget Sound, Gray's Harbor, the lower Columbia River, and San Francisco Bay—came from New England, and the prestige of their Northern dialect is apparently responsible for the concentration of Northern features in these ports and in other Western cities. Outside the San Francisco area, California—which has long received settlers from all parts of the country—has a predictably mixed dialect situation but with more Southernisms than in the Pacific Northwest.

Clearly, much remains to be learned about Western U.S. English. And it may be that studying the spread of Eastern forms westward will not yield the most interesting information. Researchers might concentrate instead on the development of Western focal areas and the regions over which their influence extends. Seattle, Portland, San Francisco, Los Angeles, Salt Lake City, and Denver are obvious candidates for this sort of analysis. Los Angeles, in fact, may turn out to be a peculiarly contemporary focal area since its influence spreads out not only locally but, thanks to the film and television industries, nationally.

REGIONAL AND CLASS DIALECTS

Researchers may also discover that in Western cities, as in Eastern cities, regional dialects can turn into class dialects. That is, the speech brought by migrants from one regional dialect area may become associated with the lower social classes, and speech from another region with the higher classes. This is exactly what has happened in San Francisco. Around 1870 New York contributed the greatest number of in-migrants to the San Francisco population. Many of them settled in the old area known as the Mission District. By 1940, however, the source for most new residents had changed to the Great Lakes region. Thus older settlers brought their New York City *r*-lessness and sometimes a New England "broad *a*," while newer arrivals brought an *r*-ful Northern or North Midland English. Currently, the New York-influenced variety, called the "Mission Dialect," is linked with older, less educated speakers—those outside the modern mainstream—and therefore stigmatized. Oddly, San

Franciscans stigmatize only the local survivals of New York speech while they hold New York itself in high esteem. Thus an originally regional dialect can be integrated into a new language environment solely as a class marker and retain none of its regional associations (DeCamp 1971).

Other examples of regional dialects becoming class dialects can be found in the eastern part of the country. The absence of *r* after vowels originally distinguished the coastal Southern dialect from the *r*-ful South Midland speech of the Scotch-Irish, whose eighteenth-century migration into the Appalachian Mountains is charted in Figure 14. But since the *r*-less coastal Southern dialect belonged to plantation owners, it soon became the prestige variety for the entire region. The *r*-ful South Midland dialect, on the other hand, belonged to the subsistence farmers who settled the hilly regions. Eventually, the prestigious *r*-less variety spread throughout the plantation states among the upper classes, while the *r*-ful variety came to be associated exclusively with lower-class whites. Until recently, *r*-lessness in these states was a prerequisite for high social standing.

Beginning in the 1950s, many speakers of this South Midland variety (also called **Appalachian English**) have migrated to Northern cities like Detroit to escape economic hardship. Before this recent out-migration, the rugged terrain and infertile soil of their home region had kept Appalachians isolated from modern urban and commercial influences and allowed them to preserve their traditional crafts, music, and folkways for over two centuries. But their folk culture did not usually equip Appalachians for immediate success in a modern urban society. When they went north, they therefore clustered in low-paying jobs and neighborhood enclaves, living—in spite of their long Anglo-Saxon heritage—as much outside the dominant society as blacks and immigrant groups have. Their close-knit neighborhoods have helped Appalachians to maintain their South Midland dialect, which has now become a class marker in the urban North, much as it did in the coastal South over a century ago.

Appalachian English deserves attention partially because out-migration has recently given it national visibility. But this variety also interests dialectologists because the isolation that has fostered traditional folk culture in this area has also preserved some archaic forms of speech. Since it has been minimally influenced by changes in mainstream society and speech habits, the Appalachian region is known to dialect geographers as a **relic area**. Such an area offers a glimpse into earlier features of American English, many of them inherited directly from seventeenth- and eighteenth-century British English. Table 7 displays some features of Appalachian English and indicates which are considered archaisms.

The examples of New York-based English in San Francisco and of Appalachian English in the coastal South and the urban North demonstrate that regional dialects can have social implications: not all of them are equally valued in American society. In fact, the most prestigious varieties of American English come from the areas with

T A B L E 7. Features of Appalachian English

Appalachian English Feature	Examples
Pronunciation:	
/əz/ plural following /-st/, /-sk/, /-sp/	test*es*, desk*es*, wasp*es*
*Intrusive /t/, especially after /s/	once*t*, across*t*
/l/absent before /p/, /b/, /f/	he'p, wo'f
Deletion of unstressed initial syllable, initial /ð/, initial /w/	'llowed, 'ccording, 'fore, 'em, 'uz, 'un
*/h/ retention in stressed positions	*h*it, *h*ain't
a before nouns beginning with vowel	*a* apple
*High rate of /ɪn/ for /ɪŋ/	tellin', huntin'
Final unstressed *ow* becomes *er*	holl*er*, tobacc*er*, yell*er*
Final /ə/ becomes /i/	sod*y*, Virginn*y*, extr*y*
Grammar:	
a prefix on *-ing* verbs	he was *a*-tellin', a bear come *a*-runnin'
Subject-verb nonconcord	we was, he don't
Irregular verbs	
regularized simple past	we *throwed* them a party
variant simple past	we *set* there one day, I *brang* one
uninflected simple past	finally the state *come* by
simple past same as past participle	that's all I *seen* of it
Perfective *done*	I *done* forgot when it opened
Comparatives and superlatives	
-er, -est generalized	awful*est*, beautiful*er*
*redundant markers	*more* old*er, most* stupid*est,* wors*er*
regularized comparatives and superlatives	baddest

(*cont.*)

T A B L E   7.   Features of Appalachian English (*Continued*)

Appalachian English Feature	Examples
*Frequent absence of -*ly* on adverbs	I come from Virginia *original*
*Nonstandard negation	I did*n't* have *nothing* to do, *no-body* did*n't* see him, did*n't* *nobody* get hurt
*Ain't (*hain't)*	I *ain't* been there; *hain't* that awful?
Plurals	
*Uninflected nouns in expressions of measure	two *gallon* of moonshine
regularized plurals	deers, wifes
-*s* added to irregular plurals	mens, oxens, childrens
Pronouns	
nonstandard variants	hisself, theirself, *them* boys, *this here* one, *his'n, y'all
object case in compound subject	*me* and my baby sleep the day
relative pronoun deleted	I got some kin people lived there
which as conjunction	I went to Cleveland *which* my cousin lives there
personal dative	we had *us* a cabin
Existential *it* and *they*	*it's* too much murder, *they's* copperheads around here
Nonstandard use of prepositions	*at/of* wintertime, *at/of* the morning, I lived Coal City, I just go *at* my uncle's, *upside* the head, etc.
Indirect questions marked by direct question word order rather than *if* or *whether*	I asked him *could I* come down

Vocabulary:
but it still didn't *learn* (teach) him anything; I *took* (caught) a virus; come and *take up* (live) with us; I been *aiming* (planning) to go down and see him; I got *blessed out* (scolded); it was just *fixing* (preparing) to bite me; I'll get *fussed at* (scolded); she *got* (became) sixteen; you couldn't *go* (travel) the road; they sometimes *happen in* (arrive) at the same time; I've *heared tell* (heard) of some; I *reckon* (guess) she's done sold it; I hollered *right* (quite) loud; the house burnt *plumb* (completely) down; would you *druther* (rather) I did something; he *ain't but* (is only) thirteen; I *yet* (still) eat a lot; it's *subject* (likely) to kill 'em; it'll get better *some of these days* (one of these days); we tromped through the woods 'til *long about* (about) six o'clock; an old horse way back up *yonder* (at a considerable distance); trees that're *pert' near* (almost) square; I'm not *for sure* (certain)

*considered archaisms
Source: Wolfram and Christian 1976.

the most economic power and cultural influence. Early in American history, these were the coastal cities that retained links with England—Boston, Richmond, Charleston. As economic patterns altered, more power accrued to the industrial North Central states, and urban centers such as Chicago, Detroit, and Cleveland set the standard for prestigious speech and became the model for broadcast pronunciation. Since the Civil War, Southern speech in general has been devalued because economic centers have been mainly in the North. With the current decline in heavy industry and consequent migration from the Great Lakes states to the newly prosperous South and Southwest, it will be interesting to see whether Southern speech again achieves high status.

CHAPTER 5

Standard American English

Wɪᴛʜɪɴ ᴛʜᴇ sᴏᴄɪᴀʟ ʜɪᴇʀᴀʀᴄʜʏ of American English dialects, a single prestigious variety, called **standard English**, occupies the top rank. Standard English can be best described as a model for acceptable or "correct" usage based on the language of cultural, economic, and political leaders. Most of us have come to feel that this respected variety has a kind of inherent validity. But actually, social and economic factors played determining roles in its development.

Standard American English traces its roots to social and linguistic events beginning in fourteenth-century London. During that century, England's rigidly class-stratified, predominantly rural social structure started to make way for a rising mercantile class whose commercial activities centered in London. This profound transformation in British society crucially affected not only social and economic relations but the relationships among varieties of English as well. Those who were attracted to London during and after this period brought with them the regional dialects of their home areas. If they then rose through the class system, it became important for them to adopt the manners, values, habits, and language of the London upper classes to which they aspired. Movement toward London and the new fluidity in class structure thus made it socially desirable for large numbers of people to learn a dialect not originally their own—the dialect of the London upper classes. No longer simply the unconscious regional speech of the London nobility, this variety gradually became an object of conscious study and adulation. When, in the fifteenth century, William Caxton introduced printing into England, he began to codify both the spelling and the grammar of this prestigious variety, making it a written standard. As printed texts became more available and as more people learned to read, knowledge of the features of written standard English spread. By writing in the standard dialect, Chaucer, Shakespeare, and other literary figures enhanced its prestige and contributed to a sense of its range and elegance.

By the time North America was colonized, standard British English, derived from London regional speech, had a firm foothold among the educated in England. And until after the War for Independence, Americans looked to upper-class Londoners for models of acceptable speech. That is what led status-conscious colonials to import *r*-lessness and the "broad *a*" from British standard into the cultured English of Eastern U.S. cities. As the United States developed its own elite class independent of England, the American version of standard English diverged more and more from British standard. Evolving along with the U.S. economy, American standard first consisted mainly of British-derived East Coast regional features, such as *r*-lessness, but with the westward shift of economic power, an *r*-ful Midwestern variety has come to dominate.

What this brief history should make plain is that standard English is the language of the powerful, nothing more. It is socially "correct" in that those who wish to belong to the upper and professional classes naturally need to sound like them. But, somewhere along the line, standard English became more than a matter of etiquette. It also began to seem linguistically "correct," so that now standard forms not only are considered socially superior but are wrongly sanctified as logically, expressively, and aesthetically superior as well. Thus, for instance, grammarians insist that double negatives (*Mary didn't want no doughnut*) are logically flawed since, in language as in multiplication, two negatives must equal a positive (supposedly, *Mary did want a doughnut*). In reality, of course, every English speaker knows that in language two negatives simply intensify the negation. Nevertheless, with such impressive social and linguistic virtues ascribed to it, standard English can hardly fail to arouse the anxiety of those who do not speak it regularly at home but feel compelled to use this exalted variety to the best of their ability in formal and public situations.

As if to deepen the insecurity of nonstandard speakers, standard American English also turns out to be something of an abstraction, whose exact features are impossible to pinpoint. Since all languages change constantly, almost as soon as a grammarian can commit the characteristics of upper-class speech to paper, some of them have altered in actual upper-class usage. For example, many standard English speakers no longer distinguish among the pronunciations of *Mary, merry,* and *marry;* for some, *dove* is an acceptable past tense of *dive*; for most, the noun *loan* can now be used as a synonym for the verb *lend.* The continual evolution of language—not to mention the inevitable changes in membership of the American upper class— makes it fundamentally impossible to capture the essence of upper-class speech.

Furthermore, unlike England, the United States has more than one cultural center, and, consequently, there are different regional standards for American English—often fanning out from such focal areas as Boston, Charleston, Chicago, or Salt Lake City. What is acceptable in the cultured speech of one area may seem uncouth in another area. Southern speakers of standard English, for example, often use *ain't* in casual conversation while educated Northern speakers stigmatize this word regardless of the context. To an extent, jet travel and mass media have lately tended to blur these regional distinctions. Newscasters are taught to use "network English," which has nearly uniform features of grammar and similar pronunciation features from coast to coast. The existence of network English causes most Americans to feel there is a national norm for English usage. Yet many personally identify more closely with the leaders of their own community than with national leaders and may therefore strive to imitate the local standard.

Inherent linguistic changes and regional variation make standard American English impossible to define with any degree of precision. But, especially for written standard, there is a clear consensus about spelling and substantial concurrence about acceptable features of grammar. For instance, subjects and verbs must agree in number (*Jake runs,* not *Jake run*); pronouns must take certain cases depending on their function (*between you and me,* not *between you and I; whom did you see,* not *who did you see*). Still, many grammatical items are disputed among users of standard written English. Some, for instance, maintain that *hopefully* should never be used as a sentence adverbial (as in *Hopefully, she will be here tomorrow*); others find it perfectly acceptable. Some decry split infinitives (*to fully appreciate*) while other standard speakers use them with relish. All such arguments are ultimately futile since standard English does not exist in any objective form but is redefined each time it is used.

American spoken standard allows for more variation than does written standard. Many regional pronunciations are acceptable, particularly those subtleties of vowel articulation that escape the notice of the average listener. Thus *bought* can be pronounced with either an /a/ or an /ɔ/, *horse* with either an /o/ or an /ɔ/, and *pen* with either an /ɛ/ or an /ɪ/. Numerous regional expressions fall within the permissible range for spoken standard too. Standard speakers from the East can say *on line* where other standard speakers would say *in line*; soft drinks can be called *pop, soda, soda pop, tonic, coke,* or *cold drink*, depending on the regional standard. But all native speakers of American English share a sense that some spoken features are always nonstandard: *dese* for *these, acrosst* for *across, pecific* for *specific,* to cite a few. Thus, for both written and spoken standard American English, there is a firm national conviction that such a variety exists but a much shakier consensus on exactly what its characteristics are.

PRESSURES TOWARD STANDARDIZATION

Despite shades of uncertainty about its features and the insecurity it can engender among nonstandard speakers, standard English remains a useful and, for American society, an inevitable concept. It is true that all dialects of American English are mutually intelligible; but a shared standard language minimizes the risk of subtle miscommunication between residents of different regions and, in general, provides a reassuring norm for use in public or formal exchanges. As the language of government, business, media, and education, it is also an essential ingredient of economic success and middle- and upper-class status.

Most Americans feel the need to control or at least approximate standard English. The same forces that impel non-English speakers to learn English also induce nonstandard speakers to learn standard. The American dream of upward mobility seems to promise wealth to anyone intelligent, ambitious, and properly trained in the language and culture of the powerful. Indeed, standard English is often considered one of the few reliable indicators of membership in the upper and professional classes. Thus speakers of nonstandard English or of non-English languages have strong incentives to learn the standard.

And American schools have tried to give them the opportunity. With the nineteenth-century surge in public education and immigration, standard American English became rigidly codified in grammar books; and, trying to boost their students into the upper classes, schoolteachers instructed speakers of other languages and dialects in standard English rules. Every schoolhouse in the United States echoed with such warnings as these: avoid ending a sentence with a preposition; use *climbed*, not *clim*, for the past tense of *climb*; never say *ain't* or *he don't*. Even pronunciation was subject to correction: *mourning* and *morning* should not have the same vowel sound; *new* should rhyme with *few*, not *zoo*. This zealous indoctrination in the schoolroom probably did not teach anyone all the subtleties of the standard language. But it did turn all Americans into true believers in a standard or "correct" form of English, whether or not they thought they could speak it.

The continuous flow of non-English speakers into the United States has also contributed to standardization. Upon arriving in this country, many immigrants have been eager for economic advancement and ready to take whatever steps are necessary to achieve it. In a typical pattern, at least for urban dwellers, first-generation Americans will strive to better themselves by learning English as a second language, even though their English will usually carry the stigma of being accented. Second-generation Americans, particularly those invested in upward mobility, often strongly reject the low-prestige English of their parents and, in an effort to avoid this stigma themselves, will set out quite intently to learn standard English and ascend further in the class structure. This paradigm for assimilation has been long and well rehearsed in the United States, and the learning of standard English has been an integral part of it. To some extent, the same cross-generational pressures work on upwardly mobile native-born Americans who speak nonstandard varieties: the first generation to go to college may react strongly against the nonstandard English of their parents and determine to sound as standard as possible themselves.

PRESSURES AGAINST STANDARDIZATION

With such powerful pressures toward standardization, why are there still so many nonstandard speakers? Linguists have discovered pressures against standardization that equal or outweigh the conditions favoring it. The most fundamental of these negative forces is allegiance to nonstandard subgroup norms. Region, ethnicity, class, and age divide the U.S. population, and each of us feels a primary loyalty based on one or more of these factors. Our subgroup identification largely determines our behavior, values, and language variety. Those who identify with subgroups that typically use nonstandard English will also use nonstandard English—at least in interaction with members of the group and possibly all of the time.

By retaining their nonstandard speech, group members demonstrate their solidarity with fellow members, their pride in belonging to their group, sometimes their desire to be accepted by the group. For them, the prestige and personal security of subgroup membership surpass the prestige of belonging to mainstream society. Thus a wealthy black entertainer with many standard-speaking friends may nevertheless continue to use nonstandard features of black English because he wishes to honor his cultural heritage and retains a strong sense of loyalty to his black audience. Or a transplanted New Yorker may show her continuing devotion to her hometown by using New York regional speech, even though her new neighbors in Denver consider her English nonstandard. Similarly, a factory worker will signal his solidarity with his co-workers by speaking to them in nonstandard English—whether or not he is capable of using the standard.

Pressures against standardization and toward peer group loyalty are particularly strong among young people. Here overuse of standard forms comes in for the severest censure. A teacher told one researcher (Labov 1972b:492):

> I had a boy of Greek parentage, and oh! he spoke beautifully in class, and I happened to hear him on the street one day. He sounded just like everybody else in Chelsea, and when I mentioned it to him—the next day—he said that he knew which was correct, but he said: "I couldn't live here and talk like that."

To "live" in the adolescent world, most teenagers will adopt the language of their peer group, not the standard English spoken by their teachers and sometimes by their families. There is even evidence that, by the time young nonstandard speakers learn to recognize standard English norms in early adolescence, it is already too late in their development for them to acquire a complete control of this prestigious variety (Labov 1972b:340 ff.). So the continued vitality of nonstandard English may be built into the very process of language acquisition in children.

Besides subgroup allegiance, another related pressure against standardization is the isolation of some nonstandard-speaking groups from the dominant society. Earlier in U.S. history, this isolation was mainly geographical, explaining, for instance, the prevalence of nonstandard forms in the inaccessible Appalachians. Now, however, isolation from the mainstream tends to be social. In large cities, ethnic and class barriers can deeply divide non-mainstream groups from middle- and upper-class whites even when they live within a few blocks of one another. Tight-knit ethnic and working-class enclaves persist partly because of group loyalty, partly because of exclusion from the power structure. Such well-insulated urban neighborhoods can ensure that members of non-dominant groups interact almost entirely within their own ethnic or working-class community. Except in school— where many of them feel alienated anyway—they thus have little chance to establish the meaningful relationships with standard speakers that might lead them to adopt standard English.

Moreover, subgroup members may feel no need or desire to learn standard English, especially if they pursue opportunities for success within their non-mainstream language community. A teenager who works in a record store will want to make use of teen jargon to sell records to his peers. Sounding like a standard-speaking adult would only convince his customers that he didn't know his business. Owners of shops and restaurants in ethnic or working-class neighborhoods know that retaining neighborhood speech patterns is good for business. Standard English would seem condescending, pretentious, or distant to their patrons. Even a standard-speaking professional will often revert to nonstandard forms if most of his friends or clients come from the ethnic neighborhood where he grew up. One New York lawyer explained (Labov 1972b:492):

> Most of the people I associate with in this area are men with very little schooling . . . mostly Italian-American . . . so that these are the men I've gone out drinking with, the ones I go out to dinner with, and when I talk to them, my speech even deteriorates a little more, because I speak the way they speak.

In general, since the United States will never be a completely homogeneous society in which everyone participates equally in mainstream culture, nonstandard forms are bound to persist simply to set one subgroup off from another.

Finally, a word about the effect of the electronic media on language standardization. The network English of most radio and television reports reaches daily into the homes of standard and nonstandard speakers alike. This massive infusion of standard English may seem to promise that eventually all Americans will become standard speakers because of constant exposure to the media. Actually, the reverse is true. Linguists have found that very few of us pattern our language on that of media personalities. Instead, we learn the dialect of our own reference group—those with whom we share ongoing and significant interaction.

Electronic media not only fail to promote standardization; they may even work against it. Ever since Caxton brought printing to England in the fifteenth century, the printed word has served as one of the great forces of English standardization. Conventions of written standard were gradually consolidated and passed from one generation to the next. Readers learned and imitated the standard spelling, usage, and sentence structure of their forebears, often using the English of great writers as a model. The more literate we became, the better we controlled standard written English.

But in the age of televisions and telephones, this paradigm for the transmission of standard English conventions has begun to alter. Speech, rather than writing, is the medium for more and more language activities, whether formal or informal. Since spoken language is known to change much faster than written, a consistent standard will be increasingly difficult to define and maintain. One linguist notes that this anti-standardizing tendency of speech has led, for instance, to changes in subject-verb agreement. Verbs now tend to agree with the nearest noun, not necessarily the subject noun, as in *The status of women are always lower* or *One-third of our lives are spent in bed*. And oral transmission has promulgated such nonstandard vocabulary forms as *half-hazard* for *haphazard, upmost* for *utmost,* and *all total* for *all told* (Bolinger 1981). By emphasizing speech at the expense of writing, then, electronic media are probably working against language standardization.

But that is not necessarily a cause for national lament. After all, differences in language use allow us to express distinctions in our personalities and backgrounds. The way we speak articulates much of what is unique about who we are. And variation in language only adds to the nation's storehouse of linguistic resources and nuances. In a way, the impressive array of forces ranged against a completely standard English are the very ones that sustain the invaluable variety of American culture and of human culture generally. Uniformity would be as dull in language as it is in life.

FURTHER STUDY IN THE DEVELOPMENT OF AMERICAN ENGLISH

READINGS

Histories of Anglo-American Dominance

BERTHOFF, ROWLAND TAPPAN. *British Immigrants in Industrial America: 1790–1950.* Cambridge, Mass.: Harvard University Press, 1953.

HIGHAM, JOHN. *Strangers in the Land: Patterns of American Nativism 1860–1925.* New Brunswick, N.J.: Rutgers University Press, 1955.

MANN, ARTHUR. *The One and the Many: Reflections on the American Identity.* Chicago: University of Chicago Press, 1979.

PITT, LEONARD. *The Decline of the Californios: A Social History of the Spanish-Speaking Californians, 1846–1890.* Berkeley: University of California Press, 1966.

SIMMONS, R.C. *The American Colonies: From Settlement to Independence.* New York: David McKay, 1976.

Regional Dialects

ALLEN, HAROLD B., and GARY N. UNDERWOOD, eds. *Readings in American Dialectology.* New York: Appleton-Century-Crofts, 1971.
Useful collection of regional dialect studies.

MARCKWARDT, ALBERT H. *American English.* New York: Oxford University Press, 1958.
Strongest on origins of American English.

McDAVID, RAVEN I., JR. "The Dialects of American English." In *The Structure of American English,* by W. Nelson Francis, pp. 480–543. New York: The Ronald Press, 1958.
On the history and features of regional dialects in the United States.

McDAVID, RAVEN I., JR. *Varieties of American English.* Selected and Introduced by Anwar S. Dil. Stanford: Stanford University Press, 1980.
Selected essays by the most prominent American regional dialectologist.

MENCKEN, H.L. *The American Language.* With annotations and new material by Raven I. McDavid, Jr., with the assistance of David W. Maurer. New York: Alfred A. Knopf, 1977.
Updates Mencken's 1919 classic on the development of an American vernacular.

REED, CARROLL E. *Dialects of American English.* Rev. ed. Amherst: University of Massachusetts Press, 1977.
Best introduction to the topic.

SHORES, DAVID L., and CAROL P. HINES, eds. *Papers in Language Variation*. Introduction by Paul A. Eschholz. University, Ala.: University of Alabama Press, 1977.
Mainly on Southern varieties.

WILLIAMSON, JUANITA V., and VIRGINIA M. BURKE, eds. *A Various Language: Perspectives on American Dialects*. New York: Holt, Rinehart and Winston, 1971.
Articles on regional, social, and literary dialects.

WOLFRAM, WALT, and DONNA CHRISTIAN. *Appalachian Speech*. Arlington, Va.: Center for Applied Linguistics, 1976.

Language Standardization

KLOSS, HEINZ. *The American Bilingual Tradition*. Rowley, Mass.: Newbury House Publishers, 1977.

SHOPEN, TIMOTHY, and JOSEPH M. WILLIAMS, eds. *Standards and Dialects in English*. Cambridge, Mass.: Winthrop Publishers, 1980.

SMITH, RILEY B., and DONALD M. LANCE. "Standard and Disparate Varieties of English in the United States: Educational and Sociopolitical Implications." *International Journal of the Sociology of Language* 21 (1979):127–40.

ACTIVITIES

1. Administer the Checklist of Regional Expressions in Table 6 to acquaintances from various parts of the country. As you read the descriptions aloud, try to avoid using the expression you are attempting to elicit. If informants respond with more than one expression, ask them whether there are differences in meaning between them. Try to establish the regional distribution of items not designated on the Checklist.

2. Ask speakers from different regions to read aloud the pairs of words below. Compare their pronunciations with those in Table 5 to see whether their speech conforms to the regional variety in their place of birth or present residence.

Harry	hairy	since	sense	vague	egg
dawn	Don	you	Hugh	do	due
tour	tore	source	sauce	can't	can
fire	far	lied	loud	root	route
hep	help	which	witch	for	foreign
				morning	mourning

3. Dialect geographers have charted many different words on maps similar to that in Figure 12 and assembled them into linguistic atlases. Look through some atlases (e.g. Kurath and McDavid 1961, Kurath 1939, Kurath 1949, Atwood 1962, Allen 1973–1975, Bright 1971) to see how regional dialect boundaries are established by comparing the distributions of individual features. Compare the linguistic atlas maps to the responses you elicited for the Checklist of Regional Expressions and the pronunciation word pairs above.

4. Study the Appalachian English speech sample in the Appendix. Look for the features displayed in Table 7.

5. Consider how pressures for and against standardization have affected your own use of English. Has anyone ever tried to correct your speech? If so, what were the circumstances and what language features were involved? Have you ever made conscious efforts to change your own speech? In what ways? What kind of language use do you associate with words like "stilted," "priggish," "highfalutin," "pompous"? What about labels like "sloppy," "ignorant," "vulgar," "country"? Have these labels ever been applied to you? Are you more or less standard-speaking than your family and friends? Why?

PART III

A Sociolinguistic Paradigm

When I first came here, to New York, they used to say, "You speak like a fairy—like they do in Massachusetts." When I kept going back to Massachusetts, they said, "Gee, you got the New York lingo."

—an Italian American

There was a girl who was always very proper . . . so she'd always walk up and say, "Pardon me." We'd all laugh, we knew it was correct, but we'd still laugh. Today, she end up successful.

—an Afro-American

CHAPTER 6

The Dynamics of Language Use

T HROUGHOUT U.S. HISTORY, monolingualism and language standardization have been promoted institutionally and in social custom. Yet, as the previous chapters show, our language remains diverse because of the persistence of non-English language communities, regional dialects, and pressures against standardization. Moreover, language use differs not only from one language community to another; it also varies within a single language community, as Chapters 6 and 7 will illustrate, using the case of American English. This variation can only be appreciated by studying language in its social context.

By its very nature language is a social phenomenon. In intimate, private conversation as in formally structured communication, speakers and listeners draw constantly on their knowledge of social and cultural norms and standards for behavior to interpret and evaluate talk. We react not only to the content of linguistic messages but also to the manner in which they are presented and to other, non-linguistic contextual cues. For communication to be well-received, these modes must reinforce each other in the listener's mind. **Socio-linguistics** is the study of the factors that affect how a message is formulated and how it is received.

Traditionally, linguistics has been concerned with describing the structure of language itself rather than the process and structure of acts of communication. Sociolinguistics has expanded the scope of language study in several dimensions. The study of phonology and syntax, briefly outlined in the Preface, has been augmented by analyses of the structure of conversations and styles of speaking. There has been initial investigation into the relation between verbal and nonverbal modes of communication and how they are used to reinforce or contradict each other. Sociolinguistics particularly has focused on the ways in which language communicates more information than the simple content of the speech. It embodies attitudes speakers hold toward themselves, their listeners, and the topic of the talk itself—all crucial elements in the interpretation of messages.

All of us strive to be clear and convincing in our speech, but the efficacy of linguistic performance depends not just on speaking ability but on assumptions of both speaker and listener about the forms of interaction. Common norms for speech events facilitate communication. If there are discrepancies in the behavioral expectations participants bring to an encounter, then the potential for misunderstanding rises. The most radically differing norms for interaction exist between speakers of two distinct languages, who face an almost insurmountable obstacle to communication. But, even among speakers of a single language, there are sharply and finely distinguished rules for appropriate language behavior and for interpretation of messages. A speaker's ethnicity, socioeconomic class, even gender determine special standards for speaking and for interpreting speech. These differences in communication conventions contribute to the success or failure of a speech event among members of a single language community.

DEFINING SPEECH COMMUNITIES

Communication succeeds most readily when interlocutors adhere to the same standards for language, both behaviorally and attitudinally. Those with whom we share a consensus about language structure, language use, and norms for interaction constitute a **speech community**, within which we expect speaker intent and listener comprehension to mesh. Members of a speech community share a common notion of what is "correct" language.

Speakers of American English form one large community, agreeing as they do on the choice of language for all public, if not all, purposes, and acceding to a single variety of English, standard American, as the most desirable form. This linguistic consensus finds expression in our national media, governmental, commercial, and educational institutions, and in the behavior of millions of speakers who employ it, to the best of their abilities, in public discourse.

In fact, however, individual approximations of standard American English vary considerably. Dialect geographers found differences in the perceived standard in their studies of regional vocabulary and pronunciations. More recent studies have found variations among American English speakers in other aspects of language as well. Syntactic structures, conversational structure, conventions for joking and story-telling, ways of expressing politeness, nonverbal communication—any significant linguistic feature—may demarcate a group of speakers. Syntactically, for instance, speakers in parts of the country form constructions like *I got me a new shirt* by analogy with such sentences as *I got him a new shirt*. Conventions for greeting vary. In some regions *hello* is *howdy* or *how do*. Equally variable are the nonverbal components of this speech event. When does a nod suffice and when is a handshake required? Is it necessary to stand? Do people shake hands only when introduced or whenever they meet?

Speakers also vary their language use according to the situation they find themselves in. Formal interviews tend to elicit speakers' best efforts to produce the standard language—that variety used in fairly formal settings to talk with strangers and official personages. Sociolinguists try to ascertain the range of linguistic forms that represent a speaker's full knowledge of the language. In fact, the style of speech reserved for casual conversation is not only the most natural but linguistically the most systematic, demonstrating speakers' true command of linguistic forms.

Part of "knowing" a language is this ability to **style-shift** according to the topic and setting of an interaction and the number and identity of the participants. All speakers of American English, for example, can distinguish ritual from spontaneous speech in certain contexts. In settings such as a marriage ceremony or the impanelment of a jury, we know that formulaic language is required. The only appropriate response to the question *will you* or *do you* in these contexts is *I will* or *I do*, not *sure, okay,* or *if you say so*, even though the latter "mean the same" in casual conversation. These highly predictable public speech events constitute the most formal part of the **verbal repertoire** of an American English speaker. They are similar to ritual exchanges that exist in all languages and cultures.

Members of a speech community agree on when ritual, formal, informal, and intimate styles are appropriate and on the linguistic and nonverbal features that serve to characterize each of these styles. As they learn a language, children gradually learn these distinctions as well as the sound and grammatical systems of the language. The markers of style are as crucial to successful functioning as the linguistic forms themselves. Part of early school training is initiation into the special, more formal style of interaction we require there. Children must learn not only how to talk but when—in school classes, usually not until given explicit instructions to do so. Adults must come to understand the linguistic markers that distinguish informal conversation with co-workers from the respectful, more reserved style to be used with the boss. It is equally important not to use an intimate style when only informal is appropriate. For instance, switching too soon with a member of the opposite sex might be construed as "too forward."

For American English, the terms of address encode important distinctions in deference and social distance and serve as a good example of the ways we all control shifts in style. Reciprocal first naming is used among intimates and close acquaintances, with the special intimacy of lovers often reflected in special terms of endearment otherwise reserved for small children—such as *sweetie, baby, pumpkin, kitten.* To strangers and to superiors title and last name are required, but superiors may address inferiors with the intimate form—first name only. Thus, using someone's first name implies personal closeness if it is reciprocal, power if it is unidirectional. The conventions for what is close enough for first-name address change from group to group among American English speakers, and each of us must make judgments daily about how to apply these rules. For example, immigrant Jews in New York may expect even long-time social acquaintances to address them as *Mr. and Mrs. Schmidt* while American-born Midwesterners might expect to be called *Chuck and Julie,* even on first meeting. Errors in judgment lead to social opprobrium while appropriate application in each new situation contributes to approval and success.

Within the speech community of American English, a number of geographical dialects have been identified—regional varieties that constitute a standard for the area. But even within a single region not all speakers act alike. Sociolinguists have discovered that the language community is structured into **internal speech communities** whose membership is determined by the entire range of sociological variables: age, class, ethnicity and race, gender, educational level, occupation, religious affiliation, and so on. Internal speech communities have their own norms for linguistic behavior, and their members have interactional modes that distinguish them as a group separate from outsiders. In informal styles such as those used in play groups and among close friends, these internal speech communities emerge most clearly. Private events reveal the internal speech communities to which a speaker belongs or wishes to appear to belong. By studying the demographic bases of internal speech communities, sociolinguists can describe the symbiotic process by which we use language to define ourselves socially and by which others evaluate us through our linguistic performance.

Speech community membership is partly a matter of birth; we are born in a specific region of the country, in an ethnic group, and at a social level that all contribute to the shape our language takes. Although most aspects of language are stabilized by late adolescence, changes may continue to take place throughout life, especially for speakers whose social reference group shifts. Geographic or social mobility may cast speakers into situations in which their language is different from that of the people with whom they come into personal or professional contact. They become linguistic outsiders whose success in their new environment is determined in part by their ability to assimilate to the new linguistic norms. Assimilation to new speech communities very much resembles acquiring yet another style, adding to a speaker's verbal repertoire a new, specialized way of talking. The number of speech communities to which we simultaneously belong is restricted only by the variety of interactional norms we encounter and our will and ability to command them.

Speech community membership is expressed both consciously and unconsciously. Some characteristics of the speech of a group will be shared and used by all; others are chosen to create a more or less close identification with a particular community. These consciously varied features are **context-sensitive**; that is, they alter in occurrence and frequency of occurrence according to when, where, with whom, and about what the user is speaking. Sociolinguists depend on unconscious linguistic forms to determine speech community membership and conscious linguistic choices to assess a speaker's attitudes about that community.

The use of terms of address can again serve to illustrate variation arising from membership in specialized speech communities. While conventions for first name versus title and last name are common to the entire speech community of American English, within that community specific groups apply the general rules in peculiar ways. In the same town one church congregation will use immediate and reciprocal first naming as a means of establishing closeness with one another and extending a sense of belonging to newcomers. Another construes titles as an expression of respect due their priest as a representative of a sacred office and the church elders in deference to their age and experience. Often the only way to discern the appropriate term of address is to overhear a parishioner's *Mr., Dr., Father, Reverend, Pastor,* or *Bill.* Across families naming conventions vary from encouraging children to use first names for all family friends and relatives, even parents, to insisting that all elders and members of older generations receive a kinship title or title and last name address.

Language functions not only to communicate social information but also to define and maintain social roles. One of the characteristics of a speech community is that its members can instantly and accurately distinguish members from nonmembers. In-migrants to New York City, for example, often pick up well-known New York vowel pronunciations in certain words such as *dog* and *coffee.* They come to sound very "New Yorky" to the folks back home, but no native New Yorker is deceived. An Englishwoman returning to her home after long residence in the United States may be told she sounds totally Americanized, though she is still immediately recognized as a foreigner here.

If all social factors were equal, we would tend to assimilate our language to that spoken by those with whom we are in steady contact. And neither we nor those we are adapting to would be aware of the process. But social factors are never equal. Assimilation is enhanced by a positive attitude toward the speakers of a particular variety. And, although there is a strong tendency to sound like those we interact with, speakers can resist this if they are strongly motivated to (Ervin-Tripp 1978). If the new resident in Manhattan admires New Yorkers and enjoys New York life, he will be more likely to adopt New Yorkisms into his own speech, taking on New York as part of his social identity. If he does not like New York or New Yorkers, he can probably live there for years with his speech quite unaffected.

LANGUAGE ATTITUDES

But positive and negative attitudes toward groups of people are not purely personal decisions. Society decrees that certain people be more highly thought of than others—because they are economically, culturally, or politically more powerful. To the extent that social identity is tied to language, actual linguistic forms become "good" or "bad" language according to the social standing of the individuals and groups who use them.

Although *ain't* was once a perfectly acceptable contraction for *am not*, most American English speakers now avoid using it because of its association with lower-class people, especially blacks and Southerners. *Ain't* has become so stigmatized that its use alone suffices as a marker of nonstandard speech. And, in turn, all the negative associations society imposes on a social group come to be extended from the linguistic form onto the person who uses it. An *ain't* user is judged not only to be speaking nonstandard English but to be ignorant, insensitive, dumb, even dirty—stereotypes of lower-class people.

Such **linguistic stereotyping** also works in the opposite direction. An American coming home after a year in London might find herself regarded as snooty and affected if she has adopted standard British ways of speaking. Americans think of English speech as cultured, educated, in some cases even effeminate and tend to associate these "high brow" attitudes and outlooks with anyone who employs those linguistic forms. Of course, high-prestige nonstandard forms can work to a speaker's advantage as well, socially and professionally, while forms considered substandard work against their users in all interactions with mainstream society.

SUBJECTIVE REACTION

Members of a speech community depend on language not only to infer a speaker's background but to make social evaluations about the speaker that have no relation to the language behavior itself. A speech community shares a **subjective reaction** to different language varieties, making judgments not only about social standing, amount of education, and profession, but character and personality traits as well. Given short, taped speech passages of various language varieties, American English speakers feel capable of rating the users on traits such as high/low intelligence, good/bad upbringing, ambition/laziness, trustworthiness/untrustworthiness, sincerity/insincerity, good/no sense of humor, friendliness/unfriendliness, in addition to good/poor education, manual laborer/professional. Speakers of low-status language varieties are judged negatively both professionally and personally. Such subjective reaction tests reveal biases toward groups of people that many of us would not ordinarily express but that influence us whenever we hear nonstandard forms in interaction.

While American English speakers exhibit remarkably similar attitudes when their subjective reactions to speech samples are tested, certain variables that mark internal speech community membership may evoke a positive response, even though they are nonstandard features. A Southerner, for instance, may rate another Southerner low on education, intelligence, and ambition because of nonstandard, Southern pronunciation, vocabulary, or grammatical forms but at the same time rate that speaker higher than a speaker with a Northern, national standard on personal variables such as friendliness, sincerity, and sense of humor. The same is often true of ethnically identifiable speech. Members of the ethnic group think poorly of their fellow speakers on indicators of social standing but sometimes react positively to the familiar speech pattern in personal terms. These splits indicate a **covert prestige** value attached to the nonstandard forms—a group feeling that is a positive incentive for the maintenance of nonstandard speech. For these speakers, public and private prestige language norms are in competition, and high levels of style-shifting can be expected in order to accommodate speech to the demands of different settings.

Sociolinguistic Markers

In a society such as ours where one variety of a language is accorded the status of a standard, every other form of speech functions in many respects in reaction to it. Since the standard is the accepted medium for public interchange, no one can expect to operate successfully without a good understanding of it and at least a minimal ability to speak it. Nonstandard speakers are often very adept at shifting their style of speaking English toward the standard form when talking with standard speakers or in formal settings.

Only certain features that differentiate the standard from nonstandard varieties achieve the status of **sociolinguistic markers**—linguistic features to which social attitudes are attached. Other discrepancies between language varieties go by unnoticed by standard and nonstandard speakers alike. It is the negative sociolinguistic markers—the stigmatized forms—that change as speakers shift styles toward the standard. For example, "dropping the *g*" in *-ing* verb endings (*fishin'* for *fishing, goin'* for *going*) is thought of as sloppy articulation by the entire American English speech community. This attitude persists despite the fact that virtually all speakers of American English use *-in'* some of the time.

Sociolinguists isolate sociolinguistic markers by studying the forms members of a speech community shift away from in situations that permit more attention to be placed on the form of their speech rather than its content. When speakers can be more careful, they approximate the standard as best they can. Figure 16 shows the percentage of *-in'* versus *-ing* endings among New York City white speakers. The lower and working class would be considered nonstandard speakers for many features of their speech, including their high rate of *-in'*—over 80 percent—in casual conversation. The drop-off in *-in'* usage in careful interview style (approximately 55 percent *-in'*) and again in even more closely self-monitored reading style (less than 30 percent *-in'*) indicates their awareness of the feature as a sociolinguistic marker and their agreement with the "correctness" of this stigmatizing attitude.

Upper-middle-class speakers are the people whom the working- and lower-class sample is seeking to emulate. The upper middle class regard themselves as standard-speaking, but even they show a significant use of *-in'* (over 10 percent) in their casual style. This disappears virtually completely, however, in reading style. Thus, even though the working- and lower-class speakers shift more profoundly from casual

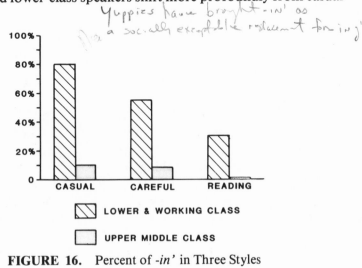

FIGURE 16.   Percent of *-in'* in Three Styles
Among New Yorkers
SOURCE: Labov 1972b:239.

to reading style, they do not achieve the targeted elimination of *-in'* and would be heard as nonstandard by the upper middle class in any case.

This same pattern of style-shifting can be found at other levels of linguistic structure as well. Grammatically, for instance, it is considered less desirable, if not incorrect, to end a sentence with a preposition. Those who wish to appear educated and intelligent may shift from their casual *Who are you going with?* to the more pretentious *With whom are you going?* if they can remember to do so. Choice of vocabulary is altered to suit the dignity of an occasion. A mother at a company picnic might tell her child to *Put that junk in the trash can* but, as entertainment announcer, remind the crowd to *Please deposit refuse in the receptacles*. We even adjust our nonverbal behavior to conform with the appropriate level of interactional style. Casual postures such as feet on stools and low tables and one ankle crossed over the other knee are avoided in business and professional encounters and punished in schools. Etiquette books give us models of verbal as well as nonverbal behavior, but no set of written rules even begins to give a complete picture. Those who come from nonstandard-speaking environments are learning the prestige norms as non-natives and lack the fluidity and ability to manipulate the variety within the prescribed behaviors in ways that mark those who grew up within the standard.

LINGUISTIC INSECURITY

Extreme style-shifting, such as exhibited by the New York City lower working class on *-in/-ing*, is evidence of **linguistic insecurity**. Nonstandard speakers come to accept the negative evaluations of their speech—and through it of their culture and characters—that standard speakers impose. They alter their usage away from their normal, casual conversational style yet still feel insecure about the acceptability of their ways of speaking. Linguistic insecurity tends to be highest among those nonstandard speakers who have had sufficient exposure to the standard to be well aware of what is stigmatized and who aspire to middle-class life, for which standard American English is a virtual prerequisite.

Pronunciation of postvocalic *r* by New Yorkers provides a clear example of the style-shift dynamic that linguistic insecurity evokes.

Figure 17 charts the increasing pronunciation of *r* in three socioeconomic groups as they shift across five styles of increasing formality. Omitting the *r* in words such as *car, beard,* and *farm* is a stigmatized feature of New York City dialect. Even upper-middle-class and professional New York natives exhibit this feature, but all are aware that it is considered nonstandard by non-New Yorkers. All the speakers in the sample from which Figure 17 is drawn recognize inclusion of *r* as national standard usage, increasing their percentage of *r* with every rise in the level of formality and the attendant attention to pronunciation.

Upper-middle-class speech is the appropriate target for the working- and lower-middle-class New Yorkers who wish to achieve an acceptable local standard. Working-class and lower-middle-class speakers use *r* in less than 10 percent of the possible instances in their casual speech while upper-middle-class speakers show about 20 percent *r* in their casual style. The upper middle class gradually increases *r* inclusion to about 60 percent when reading word lists of **minimal pairs** (that is, word pairs that differ only in one sound, in this case with or without *r*, such as *source/sauce, farther/father*). The working class raises its percentage of *r* steadily and attains an *r* rate in pronunciation of minimal pairs that approaches upper-middle-class usage. Thus their reading is at the New York City standard level. But the lower middle class increases *r* usage from 6 to 80 percent, surpassing the upper-middle-class rate of *r* pronunciation in word-list and minimal-pair reading. This group of people, living on the margins of respect-

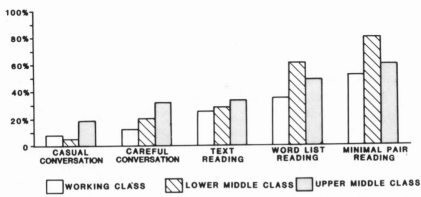

FIGURE 17.   Percent Pronunciation of Postvocalic *r* Across Five Styles Among New Yorkers

Source: Labov 1972b:125.

ability, is most linguistically insecure. The local standard is not standard enough for them; they correct their speech toward the national standard more than any other class of people.

Linguistic insecurity can also be assessed through speakers' reports about their own dialects. They can be asked to identify which of a pair of pronunciations of a word is their own and which is the "correct" pronunciation. A sample list of test words is given in Table 8. Each pronunciation pair contains a sociolinguistic marker, and the discrepancy between the speaker's two responses is an indication of sensitivity to the marker and anxiety about assimilating to the "correct" version. A linguistic insecurity test does not measure use of or even knowledge of the actual standard forms but only speakers' attitudes toward their own variety.

In the case reported in Figure 17, lower-middle-class New Yorkers would be expected to respond that they use the r-less /ban/ for *barn* rather than the "correct" /barn/ pronunciation. Their extreme style-shifting indicates that they perceive a vast discrepancy between their own speech and their standard target. But linguistically insecure people in South Carolina might report /ban/, the prestige Charleston pronunciation, as "correct" and devalue their own r-pronouncing form, even though it conforms to the general American standard. Linguistic insecurity is not necessarily tied to performance. Fairly standard-speaking individuals may still perceive themselves as speaking "wrong" by comparison with the talk around them.

Among somewhat more educated speakers **spelling pronunciations** are indicators of linguistic insecurity. When readers encounter words first learned in conversation, they may adjust their pronunciation to conform to spelling, thinking their original pronunciation must have been incorrect. Since English spelling does not fully reflect pronunciation, errors can thus be introduced into speech. Commonly mispronounced words include *salmon,* with the *l* articulated; *often*, with the *t* pronounced; and *gnu,* when the *g* is not kept silent. Vowels also can be read literally, for example producing /protiən/ in three syllables for /protin/, *protein*. Spelling pronunciations may overcome the original articulation, as has happened in *recognize*, where the *g* is now sounded. Its correct pronunciation was once /rɛkənaiz/. One of the forms currently in transition in American English due to pressure from spelling is *herb*. For the noun, the *h*-less pronunciation is still preferred. But for the adjective form *herbal*, the initial *h* has become fully accepted.

T A B L E 8. Linguistic Insecurity Test

Linguistic insecurity tests measure the discrepancy between what people perceive as "correct" language and their own usage. For these purposes it is irrelevant whether the informant selects the *a* or *b* form of the word. What matters is whether the form designated "correct" is the same as "the one I use." The greater the differences between the pronunciation speakers recognize as "standard" and their own usage, the greater their linguistic insecurity.

Test Words

1. Joseph	a. /ǰosɪf/	b. /ǰozɪf/
2. catch	a. /kæč/	b. /kɛč/
3. tomato	a. /təmeto/	b. /təmato/
4. diapers	a. /daipərz/	b. /daiəpərz/
5. aunt	a. /ant/	b. /ænt/
6. often	a. /ɔftən/	b. /ɔfən/
7. garage	a. /gəraǰ/	b. /gəraž/
8. humorous	a. /hyumərəs/	b. /yumərəs/
9. February	a. /fɛbruɛri/	b. /fɛbyuɛri/
10. avenue	a. /ævənu/	b. /ævənyu/
11. nuclear	a. /nukyələr/	b. /nukliər/
12. Missouri	a. /məzuri/	b. /məzurə/
13. sure	a. /šur/	b. /šur/
14. barn	a. /barn/	b. /ban/
15. greasy	a. /grisi/	b. /grizi/
16. roof	a. /ruf/	b. /rʊf/
17. calm	a. /kalm/	b. /kam/
18. wash	a. /waš/	b. /warš/
19. poor	a. /pur/	b. /por/
20. across	a. /əkrɔst/	b. /əkrɔs/
21. hanger	a. /hæŋgər/	b. /hæŋər/
22. get	a. /gɛt/	b. /gɪt/
23. iron	a. /arn/	b. /aiərn/
24. police	a. políce	b. pólice
25. comparable	a. cómparable	b. compárable
26. pecan	a. /pikan/	b. /pikæn/
27. acorn	a. /ekorn/	b. /ekərn/
28. salmon	a. /sælmən/	b. /sæmən/
29. herbal	a. /hərbəl/	b. /ərbəl/
30. when	a. /wɛn/	b. /hwɛn/

SOURCE: Labov 1966:601, with additions by the authors.

HYPERCORRECTION

Linguistically insecure people are prone to overestimate the difference between their own variety and the standard language. They may react to the perceived discrepancies by **hypercorrecting** their speech—generalizing a rule of standard English to cases where it does not apply. For example, in Boston certain words that are pronounced with the /æ/ vowel (as in *hand*) in standard American English have become /a/; words like *aunt, bath, can't* thus have the vowel of *spa*. Newer or lower-class residents of the city try to adopt this locally prestigious vowel but often do not fully comprehend the restrictions on its use. A common error is to generalize from *can't* /kant/ to its positive counterpart *can*. But *can* is not an /a/ vowel word; established Bostonians pronounce it not /kan/ but /kæn/, as in most of the United States. This error is, of course, instantly recognized by the Boston linguistic elite and results in extreme stigmatization of the would-be social climber.

A widespread phonological hypercorrection is the misuse of the initial /hw/ sound represented in spelling as *wh-*. In older forms of English and in certain areas of the United States today, *where* sounds different from *wear, whether* from *weather*, *which* from *witch*. In most of the country the distinction has been lost. But the older *wh-*pronouncing dialect retains higher status, especially in areas where older speakers still have distinct pronunciations and among educated speakers everywhere. Those who grew up with a marginal understanding of the distinction often misapply the *wh-* sound to non-*wh-* words, creating /hwip/ for *weep*, /hwɪtnɛs/ for *witness,* and other hypercorrect pronunciations. Those who were instructed in the distinction as part of their school training have difficulty limiting its application to just one of the sets of minimal pairs. For instance, they read *witch* as *which* or *weather* as *whether* when trying to be formal and especially "correct," while never making the distinction at all in their casual speech.

Another form of phonological hypercorrection is mispronunciation of foreign words by over-extending the sound rules of the language of origin. By only partially understanding the rules of French pronunciation, would-be users of a prestige form can create an effect on listeners that is the opposite of the one they were striving for. Consonants at the ends of words are not sounded in French, but Americans may not understand the limitations of this rule: *tête-à-tête*, "head to head," meaning "private conversation," may be rendered

/tetəte/ instead of the acceptable /tɛtətɛt/. Like spelling pronunciations, foreign-like pronunciation errors are extremely stigmatized among those who command the correct pronunciation.

Hypercorrect forms appear at all levels of linguistic structure. Grammatically, overuse of the subjective rather than objective case of pronouns is extremely common. Having been told that *It's me* and *Him and me are going to the playground* are incorrect, speakers draw the false conclusion that subjective pronouns are always "fancier." But, in fact, it is the syntactic distinction between subjects and objects that teachers and parents are trying to point out. The result of over-generalization is phrases like *between you and I, Bill went to the store with Joe and I,* even *a girl like I,* which was used to caricature Marilyn Monroe as a "dumb blonde" in the 1953 film *Gentlemen Prefer Blondes.* The film example is such an exaggerated application of hypercorrect subjective that it was recognizable by the entire movie audience, making the user an object of ridicule even for those who employ the hypercorrection in more moderate forms in their own speech.

Who and *whom* are especially problematic since their function as question words puts the objective as well as the subjective form into initial position in the sentence. *Whom* appears in the place normally assumed by a subject so is likely to be rendered as *who,* the subjective form. *Who did you talk to?* is used regularly by almost all Americans, but standard speakers shift styles to *Whom did you talk to?* or even *To whom did you talk?* (avoiding the stigmatized final preposition) in their formal interactions and in writing. Nonstandard speakers understand the need to use *whom* to sound "right" but, once again, have not acquired the case rule underlying its use. Thus a secretary in his best professional style may inquire *Whom shall I say is calling?* when the question word is actually the subject of the dependent clause and should be *who.*

Similar over-carefulness results in the adverb *well,* as in *that looks well on you* when the adjectival form *good* is required. But speakers whose *You play that real good* has been stigmatized draw the conclusion that *well* is better, not that the two are grammatically distinct. *I feel badly* for *I feel bad* has the same source.

Sensitivity to social change can also create hypercorrections. Recently, many women have objected to the use of the "generic" masculine pronoun for indefinite reference. Not wishing to offend his female listeners by implying exclusion, a male television interviewee remarked, "I'm the kind of person who does his or her own thing."

Although all members of the American English speech community experience pressures to conform to the prestige language norm, the relationship between nonstandard varieties and the standard is not entirely unidirectional. Local varieties influence what is construed as ''standard,'' creating somewhat differing targets for correct speech in each area. And in its natural setting—peer group conversation—nonstandard speech continues to evolve along its own lines in directions that the standard too may some day follow.

CHAPTER 7

Demographic Factors in Linguistic Variation

THE DYNAMICS OF American English speech communities can be comprehended as an outcome of the interactions between language use and sociolinguistic attitudes. The nature of variation and the direction of change can be understood by studying the demographic bases for linguistic loyalty. Each of the following sections describes one of the important factors influencing linguistic variation: region, ethnicity, class, gender, age, and occupation. The overlapping effects of these variables—sometimes reinforcing, sometimes contradictory—determine speakers' usage within their communities and their relation to the national standard.

REGION

The evolution of regional varieties of American English has been described in Chapter 4. Within the larger speech community of American English, regional variations continue to add a local character to oral language. Even media broadcasters, formally trained for public speaking, do not sound identical throughout the country. When a network news program inserts a clip of a tornado in Texas, a flood on the Carolina coast, a nuclear accident in Pennsylvania, or a volcanic eruption in the Pacific Northwest, the local announcer's pronunciation adds a convincing note of eyewitness authenticity to the report.

In the same ways that nonstandard dialects interact with the national standard, local speech varieties continue to be measured against the regional prestige norm. The Bluegrass country in west-central Kentucky constitutes just such a focus of prestige culture for the surrounding region. The language variety traditionally spoken by the local elite contains a number of features negatively valued elsewhere in the country, for example rendering *chimney* as *chimley* and *eleven* as *ilebem*. While speakers in other sections of Appalachia show diminished use of these nonstandard pronunciations, Lexington area speakers tend to retain them as a mark of belonging to the Bluegrass culture.

Yet national norms continue to encroach on many regional dialects, as Chapter 5 explains. Now the American standard requires articulation of *r* following vowels (as in *car, source*) while many regional standards are *r*-less. The general trend in the United States is toward replacement of *r* in *r*-less dialects. The rate of change varies greatly, however. Much of the southeastern United States is characterized by *r*-lessness while the Northeast (except eastern New England) is largely *r*-pronouncing. This North/South speech distinction has maintained itself quite stably over generations. Yet in recent years *r* inclusion has grown rapidly in certain parts of the South. The increasing industrialization of Southern cities has brought an influx of Northerners to urbanizing areas. Companies rely on the local population to provide the unskilled labor force but import managers and skilled workers from the Northeast. This economic situation brings about a new prestige speech—one with restored *r*-pronunciation—in urban centers such as Atlanta and Raleigh-Durham, North Carolina. A sociolinguistic study conducted in Hillsboro, North Carolina, reported that a cross-section of local whites increased their use of *r* by over 10 percent when shifting styles from reading sentences to the more careful style of word-list recitation (Levine and Crockett 1966). Since these very cities are traditional centers of culture and prestige behavior, a conflict between regional and national prestige has been created. The next few years will reveal to what extent Southern cities, and through them perhaps the entire Southeast region, will reorient themselves sociologically and linguistically. Variable use of *r* will be an index of social change.

Major metropolitan areas do not always function as positive

linguistic models for their region. New York City speech is highly distinct and recognizable to people in adjacent areas, as well as around the country. But it is negatively, not positively, regarded by outsiders and by New Yorkers themselves. Unlike the speech of its sister cities along the Eastern Seaboard, New York City dialect has not spread to the surrounding region but is confined to the city itself. New York vowel pronunciations are well known and markedly stigmatized, as are such features as the substitution of *n* for *ng* in words like *length*. One young woman described her experience among her husband's friends to a sociolinguist (Labov 1966:486):

> Bill's college alumni group—we have a party once a month in Philadelphia. Well, now I know them about two years and every time we're there—at a wedding, a party, a shower—they say, if someone new is in the group: "Listen to Jo Ann talk!" I sit there and I babble on, and they say, "Don't she have a ridiculous accent!" and "It's so New Yorkerish and all!"
>
> I don't have the accent. I'm in a room with fifty people that have accents, and . . . I don't mind it, but I *never* take it as a compliment. And I can tell by the way people say it, they don't mean it complimentary.

This woman evidences a clear understanding that "accent" is a relative term, asserting that the friends' speech is the nonstandard in her ears. Yet she also understands that she is being negatively evaluated for her New York City forms.

Because negative prestige has become attached to their local dialect, New Yorkers rank very high when tested for linguistic insecurity. They have come, by and large, to believe the external evaluations of their speech as "sloppy," "careless," and "distorted." Although they fear that others will judge them negatively because of their pronunciation, New Yorkers are their own worst critics. In subjective reaction tests they consistently rate outsiders more positively than their fellow New Yorkers, condemning New York features more strongly than do non-New Yorkers.

New regional prestige norms continue to evolve in the United States despite pressures toward leveling represented by mass communication and population mobility. Salt Lake City is a focal area for Utahans, linguistically as well as socially and culturally. Linguistic innovations that begin there are adopted as prestige forms throughout the state. Salt Lake City speakers are willing to go to great linguistic lengths to establish and maintain their urban identity. They act to differentiate themselves from speakers of a stigmatized, rural dialect that is spreading northward from southern Utah. This rural dialect has

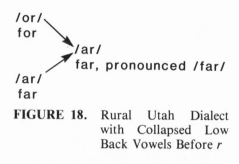

FIGURE 18. Rural   Utah   Dialect
with   Collapsed   Low
Back Vowels Before *r*

partially merged lower back vowels. That is, before *r* rural speakers
are collapsing /a/ and /o/, so that *for* becomes *far* (see Figure 18).
Salt Lake City and more educated speakers throughout the region use
this dialect as a basis for humor, just as supposed ''hillbilly'' forms are
used elsewhere in the United States. The southern rural pronunciation
of *fork* as *fark* and *Lord* as *Lard* has brought about a linguistic reaction among other Utahans. Urban and educated speakers have begun
to shift away from the vowel /a/ in all /ar/ words, so that they have no
words with the stigmatized /ar/ sequence. Thus *far* in some Salt Lake
City speakers has been hypercorrected to /fɔr/ in order to indicate
that the speaker is not a user of the *for* = *far* dialect (see Figure 19).
Salt Lake City speakers have overgeneralized their understanding of
the stigmatized feature—/or/ becoming /ar/—and have altered even
legitimately /ar/-sounding words to a new pronunciation, one that is
not found at all in the rural dialect. This hypercorrection has, in effect, created a new regional prestige pronunciation, motivated out of
sociolinguistic factors unique to Utah (Cook 1969).

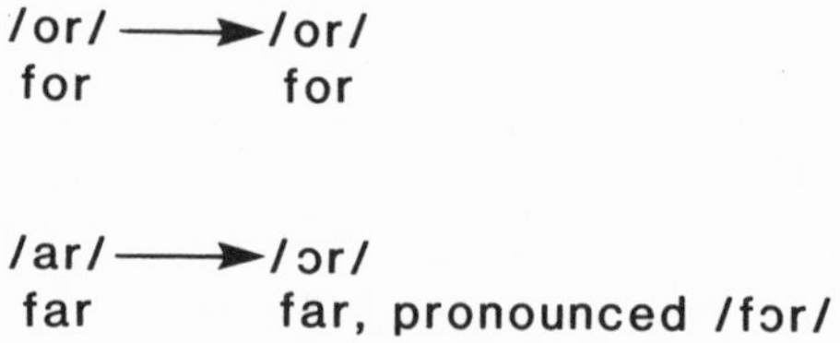

/or/ ——▶/or/
for   for

/ar/ ——▶/ɔr/
far   far, pronounced /fɔr/

FIGURE 19. Salt   Lake   City   Dialect
with   Low   Back   Vowels
Retained Before *r*

ETHNICITY

In the United States, social identity derives from a complex of
allegiances. Ethnicity's mark on speech is no less indelible than that of

geography. Although the particular mix varies, no region of the country is ethnically uniform (see Figure 8). The coastal and Deep South are largely of English and African descent but are also home to a variety of European nationalities in smaller numbers. The inland South has a core Scotch-Irish population, but only remote pockets remain unaffected by later immigrations and population shifts. The Northeast is well known for its multi-ethnicity, varying in its complexion from city to city but exhibiting many of the same inter-ethnic dynamics. The Appalachian Scotch-Irish have migrated to the Great Lakes region, further complicating the typical Northeastern pattern there. In the Midwest various European groups settled in regional concentrations. The Southwest is home to American Indians and large numbers of Hispanics as well. The Pacific Coast has the additional factor of significant Asian American populations.

The standards for American English language use are set by established long-resident northern Europeans, especially Anglo-Saxons. Descendants of non-Europeans and of immigrant groups arriving from Europe in the late nineteenth and early twentieth centuries—such as Italians, Jews, eastern Europeans—have not penetrated the upper middle class and the professions in proportionate numbers. Their speech patterns are thus associated with working-class culture and stigmatized for formal interaction. So ethnicity plays a part in linguistic insecurity and in language change.

Ethnically distinct speech is not just a social marker to outsiders but also indicates solidarity to group members. Unique speech forms, disparaged as nonstandard by middle-class speakers, may constitute a covert prestige norm, embodying and symbolizing a special culture into which only like-speakers are welcomed. Ethnically identified English serves native-born ethnic Americans as a marker of group cohesion and loyalty—a role similar to the one played by use of the homeland language for first- and second-generation immigrants. Ethnic Americans require standard English if they are to achieve social mobility and public influence, but social solidarity demands maintenance of nonstandard forms. Personal interaction and public interaction take place in different dialects of English. These conflicting linguistic loyalties differ in intensity but not in kind from the language choice problems faced by the immigrant generation.

In New York City vowel pronunciation serves as an indicator of ethnic identity. From a sociolinguistic perspective, New York City constitutes a single regional dialect, but its complex social structure finds expression in linguistic stratification according to socioeconomic class and ethnicity. The linguistic features that specifically mark New York City dialect undergo varying extremes of usage depending on speakers' class and ethnic identification. Each succeeding wave of immigrants has mimicked the English of its predecessors, adopting approximations of their ethnic English as models. But the transfer from homeland language to English has not resulted in eradication of language as a marker of ethnicity. Rather, differences among ethnic groups have been maintained by highly refined linguistic differences in their pronunciation and use of English, differences that go unnoticed by outsiders but that function as salient sociolinguistic markers to members of the New York City speech community.

As mentioned in Chapter 4, vowel raising is a characteristic of the New York City dialect. But, within the New York speech community, the phonetic heights of vowels vary in systematic ways. Among white ethnics, the degree of raising serves as an identity marker. In particular, Italians contrast with Jews in their vowel-raising behavior. Both groups raise front vowels so that the vowel of *bad* is long and close to the vowel of *bed* (/æ/ approaches /ɛ/). Italians continue this movement, raising the vowel in certain words to the point where /æ/ is almost /e/, as in *bade* (see Figure 20). Jews are distinguished by engaging in vowel raising in the back of the mouth as well. As Figure 21 illustrates, the /ɔ/ vowel of *coffee* becomes similar to /o/ so that *sawed* sounds to the outsider very much like *sew-ed* (Labov 1966).

In Boston, too, vowel heights are used to mark ethnicity among working-class whites (Laferriere 1979). Boston speech is *r*-less so that words such as *short* and *corn* are pronounced without the *r* sounded. Some Boston speakers have further altered a subset of words with the sequence /o(r)/, making the vowel lower, close to /a/. Thus *short*

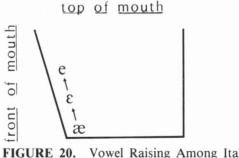

FIGURE 20.   Vowel Raising Among Italians in New York City

top of mouth

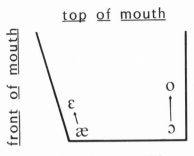

FIGURE 21. Vowel Raising Among Jews in New
York City

sounds like *shot* and *corn* like *con*. This pronunciation is called an
"Irish accent" by other Bostonians. In fact, though their speech may
have served as the model for later immigrants, the Irish are not the
heaviest users of the lowered vowel pronunciation. The three large
Boston working-class ethnic groups—Irish, Italians, and Jews—differentiate themselves from each other on the /o(r)/ variable, both in
their actual articulation of it and in their sensitivity to it as a sociolinguistic marker. Figure 22 shows this variation in pronunciation of
the lowered vowel in three styles.

In all styles Italians are the highest users of the /a(r)/ pronunciation. Jews always most resemble the Boston standard /o(r)/ articulation. Jews are also most sensitive to the negative social value attached
to the /a(r)/ pronunciation by middle-class Bostonians. They reduce
their use of the lowered articulation by 28 percent as they cross styles,
shifting somewhat more sharply than the Irish (26 percent reduction

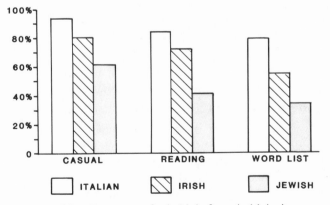

FIGURE 22. Percent of /a(r)/ for /o(r)/ Among
Boston White Ethnics in Three Styles

SOURCE: Laferriere 1979:607.

of /a(r)/) and far more dramatically than the Italians (15 percent /a(r)/ reduction). Jews, however, make their drastic shift between casual and reading style, while Irish and, especially, Italians shift away from the lowered vowel only when they are exercising extreme care. The Jews command the ability to change generally in interaction with the standard.

It is not the nature of language change that creates sociolinguistic markers, but the nature of social attitudes toward groups that employ the language forms. As changes become identified with groups of speakers, they take on positive or negative prestige, depending on the social standing of the speakers. The merger of the two low vowels /a/ and /ɔ/ has been completed in some parts of the United States—a major restructuring of the vowel system accomplished without any notice by, for instance, the whole populations of western Pennsylvania and the West Coast states. The merger is now spreading to other parts of the country. In some regions speakers of all ethnicities are merging the vowels at the same rate, but in others blacks and Hispanics appear to resist the loss of the distinction. If this trend toward ethnic stratification continues, unmerged /a/-/ɔ/ may become a vehicle for expressing our social attitudes toward these groups of speakers.

Some ethnic linguistic markers have transcended a single locale, marking users according to their ethnicity in wide regions of the country. Jews throughout the Northeast and Midwestern region tend to retain some Yiddish-derived speech features. Raising of /æ/ is common in Chicago, Detroit, Cleveland, and St. Louis as well as in New York City. In fact, outsiders often mistake such speakers for New Yorkers since this characteristic is so strongly identified with the speech of New York. In these cities vowel raising has begun to spread to other ethnic groups as well, perhaps becoming a general characteristic of urban ethnic and working-class speech. Ethnically identified Jews in many parts of the United States make use of word order change for contrastive emphasis in ways drawn directly from their forebears' native tongue. The stressed word is placed first in the sentence, as in *Hoodlums he takes up with*. Another usage characterizing Jewish-American English is *already* for *now*, as in *Be quiet already, I'm coming already*, or the set phrase, now commonly used by many Americans, *All right already*.

Ethnicity is also indicated by styles of talking such as joke-telling and by nonverbal interactional behavior. Many of the unconscious aspects of speech style and nonverbal behavior seem to survive intact in the switch from the homeland language to English.

Within ethnic groups certain ways of expressing humor are favored. Punning, for instance, is considered a very clever form of humor among some groups and scorned as low humor in others. Subtler forms of humor may entirely escape the notice of ethnic outsiders. They may not understand why a certain thing is being said at all or fail to understand that a statement is intended to mean something other than its literal interpretation. Irony—saying the exact opposite of what is meant—is frequently employed by British Americans; understatement, deprecation, and self-deprecation might be favored in the same situations by other ethnicities.

One form of humor important among black Americans is **signifying**, making a point by indirect reference. The actual point of the remark, often a criticism, is never mentioned, only alluded to in a way that makes it unmistakable. A skillful signifier manages to convey a sharp point without ever directly mentioning it. An exchange between two young women illustrates this form of humor, with Grace providing the following background to the story (Mitchell-Kernan 1972:323):

> After I had my little boy, I swore I was not going to have any more babies. I thought four kids was a nice-sized family. But it didn't turn out that way. I was a little bit disgusted and didn't tell anybody when I discovered I was pregnant. My sister came over one day; I had started showing a little by that time.
>
> The interchange took place as follows:
>
> ROCHELLE: Girl, you sure do need to join the Metrecal [a weight-loss drink] for lunch bunch.
>
> GRACE (noncommitally): Yea, I guess I am putting on a little weight.
>
> ROCHELLE: Now look here, girl, we both standing here soaking wet and you still trying to tell me it ain't raining.

This humorous indirect reference made it clear to Grace that her sister knew what she was hiding, and they might as well have it out in the open.

Ethnic groups vary, too, in their tolerance for silences and pauses in speech. Dinner party conversation among Anglo-Americans is likely to include brief unfilled lapses which, though not alarming to group members, may indicate ill-humor or boredom to an outsider. Alternatively, an Anglo-American may experience a southern European household as frenzied or confusing since talk is more continual. Even longer periods of silence pervade the interactions of English-speaking native American peoples—a carry-over from their traditional culture and conversational structure.

Nonverbal language seems to be particularly resistant to change or conscious modification. Gestures and postures impart important clues to a person's opinions, attitudes, and comfort and may convey explicit information, such as agreement and dissent, as well. Speakers tend to be unaware of this component of their communication, just as listeners absorb it without conscious attention. Subtle distinctions in group nonverbal norms may be overlooked or misread, but they are rarely comprehended as communicational differences. Nonverbal behaviors are learned early and retained largely unaltered throughout life. Thus they are often clear indicators of ethnic identity. Americans from Mediterranean cultures, for example, are widely recognized by hand gestures that accompany their more animated conversations.

Ethnic linguistic differences may be sources of profound misunderstanding in American society. Whether consciously or unconsciously perceived, they form bases for judgments about groups and individuals that may be inappropriate and inaccurate.

CLASS

Americans routinely use linguistic indicators of social and economic class to evaluate speakers' intelligence, abilities, and moral character. On the presumption that everyone aspires to upper-middle- or upper-class speech, deviation from standard English is construed negatively. Yet, as with ethnic language features, class markers in speech have the important sociological function of identifying group members and creating group solidarity.

Just as use of standard English characterizes the upper middle class in general, so many nonstandard features transcend ethnic and regional boundaries. Detroit working-class blacks and whites, for example, all frequently use double negation. *I don't know nobody* replaces standard English *I don't know anybody*. Figure 23 shows the sharp class stratification. Although whites are generally less likely to use the stigmatized grammatical structure, all lower-working-class speakers have it more often than not, while it virtually disappears among the upper middle class of both races. Blacks and whites show parallel patterns of style-shifting as well. Both groups are sensitive to double negation as a stigmatized marker of lower-class speech and shift away from it in their careful speech and reading style. Likewise, attitudes about sociolinguistic markers are stratified by class. It is

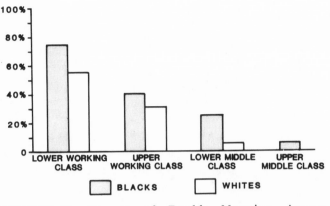

FIGURE 23. Percent of Double Negation Among Detroit Blacks and Whites

Source: Shuy et al. 1967:20–21.

speakers who employ nonstandard features whose subjective reactions to them may be most negative.

Regional dialects and ethnic linguistic markers often have a class component that contributes to their evaluation by standard speakers. Appalachian English is not an object of scorn because its users come from remote valleys. Rather, it is the poverty of Appalachian speakers that makes others distance themselves from the dialect. Likewise, inner-city white ethnics are the core of the urban working class. Ethnic linguistic markers become stigmatized because their users have low socioeconomic status.

Linguistic change often originates in a single socioeconomic class—frequently the working class, whose speakers are less firmly tied to the conservative literary standard. In the raised vowel pronunciation that characterizes urban populations in many parts of the Northeast, working-class speakers, especially young people, have the highest variants. Although this vowel shift continues to spread to other classes and to suburban areas, it is often stigmatized as working-class and thus stereotyped as inferior.

Language features can be used to maintain class identity as well. Working-class young men employ nonstandard markers to sound "tough" and masculine. There are also linguistic indicators of upper-class status by which members of traditionally wealthy families identify one another. Throughout the United States, the society set uses an intonation pattern that lends a "bored" quality to the voice by flattening pitch on stressed words. Understatement is also a characteristic of upper-class speech. *I'm rather tired* would be favored over *I'm very tired*. Certain words and constructions outdated in other classes are maintained by the elite. For instance, *awfully* is still used as a modifier of verbs: *My parents ridiculed it awfully*. The upper class, secure in its social position, can afford to take a more relaxed attitude toward the use of standard American English than can lower- and middle-class Americans. Thus New York City upper-class speakers readily employ the raised vowels that characterize city and especially working-class speech. Middle-class speakers shift away from the stigmatized raised /æ/ and /o/ in their careful speech in order to sound more respectable, but upper-class speakers use them unself-consciously (Nunberg 1980).

Language often remains as a social marker long after economic status has changed. A working-class family may earn a middle-class income, but nonstandard speech patterns can create a working-class social identity nonetheless. Similarly, it is only in the "right" social circles and private schools that upper-class speech can be acquired; money is not sufficient entree into upper-class society.

GENDER

Social differences create linguistic differences even between people who share constant contact. A live-in servant may retain nonstandard speech patterns in spite of daily, primary contact with standard-speaking employers, for language serves as a means of maintaining social boundaries. And speech variation consistently appears within a family itself, most obviously across generations and between the sexes.

Stereotypes of female and male language differences are especially rampant, often used as a source for humor. But stereotypes provide a more accurate index of attitudes than behavior, as men's and women's language use demonstrates. Differences there are, indeed, but the customs of women and men do not conform entirely to the common images of linguistic sex-role behavior.

Vocabulary differences between women and men are a direct result of, and an excellent indicator of, the roles which each sex has been assigned in our society. Women are more likely to be familiar with the terms necessary for working with fabrics, food, or children, while men know the terminology of sports and mechanics. A number of adjectives and adverbs are attributed almost exclusively to women:

adorable, charming, lovely, divine. Women are expected to intensify their expressions with terms such as *delighted, thrilled, so (very),* and *such (a).* These vocabulary choices are appropriate only in women's traditional sphere, however. *That was such a lovely party you gave last night!* seems fine, if very feminine, but *That was such a lovely report you turned in!* would seem odd and unprofessional. On the other hand, men's intensifiers tend to be "four letter words." There has been a virtual taboo against use of obscenities by women, at least in middle-class society, although this seems to be breaking down as sex roles and life styles change. Since "strong language" does just what it says—underlines a strongly held opinion or emotional reaction—women who want to be heard as serious, independent people have found themselves shifting to male intensifiers.

One stereotype of women's language behavior is the "schoolmarm" forcing innocent young children to learn antiquated pronunciations and incessantly correcting their grammar. In part this stereotype holds true. Women are sometimes linguistic conservatives, but they are radicals as well. Although both sexes usually are moving in the same direction in linguistic changes, their rates are not identical. Since features undergoing change are often sociolinguistic markers, this male/female difference, too, is an indication of social role and social awareness.

Perhaps because of their continued interaction with children throughout their lifetimes, women may be over a generation ahead of men in cases of language change. That is, a woman in her mid-thirties will use a new feature as extensively as a small boy in her speech community. The rate of the merger of the low vowels /a/ and /ɔ/ reflects this gender stratification. The opposite is true, however, if a change has become stigmatized. Then women are less likely to be in the vanguard than are men. One of the most highly stigmatized markers of black speech is the pronunciation of word-final *th* as *t* or *f* or its deletion. That is, *tooth* is rendered as *toot, toof,* or *too.* Figure 24 shows the effect of this sociolinguistic discrimination on Detroit blacks. In all classes men use the nonstandard pronunciation more often. The discrepancy is most striking—almost two to one—between men and women of the lower middle class, those generally most linguistically insecure. Upper-middle- and upper-working-class speakers show a difference of about 50 percent. On this and other sociolinguistic variables, only men and women of the lower working class perform very similarly, a consequence of reduced contact with standard English and limited socioeconomic expectations.

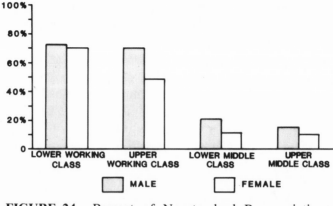

FIGURE 24. Percent of Nonstandard Pronunciations for Final *th* Among Detroit Black Women and Men
SOURCE: Wolfram 1969:92.

Men who wish to participate in the vernacular culture often find themselves in situations in which nonstandard language forms are necessary to maintain credibility. One New York small businessman explained that, while he uses standard English with his office staff, he chooses working-class features to create rapport with customers who share that background. He reported the following conscious downward style-shift, unconsciously also using *d* for *th* (Labov 1966:491–92):

> I said, "Thank you" for something, and he was annoyed, 'cause I thanked him— 'cause he's a rough, tough kinda guy, y'know. So he says, "Aaah, ya fuckin' gentleman, you!" 'Cause basically I am—he resents the fact that I'm courteous to him. So what I did was to put my head back in the door and say to him, "You know Jack, you're quite a character." He had a bunch of people—they're all close people, and he had made the remark in front of them. "What would you want me to do, take that thing from you, and call you a dirty name? Would that (/dæt/) be a sign of respect to you?" . . . So he smiled and says, "Go on, kiddo, I'll see ya."

This same businessman insisted that he would not hire anyone into his office who employed nonstandard features, such as the one he himself uses.

Women do not have opportunities to be confirmed by use of nonstandard language. Their role is to socialize children to upward social mobility and to serve as examples of correct behavior. Thus women, while apparently more sensitive than men to linguistic differences and their social import, are more firmly identified with the standard. Women are more severe in their judgments of nonstandard speakers on subjective reaction tests. They are generally more linguistically insecure, exhibiting extreme style-shifting and, more frequently than men, hypercorrection.

Linguistic gender models are adopted early. Boys and girls as young as grammar school age differ in the frequency with which they use sociolinguistic markers. Among small town, middle-class New England children, boys were discovered to use "dropped *g*" pronunciations of verbs like *runnin'* and *comin'* significantly more often than girls. Style-shift differences even emerged. Little girls shifted markedly away from the *-in'* pronunciation when placed in a formal interview situation, while boys' speech remained largely unchanged (Fischer 1958).

Just as women tend to speak more standard varieties of English, they exceed men in their use of explicitly polite forms—likewise markers of elevated style (Lakoff 1975). If men's speech is characterized by directness, women's is characterized by indirectness and circumlocution. Rather than *Let's eat!* a homemaker might say to her family *Can we eat now?* or *Are you ready to eat?*, even though the timing of the meal is the consequence of her own labor and decision-making. A command in question form offers the listener the illusion of consenting or even deciding. A stereotype of women in helping professions such as nursing or childcare is the use of *we* forms for commands. A nurse can legitimately request that a patient submit to a temperature measurement. But *We're going to have our temperature taken now, aren't we?* identifies the requester with the object of the command, making it appear less like an *I order you* interaction. Indirect requests constitute failures or refusals to accept power or authority. Women who speak excessively indirectly may, often legitimately, fear a negative response to assertion of authority on their part. Polite forms are employed toward superiors by inferiors, and women's use of politeness markers is an indicator of the status discrepancy between the sexes.

Language used toward women also reflects sex roles. For example, many women work in occupations in which first-name address is applied, even by total strangers. Administrators address clericals by first name, a privilege rarely reciprocal; retail sales personnel, overwhelmingly female, even wear badges stating their first names only.

Men's higher social status finds expression in the structure of their conversations with women. In a dialogue two people take turns speaking and listening, giving clearly interpretable cues as to when they think the turns should rotate. Refusal to observe the turns creates an imbalance in the interactional rights of the conversationalists. Contrary to the stereotype of women as excessive talkers, in cross-sex interactions it is men who do most of the talking. Table 9 displays the relative amount of time the partners in a series of interactions were silent. Women talking with each other were generally fair in their distribution of talking and listening time. Men speaking with other men, while somewhat less egalitarian than women, granted the floor to each other in a fairly democratic fashion. But in conversation between male-female pairs there was a radical discrepancy in the amount of time spent listening. Men consistently dominated the talk.

When interruptions of the speaker are calculated, sex differences emerge even more strikingly. Interruptions constitute a violation of the speaker's turn to hold the floor. Table 10 summarizes the occurrence of overlaps and full interruptions in the conversations of the same-sex and cross-sex pairs whose silence and speaking times were calculated in Table 9. In overlaps, a listener starts to talk while his partner is just finishing the final segment of her speech. Full interruptions break the speaker off in mid-thought. Both speaking too soon and cutting off the talk in mid-flow are fairly evenly distributed between two men and two women, but not between women and men. It is men who violate women's conversational rights, not vice versa.

The stereotypes of men as "strong, silent" figures and women as "chatterboxes," brimming with effusive talk, clearly do not reflect conversational reality. They probably derive more from the import attached to the content of men's and women's talk. Since men make the

T A B L E 9. Distribution of Silence Between Partners

LENGTHS OF SILENCES OF ONE PARTNER COMPARED TO THE OTHER	LEAST EQUAL	MOST EQUAL
Same-sex dialogues:		
Female-female (number of conversations = 10)		X XXX X XXX XX
Male-male (number of conversations = 10)	X XXX X	XX XX X
Cross-sex dialogues* (number of conversations = 11)	XX X XX XXX XX X	

* In all cases of cross-sex conversation, women were the more silent partners.
SOURCE: Zimmerman and West 1972:119.

TABLE 10. **Interruptions in Two-Party Conversations**

	OVERLAPS	FULL INTERRUPTIONS
Same-sex conversations:		
Speaker A	55%	43%
Speaker B	45%	57%
Cross-sex conversations:		
Males	100%	96%
Females	—	4%

SOURCE: Zimmerman and West 1972:115–16.

important economic and political decisions in most families, their remarks have more weight and interest, regardless of how they are conveyed. Women's concerns, and therefore women's ways of speaking, are trivialized. In cross-sex interactions men dominate in choice of topic as well as in talking time. This aspect of male-female conversation also contributes to the silent-man/chattering-woman stereotype. Between partners (although not between strangers, of course) it is women who initiate the majority of conversations. But women succeed in creating ongoing interactions only if the men find the topic of interest. If men initiate talk, their wives or women friends usually follow up with active conversation on the topic, regardless of their personal interest in it. But men respond only when they choose. Linguistic reality is captured in cartoons depicting an occasional "umhmm" emanating from behind the newspaper while the wife tries vainly to get a dialogue going on a topic of her choice. Several such minimal responses force her to abandon the topic. Determining the topic, too, is an indicator of the relative social status of men and women. The same rules hold true for conversation between employer and employee, lower- and middle-class speakers, ethnic minorities and members of the dominant group.

Deferential interactional patterns by women and dominance patterns toward them have correlates in nonverbal language as well. Men touch women more frequently and over more extensive parts of their bodies than women do men. This is well known to be true between strangers or in work situations, where its excesses have recently received the label sexual harassment. But even between heterosexual partners, it is the male who more often initiates touching. Especially in situations in which sexual intimacy is inappropriate, touching becomes a signal of dominance: employer touches employee, adults touch children, superiors touch inferiors. Racial minorities have become particularly vociferous in denouncing this form of interactional inequality. Just as adults object to being called "boy," they find a pat on the head or the shoulder demeaning when it cannot be reciprocated. Eye contact between men and women also functions as a status marker. Among middle-class whites, for whom it is a signal of attentiveness, women watch men's eyes more closely than men do women's. But men hold their gaze longer, forcing women to avert their glance. Extended gaze is deemed an expression of authority in all cultures (Henley 1972).

Women are also more adept at interpreting nonverbal behavior, assigning a correct emotional interpretation to a message, even when they cannot hear the speaker. This ability is a common component of linguistic insecurity. Nonstandard speakers can readily understand standard speech and the gestures that accompany it, not only because they are exposed to this variety of verbal and nonverbal behavior in the media, but also because they need to know how people with power over them are feeling. Standard speakers do not require a fine-tuned sensibility to the language of the nonstandard speaker, since they are rarely directly affected by the latter's actions. The same relation holds true for men and women: between the sexes the man is the standard.

AGE

Every American family is acquainted with at least some effects of language change. Grandpa's style of talk and word choices are quaint or old-fashioned, sometimes a source of embarrassment to young people. Out-of-date slang and usages like the sentence modifier *why*, as in *Why, I remember when we went to the lake every summer*, are construed as a sign of being out of touch with the contemporary world. Adolescent speech is a common cause for parental criticism and concern. Many family squabbles take place over new slang expressions, "sloppy" pronunciation, and "bad" language.

Language is an important component of youth culture. Adolescents make conscious use of linguistic forms deviating from their parents' and teachers' as part of their struggle to establish separate, adult identities, just as they use popular music and styles of dress. Expressions and gestures go in and out of vogue, shifting as rapidly as they become known to the adult community. Middle-class teenagers often draw their style of talking from ethnic nonstandard speech, varieties which they know their parents neither command nor approve. *Foxy, laid back,* and *ripped off,* for instance, all originated in urban black English.

By grammar school age, children have shifted their linguistic models from their parents to their playmates, mimicking especially children just their senior. It is in the grammar school years that articulatory motor control becomes set; the language variety learned then forms the ineradicable native pattern of speech. And its model is peers, not parents. After this age genuine native fluency in another dialect (or language) is far more difficult to attain.

But it is not until the mid-teens that the ability to recognize and manipulate speech styles becomes fully developed. Adolescents learn to shift styles depending on the situation and their conversation partners. They come to understand the social importance of linguistic markers and can, if they are so motivated, adjust stigmatized features in their own speech. Teen language is in part exercise and enjoyment of this newly acquired language capability. Thus by the time young people are old enough to comprehend the meaning of sociolinguistic stratification and its implications for their own life futures, they are too old to change completely their fundamental speech patterns. It is this age-grading in acquisition of linguistic ability that creates the patterns of incomplete style-shifting and hypercorrection that have been reported in Chapter 6.

But generational differences may also be the effect of genuine language change. Living languages are never static; children's speech cannot duplicate their parents'. Although many linguistic changes take place very gradually, sometimes complete shifts are accomplished in only three or four generations. In some eastern Pennsylvania families, for example, grandparents have /a/ and /ɔ/ totally distinct, the adult generation has a partial collapse—*Don* and *dawn* may be pronounced differently, but *hock* and *hawk* the same—while children in the same households have complete systemic merger of the two vowels. Teachers rail in vain against the use of *lie* and *lay* interchangeably. The teachers' parents learned the distinction as a natural part of their language acquisition. They themselves were taught it early on as a mark of "good English." For today's youth the distinction has virtually passed out of the language.

Linguistic attitudes may also undergo rapid change. A subjective reaction test given to New York City boys and men illustrates both the acquisition of sociolinguistic discrimination and attitudinal change. Table 11 summarizes the responses to two taped versions of the same

TABLE 11. **Positive Attitude to *r*-Pronouncing Speech by New York City Boys and Men**

Age	Lower Class	Lower Working Class	Upper Working Class	Lower Middle Class	Upper Middle Class	Total
8–17	16%	57%	67%	89%	50%	61%
18–19	100%	no data	100%	100%	100%	100%
20–39	100%	100%	100%	100%	100%	100%
40+	63%	67%	50%	70%	57%	62%

Source: Labov 1972b:149.

sentence. Listeners were asked whether they preferred the pronunciation including the phrase *He got hit* /hard/, with *r* pronounced as in standard American English, or the *r*-less New York pronunciation *He got hit* /haad/. Approximately a third of the respondents over forty years of age still preferred the local *r*-less pronunciation. But none of the adults under forty chose that version. Their condemnation of the traditional New York accent was categorical. Once again, members of the lower middle class proved most conscious of the sociolinguistic change; only 30 percent responded positively to *r*-lessness. The boys in the eight- to seventeen-year-old group have partially formed sensitivity to the sociolinguistic marker. Like their elders, the boys in the lower middle class are most linguistically alert. Only 11 percent fail to identify with the national standard, although their own speech is *r*-less.

Where language change occurs at differing rates within a single speech community, it serves as a mirror of social values. A generational study of the speech community of Martha's Vineyard, a small island off the coast of Massachusetts, provides just such an example (Labov 1972b:1–42). Martha's Vineyard is a relic area, retaining speech patterns long abandoned in the rest of eastern New England. Most notably it is *r*-pronouncing, unlike the regional focal area, Boston. Antiquated words such as *tempest* for *storm, buttery* for *pantry*, are still in common use. Vineyard speech is also characterized by extreme vowel centralization—an articulation lost on the mainland before 1850. Vowels ordinarily pronounced at the extremes of the mouth, especially /a/, /i/, and /u/, are shifted inward, toward /ə/. This closed-mouth, "Old Yankee" articulatory style is considered very quaint and colorful by summer visitors.

Martha's Vineyarders vary greatly from each other in their actual vowel articulation. The diphthong /ai/ is centralized almost to /əi/ in some speakers, but pronounced fully lowered by others. Thus *wife* is heard as both /wəif/ and /waif/ from island natives. When the Vineyard population is categorized according to age and ethnicity, the social meaning of this linguistic choice becomes apparent. From this single pronunciation feature alone, dramatic conclusions can be drawn about the future of the island and of individual islanders.

Centralization of /ai/ is measured by instrumental analysis of the exact location in the mouth at which the first component of the diphthong, the /a-/, is produced. Relative centralization can thus be precisely scaled, with zero representing a fully lowered, /ai/ pronunciation and 100 representing full centralization, /a-/ having become /ə-/. Table 12 shows the degree of centralization graded by age. Each succeeding age group has acquired its articulation at a more recent time, thus offering historical evidence of the rate and direction of the pronunciation shift. Clearly vowel centralization increased rather than decreased over several generations. In the fifty-year period represented by the speakers aged thirty-one through seventy-five /ai/ grew more and more centralized; Vineyard pronunciation became more markedly unlike mainland speech. The /ai/ of the youngest men, those fourteen through thirty years old, is less extreme than their fathers' generation but more centralized than in their grandfathers' speech. In order to explain this shift in the pronunciation trend, ethnicity must be considered as well as age.

In spite of its tiny population of 6,000, Martha's Vineyard is stratified ethnically. Almost two-thirds of the island's residents are of very old Yankee families—English colonists who came out from the mainland in the seventeenth and eighteenth centuries. Twenty percent are English-speaking Portuguese, both recent arrivals and long-settled islanders. The Yankee families have never wished to accept the Portuguese as true Vineyarders, preferring to identify islander status with English ethnicity. The history of the relations between these two groups can be traced in their vowel articulation.

Table 13 breaks the speech community down by ethnicity. Portuguese men have a less centralized articulation, but the age-grading in the two groups is strikingly parallel. Both English and Portuguese

TABLE 12. Percent of Centralization of /ai/ by Age

Age in years:	14–30	31–45	46–60	61–75	Over 75
	19	41	31	18	13

SOURCE: Labov 1972b:22.

**T A B L E 13. Percent of Centralization of /ai/ by
Age and Ethnicity**

Age in years:	Under 30	31–45	46–60	Over 60	All ages
English	18	54	43	18	34
Portuguese	17	37	19	13	21

SOURCE: Labov 1972b:26.

have centralized increasingly over time down to the youngest adult generation. Among the English, centralization in the young men has receded to the level of the very oldest speakers. Young Portuguese, while they have reduced centralization, fall back, not to their grandfathers' generation, but to the same level used by the young Yankees.

Since vowel centralization has been a critical distinguishing mark of native island, Yankee speech, centralized /ai/ constitutes an assertion of Vineyard identity. Increasing centralization among the middle-aged men took place at a time when tourism to the island soared; the vowel pronunciation represents their efforts to differentiate themselves from the invading "summer people." But in recent years the traditional economy—farming and fishing—has suffered severe decline, forcing many young men to seek jobs off the island. Thus their reduced centralization. The young men's positive reorientation to the mainland makes them identify with the Boston sphere, not the Vineyard.

This economic hardship has especially affected the old English families. Traditionally elite and exclusive, they have suffered economic and, subsequently, social decline. As a result, they are increasingly unable to maintain a separate social identity from the less advantaged Vineyard population. The young Portuguese men are finally attaining social equality and "island native" status and express their common bond with their Yankee age-mates by identical vowel articulation.

Once the direction of linguistic change and the social variables affecting it are understood, language use can serve as an indicator of social attitudes and, perhaps, behavior. The seemingly obscure and abstract variation in articulation of /ai/ actually predicts an islander's attitude toward his home and his likelihood of moving off-island. Table 14 demonstrates a direct correlation between degree of centralization and attitude toward the Vineyard. Those who plan to leave reveal their intentions by near-zero centralization. Those who wish to stay show strong centralization. Members of each group have restruc-

T A B L E 14. Percent of Centralization of /ai/ and Orientation Toward Martha's Vineyard

POSITIVE ATTITUDE	NEUTRAL	NEGATIVE ATTITUDE
32	16	3

SOURCE: Labov 1972b:39.

tured their language to conform to their probable on-island or off-island futures and the speech communities in which they will find themselves.

Adult members of a speech community share comprehension of the social meaning of linguistic markers. Study of speakers' language use is a reliable index of their conscious and unconscious attitudes toward the several communities in which they interact.

OCCUPATION

Each occupation has its own jargon and, as every worker knows, the ability to manipulate technical terminology and informal on-the-job slang can be as critical to getting hired and maintaining a good image as is actual work performance. Technical terms are necessary to describe tasks efficiently and accurately. On any new job the first thing that must be mastered is the set of terms for the tools of the trade, be they wrenches, drawing pens, scalpels, or purchase-order forms. Technical terms proliferate especially in occupations for which extreme precision is required. The legal profession, for instance, uses Latin words and phrases such as *habeas corpus, de facto,* and *de jure* in its casual office interactions because they directly designate specific points of law. Latin terms are used in the taxonomy of botanical and zoological species in order to indicate each type, uniquely and internationally.

No occupation is without technical terms, however. Homemakers study decorator magazines to learn the varieties of "window treatments": *cafe curtains* (*single* or *double*), *Roman shades* (*tailored* or *Austrian-folded*), and *pleater drapes* (*pinch-* or *accordian-pleated*), these last hung on *traverse rods*. Just doing the family laundry requires command of the fine distinctions among clothing that is *perma-press, wrinkle-resistant, wash-and-wear,* and *iron-free*. Office work is so rife with technical designations that critics joke of "Bureaucratese" as a special language. Many bureaucratic terms are initials or abbreviations used as though they were words: *ICV* [*identify-clarify-verify*] *this* means "do a full check on this information"; a half-time employee is a *point-five-FTE* [*full-time equivalent*].

Workers also make up special vocabulary and use words in innovative or odd combinations as an expression of group solidarity and their personal identification with or contempt for their jobs. An office worker keeping right to schedule is *on-task* or *jogging*; one who does unnecessary paper shuffling is a *make-worker*. In "Legalese," too, there is English slang as well as Latin. A clerk can be asked to *blue sky* a real estate document, that is, run it through a check of state securities laws to assure it is what it says and that it is not just a piece of "blue sky" that is being sold. *Mother Hubbard* clauses are written into leases to cover all unnamed contingencies—a reminder from the nursery rhyme that unchecked cupboards can hide a multitude of unpleasant surprises.

Manual laborers are well known for their colorful terminology. Railroaders speak of themselves as *gandy dancers*; a yard crew on catch-all assignment works as *roustabout*. Some of these words have become popular among the general population, functioning sociolinguistically as "tough" or "masculine" terminology because of their origins among working-class men. Heavy work shoes are commonly called *shitkickers*. Construction workers are called *hardhats*, a reference to their required safety headgear, but *hardhat* types are any burly, independent-minded working-class men.

General popularity of terms, both slang and technical, is an indication of the profession's influence over the public imagination. Show business is a traditional source for metaphors: the main topic is *center stage*; a person can be *upstaged* by another person, especially a *star*; a delicious dessert deserves an *encore*; a good story is *rerun* for another listener. In many business settings non-sports fans are at a distinct disadvantage. Sports metaphors have become common: success comes from *hitting it right on the numbers*; a shrewd manager may need to *lateral* a problem, that is, solve it by an indirect route; a research team leader needs to increase *momentum* or *big Mo* in the same sense as does a coach; a new employee should get a good start *right out of the gate* and *hit the ground running*, the latter expression borrowed into sports from parachute troops and thence into general use.

The increasing popularity of computers for work and recreation is bringing a whole new jargon into vogue. Home hobbyists and even schoolchildren speak of *ICs* [*integrated circuits*]; *VDTs* [*video display terminals*]; *on-line* versus *batch; time-sharing; software, hardware,* and now *firmware.* Professional programmers have long demonstrated ironic self-mockery by choosing extremely non-technical terms to describe their highly technical work. Rather than Latinate vocabulary, programmers speak in terms of *bugs* (program errors), *bits* (units of data), *glitches* (errors), *kludges* (fixes that have not solved a fundamental program error), and *gigo* (from *garbage-in-garbage-out* for input errors that result in gibberish output). They derive sufficient professional respectability from the nature of their work; their occupational jargon can be workman-like and down-to-earth.

Professions sometimes determine other aspects of language use than vocabulary. Within a highly stratified speech community such as Martha's Vineyard, occupation may be a determinant in language change. Table 15 ranks Vineyarders by occupation—the traditional island occupations, fishing and farming, and all other employment. Fishermen as an occupational class radically centralize their /ai/ diphthong. Farmers are most assimilated to mainland pronunciation. The two traditional occupations have suffered decline in recent years, but their linguistic reactions have been opposite. The few remaining fishermen hold the most negative attitude toward the tourist influx, since population increase and the attendant ecological damage exercise a direct negative effect on their livelihood. They have become popular models of old-time island life, both socially and linguistically. One woman observed of her fisherman son (Labov 1972b:31):

> You know, E. didn't always speak that way . . . it's only since he came back from college [on the mainland]. I guess he wanted to be more like the men on the docks. . . .

This man has, in fact, hypercorrected his diphthongs, centralizing them beyond others in his age group.

Sociolinguistic variation within or across speech communities is determined by the entire complex of demographic factors. Occupation frequently segregates speakers by socioeconomic class, gender, or ethnicity or reinforces class, ethnic, or regional stratifications. Occupation and its determinant, education, may also be indices of

T A B L E 15. Percent of Centralization of /ai/ by Occupation

FISHERMEN	FARMERS	OTHERS
50	16	21

SOURCE: Labov 1972b:26.

linguistic behavior, sometimes more accurate than income-related indicators of class and social standing.

Table 16 reports variation in postvocalic *r* pronunciation among
whites in the Raleigh-Durham area of North Carolina. As detailed in
the section on regional variation, *r*-lessness is being replaced by
r-fulness due to increasing presence of Northern managerial and
skilled workers. The data in Table 16 represent the percentage of
r-pronouncing in full sentence context and in recitation of individual
words from lists, the most carefully monitored style of speech. The
right-hand column records the increase in *r*-usage between the two
styles. All speakers increase *r*-pronunciation, indicating that each is
aware of the social significance of the variable. Compared to older
people, young adults increase *r*-pronunciation both absolutely and
stylistically, demonstrating the direction of the linguistic change and
its growing sociolinguistic salience. Women are more *r*-pronouncing
than men and shift their styles further (8 percent increase, compared
to men's 5 percent increase). This gender discrepancy is consistent
with female behavior on other non-stigmatized linguistic changes—an
expression of their heightened linguistic sensitivity. The variables of
occupation and education also show a spread in absolute *r*-pronounc-
ing and in style-shifting. Nonmanual laborers, those for whom up-

T A B L E 16. **Percent of *r*-Pronunciation in Sentence Style and
Word List Recitation**

	SENTENCES	WORD LISTS	*r* INCREASE
Age in years:			
21–39	57	65	8
40–59	54	60	6
over 60	44	49	5
Gender:			
Female	53	61	8
Male	52	57	5
Occupation:			
Nonmanual	53	62	9
Manual	54	60	6
Education:			
Some college	53	59	6
High school diploma	55	66	11
Some high school	50	57	7
0–6 years	52	57	5

SOURCE: Levine and Crockett 1966:223.

ward social and economic mobility is a possibility, move slightly further from *r*-lessness than manual workers. But it is the education variable that is most strikingly stratified. Speakers with a high school diploma but no further education are the single most *r*-pronouncing group, surpassing even the young adult group in word-list style. The 11 percent increase of *r* constitutes extreme style-shifting, extreme linguistic insecurity. College-educated speakers are more secure linguistically; those without high school diplomas can hold out little hope for skilled or semiprofessional employment.

These samples of sociolinguistic behavior illustrate how members of the American English speech community function in everyday interactions. In the manner of giving and receiving information; expressing respect, contempt, and intimacy; gesturing, talking, and keeping silent we act out the values of the society in which we live. In each encounter speakers draw on their vast pool of knowledge about how best to present themselves and how to judge the self-presentation of others. This knowledge is no less real because it is largely unconscious. Rather it is more powerful than consciously acquired knowledge since it seems to be "natural." It is an automatic pattern of behavior and reaction.

FURTHER STUDY IN SOCIOLINGUISTIC ANALYSIS

READINGS

CAZDEN, COURTNEY B., VERA P. JOHN, and DELL HYMES, eds. *The Functions of Language in the Classroom*. New York: Teachers College Press, 1972.
Collection of essays focusing especially on interaction across speech communities.

CONKLIN, NANCY FAIRES. "The Language of the Majority: Women and American English," *A Pluralistic Nation: The Language Issue in the United States*, edited by Margaret A. Lourie and Nancy Faires Conklin, pp. 222–37. Rowley, Mass.: Newbury House Publishers, 1978.

FISHMAN, JOSHUA A., ed. *Readings in the Sociology of Language*. The Hague: Mouton, 1968.

GUMPERZ, JOHN J., and DELL HYMES, eds. *The Ethnography of Communication*. Special issue of *American Anthropologist* 66, no. 6, pt. 2 (1964).

HUDSON, R.A. *Sociolinguistics*. Cambridge: Cambridge University Press, 1980.
Careful definitions; good reference work.

LABOV, WILLIAM. *The Social Stratification of English in New York City.* Washington, D.C.: Center for Applied Linguistics, 1966.
First large-scale sociolinguistic survey.

——. *The Study of Non-Standard English.* Urbana: The National Council of Teachers of English, 1970.
Booklet prepared for classroom teachers.

——. *Sociolinguistic Patterns.* Philadelphia: University of Pennsylvania Press, 1972.
Collection of the author's major studies in language variation.

LIEBERSON, STANLEY, ed. *Explorations in Sociolinguistics.* Special issue of *Sociological Inquiry* 36, no. 2 (1966).

SHUY, ROGER W., WALTER A. WOLFRAM, and WILLIAM K. RILEY. *Field Techniques in an Urban Language Study.* Washington, D.C.: Center for Applied Linguistics, 1968.
Describes the procedures used in the Detroit Dialect Study, offering sample questionnaires, interviews, and methods of analysis.

THORNE, BARRIE, and NANCY M. HENLEY, eds. *Language and Sex: Difference and Dominance.* Rowley, Mass.: Newbury House Publishers, 1975.

TRUDGILL, PETER. *Sociolinguistics: An Introduction.* Baltimore: Penguin Books, 1974.
Readable introduction to the topic, using British and American data.

WOLFRAM, WALT, and RALPH W. FASOLD. *The Study of Social Dialects in American English.* Englewood Cliffs, N.J.: Prentice-Hall, 1974.
Introduction to the topic, emphasizing sociolinguistic survey techniques.

ACTIVITIES

1. Administer the linguistic insecurity test in Table 8 to acquaintances. Try to select twenty of the test words for which you have heard different pronunciations. Study the words in advance so that your pronunciation is natural. You may need to adapt the phonetic form given in the table to your own speech, but be sure that the forms you offer the informant differ from each other in only one sound. Read the alternate pronunciations aloud, speaking slowly and pausing between words. Disregard answers in which the informant indicates one of the forms is unknown.

2. Question people about their attitudes toward their own speech and the speech of others. Ask such questions as: What do you think of local speech? Do you want other people to think you speak it? How do you think local speech compares with speech from other parts of the country? Are you identified by your speech when you travel? What do you think of

the speech of other local people? (Specifically, solicit opinions about other ethnicities and classes.) Name well-known local standard and nonstandard speakers and ask for reactions to their speech.

3. Assess attitudes toward language use by testing subjective reactions of listeners within your speech community. Assemble an audiotape of speech samples representing different varieties of American English, standard and nonstandard. Play the samples for acquaintances and ask them to evaluate the speakers according to personal characteristics (intelligence, friendliness, self-confidence, trustworthiness) and socioeconomic standing (occupation, education, income). You may record acquaintances of different ages and backgrounds and supplement the sample tape with voices from radio or television broadcasts. Be sure samples contain representative pronunciations, vocabulary, or grammatical features. Negative reactions to samples similar to the listener's own dialect may indicate linguistic insecurity.

4. Interview speakers from three different generations about their language use and attitudes. Ask them questions such as the following: When you were young, was your speech ever corrected by your teachers? What forms did they find objectionable? What favorite slang expressions do you use with your friends? Where and when did you learn them? What settings do you use them in? What do you think about current slang? What sorts of expressions do you consider to be strong language? When do you think it is appropriate to use such words? For men? For women? Solicit stories from your informants. Do they use any words or expressions you would not use yourself? How do they sound to you—more or less formal, old-fashioned, vulgar, polite? Good topics for stories might be a school, family, or social event, a funny or embarrassing encounter, a frightening experience.

5. While talking with informants and administering tests, note discrepancies between the ways they perceive or represent their speech and their actual usage. Are they aware of nonstandard features in their own speech, retaining them as expressions of covert prestige? Or do they hear themselves as using standard forms when in fact they do not? Tape recording interviews will enable you to compare test results with samples of spontaneous speech.

PART IV

American Languages in Contact

I'd love to go in Italia *again before I die. Now I speak English good like an American I could go anywhere—where million-aires go and high people. I would look the high people in the face and ask them what questions I'd like to know. I wouldn't be afraid now—not of anybody; I'd be proud I come from America and speak English.*

—Rosa Cavallieri, an Italian immigrant

My father asks me a question in Spanish. He won't take it in English. I have to answer him in Spanish 'cause he says, "I'm not an Italian and I'm not a Negro, but I'm a Puerto Rican and you have to speak to me in my language . . . I was born in Puerto Rico and . . . I'm going to raise you like Puerto Ricans." So if we speak English, in front of him, . . . it's like cursing in front of him.

—a New York Puerto Rican teenager

CHAPTER 8

Multilingualism and Language Change

SINCE EARLY IN THE European colonization of North America, the English language has been the dominant speech of those in political and economic power. English monolingualism has been encouraged by rewards of social approval and advancement, promises of better jobs and higher wages, and awarding of U.S. citizenship. It has been enforced by ridicule, denial of access to employment and education, confiscation of "foreign" language presses and publications, and beatings of schoolchildren for the use of other languages. Multilingualism has been mistakenly perceived as a dangerous threat to national unity. While certain forms of ethnic expression have been generally accepted, linguistic nonconformity continues to be viewed with considerable suspicion.

American multilingualism, like other language contact situations, has required linguistic adjustment on the part of all the communities involved. Communication beyond the level of rudimentary trade relations always brings about major changes in language use. The specific outcome may be maintenance of both languages, with some or all members of the speech communities becoming bilingual; extension of one language to all speakers; the formation of pidgin or creole languages, which combine elements of the languages in contact; or some other type of accommodation falling between language maintenance and language loss. The nature of the adjustment depends more on social factors than on linguistic structure. There are, however, linguistic processes that characterize all ongoing language contact situations. The various responses to the American linguistic environment are outlined in the pages that follow.

MULTILINGUALISM

Multilingualism is the first stage in adjustment to linguistic contact. In the usual case—contact between two language communities—some individuals become bilingual, so that exchange can take place. As long as contact remains limited, a few interpreters suffice to link the communities. But continuing and extensive interaction leads to larger-scale bilingualism, encompassing much or even all of one or both contact communities.

Ideally, members of each language community would learn the language of the other, but if one community is numerically, socially, economically, or politically dominant, the adjustment may go in only one direction. Bilingual situations can be **stable**, lasting for centuries, neither language encroaching drastically on the domain of the other. Often, however, bilingualism is **transitional**, a phase through which one of the language communities passes as it assimilates to the other.

Bilingual parents, such as U.S. immigrants, may choose to pass on to their children their own mother tongue or an acquired language. If they choose the former, the children will grow up bilingual, learning one language in the home and another in school and public life. An ethnic group repeating this choice generation after generation creates a stable bilingual community. Once a generation of parents chooses the latter option, however, the acquired language becomes the first language of the community's youth and the shift to monolingualism in the dominant language begins.

The majority of the world's peoples are members of bi- and multilingual societies. A standard variety of the nation's related dialects, a colonial language, or the language of one dominant indigenous ethnic group may serve as a national **lingua franca**, the shared speech for commerce and public affairs. Speakers remain conversant in their native tongues as well. Only in recent times has multilingualism come to be considered an undesirable social condition, and this view is held primarily in the Western, industrialized world.

As Chapter 6 demonstrates, the prestige of a language derives from the social status of its speakers, not from the language itself. Thus entirely egalitarian bilingualism is possible between communities with mutual respect and equivalent resources. In such situations both languages are fully accepted for discourse in the public sphere, while each remains the choice of one ethnic group for its private interactions. Egalitarian bilingualism was not uncommon among North American native peoples. In many tribes it was an important courtesy to be able to carry on meetings and entertain guests in the language of neighboring speech communities.

After British hegemony was established, however, English took on a special prestige that made true egalitarian relations among speech communities impossible. Many individuals were committed to democratic multilingualism, but their efforts rarely outlived them. William Penn, for instance, declared the native and immigrant languages in his territories equal in the sight of God and the law, but his successors in Pennsylvania colonial and state government worked actively not only to Anglicize the Indians but to prevent official recognition of German as a state language.

DIGLOSSIA

Bilingualism may take the form of **diglossia**. Rather than competing, diglossic languages have complementary uses. Each is specialized situationally, one serving as the common language of the entire speech community in public affairs and on formal occasions and one or several others used in private and informal interactions by most or all of the community. The public, or **high**, language is the medium for written communication and often a national or standardized variety. It may be an internationally important language. The private, or **low**, language tends to be a more local variety. It may also be unwritten. Speakers experience the low language as more expressive and comfortable for their personal lives; they may value it particularly because it is not used in the public sphere. Diglossia exists in many parts of the world. In Latin American nations Spanish and indigenous languages exist in parallel relationships. Spanish is the primary language of public affairs in Peru and Paraguay, for instance, but Quechua and Guarani—the tongues of a large portion of the indigenous population—have recognized status and are preferred by many for private use.

Diglossia would seem well suited to a multi-ethnic society such as the United States. However, negative Anglo-American attitudes toward multilingualism preclude the acceptance of other languages as legitimate media for private as well as public use. Such attitudes, as well as the geographic and social mobility that characterizes American life, have hindered stable bilingualism. Though denied recognition, essentially diglossic communities have existed at various times and places in American history. Bilingual communities in which public (i.e. English) and private (i.e. native) language use is situationally demarcated often formed the bridge between monolingualism in the native tongue and monolingualism in English. Among groups prevented from assimilating into mainstream American society, quasi-diglossic language use has continued over generations. For Chinese Americans, for example, language maintenance derives from loyalty to family custom and also from enforced residential and occupational ghettoization.

Overwhelming numbers of Americans of every ethnicity, indigenous and immigrant, urban and rural, have found it necessary to learn English. Minority language speakers must use English in contacts with mainstream society and also with other non-English speakers. In the Pittsburgh and Buffalo steel mills, Hungarian, Czech, and Croatian immigrants learned English not only to understand their bosses' orders but to converse with their fellow workers. Even in predominantly non-English-speaking factories, labor unions found English the best choice for their large-scale organizing efforts. The Indian tribes removed to Oklahoma from all across the Eastern and Midwestern states have one language in common—English.

Spanish—the original colonial language of the Southwest—has long served as the lingua franca among Chicanos and Indians and retains its currency despite the large influx of Anglos in recent years. Yet even these people require competence in English for interactions with Americans from outside that region. Southwestern Indians thus are often trilingual, commanding their tribal language, Spanish, and English. The enormous linguistic diversity in urban areas and Indian territories reinforces the social and economic pressures to become bilingual in English.

Many first-generation immigrants to the United States develop functional bilingualism, but few become truly fluent bilinguals. Their use of English is often limited to necessary contact situations. But their children, educated by and large in multi-ethnic English-language schools, have the opportunity to become fully competent speakers of two languages. Second-generation immigrants are typically diglossic, employing their parents' mother tongue in family, neighborhood, and religious life, and speaking English with native or near-native ability in their work and educational lives. Such speakers have well-defined domains in which each language is appropriate.

CODE-SWITCHING

In stable bilingual communities the linguistic dynamics may be slightly different. When a community has been living in a contact situation for multiple generations, both parents and children may be fluent in two languages. Within the community, then, choice of language can be less closely tied to social domain and coparticipants and more a factor of choice among speakers who would understand each other in either language. All fully **equilingual** bilinguals, those who genuinely command two languages equally well, have the ability to **code-switch**, alternating from one language to the other out of communicational convenience or preference. Code-switches may take place between conversations, as a new speaker takes a turn, from one sentence to another, or even within sentences.

Code-switches are important mechanisms for style-shifting among bilinguals and are subject to the social and attitudinal factors motivating monolingual style-shifts toward and away from standard English that were described in Chapters 6 and 7. Bilinguals switch codes in reaction to changes in the participants, the setting, and the topic of an interaction. Although bilingualism arises out of situations beyond the control of the individual speaker, bilinguals actively manipulate their language choice according to both social constraints and their individual feelings and intentions. Thus language choice serves as a sociolinguistic marker in bilingual communities, revealing speakers' feelings about themselves, their interlocutors, and the topics they are discussing.

Hispanics constitute our largest stable bilingual population. Spanish/English use is partially diglossic—Spanish associated with ethnicity, family, and friends and English with the realms of business and education. Thus language choice is determined in part by setting. Two Hispanics meeting in a private home or ethnic restaurant or club would more certainly speak in Spanish than if they met in their children's English-speaking school or at a business luncheon among Anglos. When non-Spanish speakers participate, bilinguals naturally switch to English in order to make themselves understood. But Spanish may be retained if individuals wish to assert ethnic identity or maintain privacy.

Bilingual Puerto Rican children in New York learn early to use the language appropriate to the participants in a particular conversation. By the age of eight, they can accurately discern the language preference of fellow students and will speak in Spanish or English accordingly. They report speaking Spanish to adult monolingual Spanish speakers and to younger siblings but both English and Spanish to older siblings and sometimes to their fathers. They also prove adept at code-switching in response to code-switches by their interlocutors. Interestingly, girls show more facility at code-switching than boys (Zentella 1981:234).

But language choice for Hispanic children can be complicated by the ethnicity of the people they converse with. While young Chicano children in bilingual education programs readily interact in Spanish with Hispanic staff members, they identify all non-Hispanics as English speakers, including their Spanish-speaking Anglo teachers. In one classroom children used 61 percent English with their bilingual Anglo teacher but 95 percent Spanish with their bilingual Chicana teacher's aide. Their boundaries between the two languages became blurred in the "abnormal" situation of speaking Spanish to an Anglo, so they inserted English words and phrases into their Spanish. In conversation with the Anglo teacher, 10 percent of their Spanish utterances had these English elements, compared with 1 percent mixed utterances in conversations with the Hispanic aide (McClure 1977:104).

When participants share ethnic background, language switches signal changes of topic or attitude toward the topic. In the following conversation between two bilingual Chicano educators, a shift in topic from the language of dreams to cigarette smoking is accompanied by a code-switch (Gumperz and Hernández-Chavez 1975:155):

> M: I don't think I ever have any conversations in my dreams. I just dream. Ha. I don't hear people talking: I jus' see pictures.
> E: Oh. They're old-fashioned, then. They're not talkies yet, huh?
> M: They're old-fashioned. No. They're not talkies, yet. No. I'm trying to think. Yeah, there have too been talkies. Different. In Spanish and English both. An' I wouldn't be too surprised if I even had some in Chinese.
> (Laughter)
> Yeah, E. *De veras*. (Really).

(M. offers E. a cigarette which is refused.)
Tú no fumas, ¿verdad? Yo tampoco. Dejé de fumar. (You don't smoke, right? Neither do I. I quit smoking.)

The English portion of the conversation concerns their common professional interest in bilingualism. When the topic changes to a personal habit that M. feels ambivalent and perhaps embarrassed about, she employs Spanish to mark the shift to greater informality and intimacy.

Speakers make use of language choice to achieve specific effects as they change topics. A group of bilingual Mexican American mothers, for example, expressed different language preferences for four common types of interaction with their children, as Table 17 indicates. The two strongly emotional interactions, scolding and consoling, elicited the ethnic language. Overwhelmingly preferring Spanish for scolding, mothers commented that their children take the rebuke more seriously when it is rendered in the traditional language. Like many bilinguals, they employ their first, most culturally charged language when they experience or express strong emotion. Consoling, too, tended to take place in Spanish, evoking the comfort of native culture. But praising took place in either language. Labeling— teaching children the names of things—is a far more conscious linguistic act, and these women made an effort to offer their children names in both languages. Thus they actively encouraged native bilingualism in their children.

Language switches may serve as cultural abbreviations as well as sociolinguistic markers. Bilinguals switch codes for the convenience of expressing a concept native to only one of the two speech communities whose languages they command. The English expression *talk business* in *No van a aceptar a una mujer que* (They are not going to accept a woman who) *can't talk business* is a practical way of express-

T A B L E 17. **Mothers' Preference of Spanish or English for Interactions with Their Children in the Home**

	SPANISH	ENGLISH	BOTH/EITHER
Overall home use	40%	28%	32%
Scolding	80%	16%	4%
Consoling	44%	28%	28%
Praising	32%	28%	40%
Labeling	16%	16%	68%

SOURCE: Redlinger 1978.

ing a notion foreign to Hispanic life (McClure 1977:98). Likewise, the query *¿Comieron turkey pa Christmas?* ("Will turkey be served on Christmas?") indicates that an Anglo-style celebration may be planned (Espinosa 1975:104).

While the above examples demonstrate cultural integration, some code-switches function to underline a separate ethnic identity. In the following dialogue, English *children* and Spanish *criaturas*, although they have the same literal meaning, clearly have different associations and referents. M. has been asked whom her children play with in the neighborhood (Gumperz and Hernández-Chavez 1975:160–61):

> M: There's no children. The Black Panthers next door. You know what I mean.
> E: Do they have kids?
> M: Just the two little girls.
> E: No, no. I mean do some of the other people in the neighborhood have kids?
> M: They don't associate with no children . . . There's no children in the neighborhood. Well . . . *sí hay criaturas* (yes there are children) . . .

E. does "know what she means," that only Chicano children are suitable playmates. When speaking in English, M. thinks only of English-speaking children. When she recalls the Hispanic children, she switches language. The original statement *There's no children* cannot be interpreted without reference to the speaker's cultural framework.

TRILINGUALISM

Many language communities in the United States have made use not just of two languages but of three or more. Within a single kin and friendship network of immigrant Jews Yiddish, Russian, Polish, and English can all be heard, in turn and in concert. Their multilingualism reflects the politics and race relations of north central Europe in the first half of this century.

Immigrants who arrive speaking a nonstandard regional dialect often come under immediate pressure to learn the standard variety of the homeland language, so they can function more widely in the ethnic community. Tuscans, Calabrians, and Lombards, for example, all become "Italians," acquiring a national variety and assuming an identity that conforms to outsiders' perceptions of their ethnicity. During this assimilation process, individuals and communities are transitionally trilingual—in their native dialect, the standard language of their homeland, and English. This distancing from the actual native language variety may also facilitate later movement away from the mother tongue, leading to monolingualism in English.

Fairly stable trilingual communities exist as well. The Yaqui are one example of the numerous Indian communities in the Southwest whose members command a native American language, Spanish, and English. A 1952 study of language choice among men in the Yaqui community at Tucson demonstrates the social functions of each language for the community as a whole and for individuals (Barber 1973). The men learned both Yaqui and Spanish as very young children and English at school. They used Yaqui for family and informal conversations and in tribal ceremonies. Spanish also served as a home and informal language and, formally, as the language of Catholicism. Most families were bilingual, code-switching between Yaqui and Spanish. English was primarily an "outside" language, used only when necessary with Anglos and otherwise viewed with some suspicion.

Spanish and Yaqui, on the one hand, and English, on the other, functioned essentially diglossically, with English limited to specific settings and topics in interactions with Anglos. However, more subtle rules governed the choice between the two community languages. While home life was bilingual, Spanish was the primary language of nontribal social life—dancing, drinking, and dating. Preference for Spanish was stratified by age and gender as well. Women were more likely to speak Yaqui than men. One wife regularly spoke Yaqui to her husband, who answered in Spanish. With older family members, especially women, the men tended to use Yaqui; with their children, both Spanish and Yaqui or primarily Spanish.

Such age-grading in language choice often points to language loss, in this case a decline of Yaqui in favor of bilingualism in Spanish and English. Observation of the community twenty years later, however, did not confirm this. The Tucson Yaqui continue to maintain their tribal language in addition to Spanish and English, much as in the previous generation. The Yaqui tribal tongue continues as an active language because it is a critical marker of ethnic identity. It is crucial to participation in ceremonial life, but, perhaps more importantly, ethnic Yaquis who do not speak the language regularly are not considered members of the tribe. Of a Spanish-speaking Yaqui family, one trilingual observed (Barber 1973:313), "*So mexicanos, no hablan la lengua.* (They're Mexicans, they don't speak the language

[Yaqui].)'' With these attitudes the Yaqui language may continue as long as the tribe exists.

MULTILINGUALS AND LANGUAGE ATTITUDES

Multilinguals control their choice of language, expressing themselves according to social context and intended individual effect. But the cultural assumptions associated with each language do not fail to leave a mark on the nature of their utterances. Choice of language influences what is said in content as well as form. For example, Japanese "war brides" in conversation with Japanese American interviewers expressed different opinions depending on the language choice (Ervin-Tripp 1968). Their ideas tended to conform to prevailing expectations of the culture whose language they were using. One woman's responses to questions about independence and self-definition for women illustrate her adjustments to Japanese and American social norms. Asked to complete the sentence, "When my wishes conflict with my family . . . ," she answered, in Japanese, "It is a time of great unhappiness" and, in English, "I do what I want." To "I will probably become . . . ," she responded, in Japanese, "a housewife" and, in English, "a teacher." This woman is acting biculturally as well as bilingually.

Language choice also affects how speakers are perceived by members of their speech communities. As noted above, the Yaqui do not approve of tribal members who use either too much English or too little Yaqui. Language switching is thus constrained by community standards. Opinions about the mother tongue reveal the extent of ethnic group identification and attitudes toward mainstream society.

Subjective reaction tests that evaluate social attitudes toward dialect speakers have been described in Chapter 6. Similar tests can be used effectively to gauge linguistic and ethnic loyalty in bilingual communities. In **matched guise** studies bilinguals are tape-recorded in each of their two languages. The tapes of several such double presentations are played for ethnic group members, who evaluate the voices on scales of social and economic standing (e.g. occupation, education, income) and personal qualities (e.g. intelligence, friendliness, self-confidence, trustworthiness).

A matched guise study in Detroit's Polish community revealed strong sociolinguistic discrimination (Czarnecki 1973). When using Polish, each speaker was judged friendlier and more trustworthy but less intelligent, less educated, and more likely to be a blue collar than a white collar worker. The community preferred the Polish-speaking voices for neighbors or friends—strong positive ethnic identification. But they also revealed their association of Polish ethnicity with lack of economic success and social prestige. This ambivalent attitude toward the mother tongue presents community members with the dilemma of choosing between personal and professional satisfactions. When intelligence and socioeconomic success are equated with speaking English, ambitious families may feel forced to choose monolingualism for themselves and their children.

BORROWING

The transition from multilingualism to monolingualism in the dominant tongue often begins with **borrowing**. Borrowing can take place at all levels of linguistic structure but occurs most readily—if most superficially—at the level of vocabulary. Commonly, it begins when cultural contact creates vocabulary deficiencies in the native tongue as its speakers encounter new objects and ideas. Italian immigrants, for example, borrowed the English word *job* to describe the anonymous day labor they performed on American construction sites—a concept of employment foreign to people from tightly-knit village economies.

Most language communities in the United States have borrowed vocabulary mainly from English because of its prestige, but sometimes one non-English community will borrow expressions from another with slightly higher standing. Thus, in their native tongue and in English, Italian immigrants used words borrowed from Yiddish. Eastern European Jews were their immediate predecessors in the inner cities of the urban Northeast and their models for assimilation and advancement.

In American English itself, lexical borrowing shows the presence of other languages in the society. As described in Chapter 4, English has received a large number of words for items particular to ethnic life—for example, *succotash, yam, spaghetti, taco, quiche*. The lexical richness of American English indicates the wealth of this country's cultural resources.

Borrowed words tend to be nativized phonologically in the course of their transfer. The American English pronunciations of *lingerie, guacamole*, and *sukiyaki* may mystify speakers of French, Spanish, and Japanese, respectively, just as English words may go unrecognized when they are embedded in the speech of another language community. In the borrowing language, loan words are assigned the sounds that most closely approximate their pronunciation in the lending language. Nativizations such as American Norwegian *blakkvalnot* ("black walnut"), Louisiana French *giumbleur* ("gambler"), American Portuguese *alvarozes* ("overalls"), American Italian *Brokolino* ("Brooklyn"), American Romany *anytin* ("anything"), Hawaiian *laiki* ("rice"), American Serbo-Croatian *shtof* ("stove"), and Hopi *kóvermént* ("government") offer clues to the sound and syllable systems of the borrowing languages (Weinreich 1974, Hancock 1974, Kennard 1963).

Borrowed words often become integrated enough to take on native inflectional endings, as, for example, American Portuguese *treno* ("train" with a noun suffix), American Serbo-Croatian *kitchna* ("kitchen" with a noun suffix), Pennsylvania German *gemixt* ("mix" with a verbal prefix and suffix, meaning "mixed"), Hopi *inláfti* ("in love" with a verb suffix). Agent nouns designating "one who does" are particularly common **hybrid loans** (i.e. part native, part imported) in ethnic American speech: American Yiddish *holdopnik* ("robber," from *hold up*) and *olraitnik* ("self-satisfied person," from *all right*), American Polish *butlgerów* ("bootlegger"), American Greek *bossis* ("boss"). As Hopi *inláfti* and Yiddish *olraitnik* illustrate, boundaries between words are often lost when set expressions are imported. American Italian similarly shows *azzoraiti* from *that's all right* (Weinreich 1974, Kennard 1963).

Alternatively, hybrid loans may indicate what is culturally foreign in an object. For example, Pennsylvania German *fleeshpai* ("meat pie") incorporates the native word for *meat* with the Anglo mode of preparing the dish. Florida Spanish *home plato* matches the native *plato* with a borrowed English word to form a cognate to the baseball term. Hybrids may contain redundant elements, evidence that the borrowers did not fully comprehend the structure of the lender language. American Italian *canabulldogga* ("bulldog") combines the Italian word for dog, *cana*, with the English breed name, *bulldog*, and completes the word with an Italian noun suffix, *-a*. The term is built on analogy with other English breed names such as *spaniel (canaspaniela)* in which the species name is not already incorporated (Weinreich 1974).

Many American languages also employ **loan translations**. When the constituent parts of a foreign word or expression are understood, they can be translated directly into cognate terms in the native language. Loan translations are often words learned from print—signs, newspapers, announcements. Louisiana French speakers created *marchandeses sèches* (literally, "merchandise dry" for "dry goods") to designate that variety of general store (Weinreich 1974). Wisconsin Germans have substituted the loan translation *Pferdsrettich* ("horse-radish") for the conventional German *Meerrettich* ("sea-radish").

Cultural contact and linguistic borrowing can bring about changes in word meaning in the immigrant languages as well. Urban American Italians have shifted the meaning of *fattoria* from "farm" to "factory," creating a word needed in their new environment and approximating the sound of the English word at the same time. American Greek *grihonnis*, from "greenhorn," is applied not to workers new to a job but to newly arrived immigrants. American Romany *office* denotes a fortune telling parlor. Under pressure from the English cognate, American Portuguese *livraria* and American Italian *libreria* have lost their original meaning, "bookstore," and come to mean "library." French, Italian, and Portuguese Americans have all shifted their forms of the verb *introduce* from the Romance language family meaning "to bring in" to the English "to make acquainted." When non-English words must compete with a loan word, they may be replaced or may take on a more limited semantic range. In American Yiddish *advokat* is the native word for "lawyer." But once English *lawyer* was imported, *advokat* came to be used contrastively, the English term applied to professionals trained in this country and the Yiddish word reserved for immigrants who had been educated outside the United States and who were often not eligible to practice law here but continued to serve the ethnic community. As these individuals disappeared, the English term simply replaced *advokat* as the general word for "lawyer" (Weinreich 1974).

When interaction with another language community is frequent and ongoing, borrowing may be so extensive that users of the American variety cannot understand speakers of the homeland variety. At this point, borrowing has become **language mixing**. Language mixing is always characterized by the wholesale importation of foreign vocabulary into mother-tongue structures. In some cases of language mixing, the phonological system of the recipient language takes on features of the lending language as well. American German dialects include sounds that did not exist in any homeland variety. The *j* sound (/ǰ/) in *jump* or *gin* is rendered as *y* or *sh* by European Germans. But immigrant Germans learned to say *gejumpt* rather than *geyumpt* or *geshumpt* for *jumped* and *cotton gin* instead of *cotton yin* or *cotton shin*. Even among monolingual German speakers, native sound systems have undergone restructuring due to language contact.

In more advanced cases of language mixing, syntactic structures can also be slightly affected. The case endings of continental European languages have been reduced in some of their American vernacular varieties to a two-case system corresponding to the subjective/objective dichotomy in English. Texas German dialects exhibit some confusion on this point (Gilbert 1972). In German, *with me* requires the dative case, not found in English. Some Texas Germans have replaced the dative *mit mir* with the objective case *mit mich,* paralleling English syntax. Others have combined the dative and objective pronouns into a reduced form, phonologically like English *me,* by entirely dropping the final consonants of *mir* and *mich*. Some of these same speakers have taken up English grammatical markers, such as *-s* for the plural of nouns. *Zimmer* ("room"), a noun whose singular and plural are the same in European German, can appear in Texas German as *Zimmers*—with a redundant English plural suffix added. In Romance languages adjectives generally follow nouns they modify, but English influence has displaced them to pre-noun position in some American varieties. A Rhode Island ethnic club, for instance, bears the name *Português Recreativo Club* instead of *Club Português Recreativo* (Weinreich 1974).

Like any linguistic feature that varies from speaker to speaker or from one conversation to another, borrowings often take on the value of sociolinguistic markers. A borrowing language is more or less "pure," depending on the speakers and the social constraints on the interaction. Young people, for instance, may make more frequent use of loan words than their elders. Formal language, such as that for religious services, is more resistant to foreign borrowings than casual speech. A study of English loans into American Yiddish newspapers indicates this stylistic spread. Twenty percent of the advertising copy consisted of English borrowings, while the news pages included only 5.3 percent English loans. Usages permissible for commercial announcements were excluded from news writing. And editorials and the magazine page—the material drawn directly from Yiddish life and opinion—had just 2.1 percent English (Weinreich 1974:66).

All of these contact effects can appear in the language of speakers who remain fundamentally monolingual. If groups of speakers are isolated from their larger language community, their speech often retains forms current at the time of separation but since abandoned by the main language community. In such communities speakers integrate foreign elements into their language just as they naturally adapt to linguistic changes motivated from within their native language and speech community. Isolated communities evolve new forms out of the other languages around them, eventually creating a new, contact-influenced dialect. Ultimately, it can become so unlike the language of the home community that interaction with the "old country" becomes difficult.

Borrowing need not bring about language loss, though it necessarily contributes to the speed and direction of linguistic change within the affected language communities. If the recipient community is stable, foreign imports are integrated unself-consciously. If the community is in transition, with members shifting their linguistic identification away from the native language, borrowings may indicate displacement and obsolescence of the native tongue.

In some communities, foreign words and even foreign structures have been borrowed into the native language without becoming sociolinguistic status markers. Thus they indicate linguistic accommodation but not language shift. For instance, Pennsylvania German has borrowed heavily from English. Its vocabulary, sound system, and grammatical structure have all been influenced by the dominant language. Yet it continues to exist as a separate language because its speakers prefer it as their primary means of communication.

On the other hand, loan words, imported expressions, and foreign grammatical structures may come to be viewed as indicators of social prestige, education, and economic advancement by the borrowers themselves. When positive social value becomes attached to maximum use of borrowed forms, the effect is to limit the usefulness of the native tongue within the community. Such a community is likely to undergo loss of the native language.

LANGUAGE LOSS

Many speech communities in the United States have shifted from exclusive use of their ethnic mother tongue to exclusive use of a dominant language—often after a period of extensive borrowing. Since such communities stop using the ethnic tongue, this process is called **language loss**. In most cases English replaces indigenous and other immigrant languages, though some Southwest Indian communities have adopted Spanish. When American Indians abandon their tribal language, the result is **language death**—total extinction of the tongue. The history of linguistic resistance and attrition is briefly sketched in Chapters 1 and 2.

Language loss may take place over many generations. The mainstream language may first slowly come into use in restricted, public domains, then gradually encroach on family interaction. Or the shift may be rapid and generalized, with parents encouraging children to speak the dominant language. In such cases, members of the younger generation hear the ethnic tongue spoken to monolingual elders but respond in the mainstream language, thus gaining at best partial and passive bilingual ability. In just three generations a community can pass from monolingualism in one language to monolingualism in another. Typically in these situations, the third or fourth generation—the monolinguals or their children—come to mourn the loss of their linguistic heritage and their missed opportunity for native bilingualism.

Table 18 outlines the many factors affecting language retention and language loss. They range from cultural and emotional associations with the language to family and community structure, number and proximity of speakers, and outsiders' attitude toward the speakers. Demographics, social and political context, cultural values, and language factors all contribute to create an environment that encourages or inhibits language shift. A single factor may have one effect in one community and the opposite in another. Racism and nativism, for example, isolate minorities and immigrants. Targeted populations may respond by retaining a separate and supportive ethnic and language community or by seeking rapid assimilation into mainstream society. This latter option is open only to peoples who resemble the majority population in physical characteristics.

Within any community some individuals will choose rapid assimilation while others continue regular use of the mother tongue long after their contemporaries have shifted. Among adults, men generally acquire the new, second language before women, since they are more likely to be employed outside the ethnic community. Personal aspirations, especially ambitions to professional careers, lead individuals to shift languages, since fluency in English is a prerequisite to higher education throughout the United States. For such socially mobile people, language loss may occur before it does in the rest of the ethnic community.

Some communities survive language loss with a continuing firm sense of ethnic identity, maintaining strong ties to family, homeland, custom, and ritual. For others loss of language leads to cultural assimilation. Polish Americans, for instance, continue to think of themselves as Poles, though many are no longer fluent in Polish. Their definition of ethnicity is not tightly bound up with language use. As noted above, the Yaqui represent the opposite case. Ethnic Yaquis who no longer speak the language are not considered tribal members. Ethnic maintenance, then, is related to language retention but may outlive the mother tongue.

Like the Poles, American Finns offer an example of ethnic identity surviving language loss. Between 1880 and 1920 as many as 300,000 Finns settled in the region north of the Great Lakes. The Finland-born generation developed a mixed Finnish-English variety called "Finglish," which consisted primarily of Finnish structure with extensive borrowings from English vocabulary (Karttunen 1977). Oldest children in the first American-born generation often learned this mixed language from their parents, and it is still heard among older speakers today. Yet, despite maintaining their mother tongue more successfully than other Scandinavian Americans, Finns virtually abandoned their language in the first half of this century. Derogatory attitudes toward Finns encouraged them to assimilate, and their physical resemblance to native white residents made this process relatively easy. Linguistic factors also contributed to language loss. Since Finnish, with its many loans from Swedish, had long incorporated foreign words, immigrant Finns were open to English borrowings. The American dialect, even that used by Finland-born speakers, was originally based on conservative rural varieties and, once in the United States, diverged rapidly from standard Finnish. Immigrants were thus reluctant to keep up their mother tongue by using it with European Finns. Ethnic identity, however, has survived language loss. Finns recognize one another by their ethnic names and remain conscious of their nationality. They maintain active social clubs and ethnic customs in rural and now urban areas throughout the Great Lakes region.

Slovenes who immigrated to Minnesota also underwent complete language loss in just three generations but with more profound effects on their sense of ethnic identity (Paternost 1976). In the 1890s they left their Mediterranean farms to settle as miners in the towns of far northern Minnesota. They quickly incorporated English words for the new artifacts and conditions that made up their lives. A second wave of immigrants, refugees from World War II, found the antiquated, English-influenced rural dialect spoken by their predecessors very

TABLE 18. Factors Encouraging Language Retention and Language Loss

Language Retention	Language Loss
Political, Social, and Demographic Factors:	
Large number of speakers living in concentration (ghettos, reservations, ethnic neighborhoods, rural speech islands)	Small number of speakers, dispersed among speakers of other languages
Recent arrival and/or continuing immigration	Long, stable residence in the United States
Geographical proximity to the homeland; ease of travel to the homeland	Homeland remote and inaccessible
High rate of return to the homeland; intention to return to the homeland; homeland language community still intact	Low rate or impossibility of return to homeland (refugees, Indians displaced from their tribal territories)
Occupational continuity	Occupational shift, especially from rural to urban
Vocational concentration, i.e. employment where co-workers share language background; employment within the language community (stores serving the community, traditional crafts, homemaking, etc.)	Vocations in which some interaction with English or other languages is required; speakers dispersed by employers (e.g. African slaves)
Low social and economic mobility in mainstream occupations	High social and economic mobility in mainstream occupations
Low level of education, leading to low social and economic mobility; *but* educated and articulate community leaders, familiar with the English-speaking society and loyal to their own language community.	Advanced level of education, leading to social and economic mobility; education that alienates and Anglifies potential community leaders
Nativism, racism, and ethnic discrimination as they serve to isolate a community and encourage identity only with the ethnic group rather than the nation at large	Nativism, racism, and ethnic discrimination as they force individuals to deny their ethnic identity in order to make their way in society

Cultural Factors:

Mother-tongue institutions, including schools, churches, clubs, theatres, presses, broadcasts	Lack of mother-tongue institutions, from lack of interest or lack of resources
Religious and/or cultural ceremonies requiring command of the mother tongue	Ceremonial life institutionalized in another tongue or not requiring active use of mother tongue
Ethnic identity strongly tied to language; nationalistic aspirations as a language group; mother tongue the homeland national language	Ethnic identity defined by factors other than language, as for those from multilingual countries or language groups spanning several nations; low level of nationalism
Emotional attachment to mother tongue as a defining characteristic of ethnicity, of self	Ethnic identity, sense of self derived from factors such as religion, custom, race rather than shared speech
Emphasis on family ties and position in kinship or community network	Low emphasis on family or community ties, high emphasis on individual achievement
Emphasis on education, if in mother-tongue or community-controlled schools, or used to enhance awareness of ethnic heritage; low emphasis on education otherwise	Emphasis on education and acceptance of public education in English
Culture unlike Anglo society	Culture and religion congruent with Anglo society

Linguistic Factors:

Standard, written variety as mother tongue	Minor, nonstandard, and/or unwritten variety as mother tongue
Use of Latin alphabet in mother tongue, making reproduction inexpensive and second language literacy relatively easy	Use of non-Latin writing system in mother tongue, especially if it is unusual, expensive to reproduce, or difficult for bilinguals to learn
Mother tongue with international status	Mother tongue of little international importance
Literacy in mother tongue, used for exchange within the community and with homeland	No literacy in mother tongue; illiteracy
Some tolerance for loan words, if they lead to flexibility of the language in its new setting	No tolerance for loan words, if no alternate ways of capturing new experience evolve; too much tolerance of loans, leading to mixing and eventual language loss

unlike their own educated standard variety. They could not employ American Slovenian as their native tongue. Thus renewed immigration failed to halt language loss. Although Slovenian urban communities developed newspapers and other mother-tongue institutions, Minnesota Slovenes' cultural life centered primarily on the Slovenian Catholic Church. However, the American Catholic Church was urgently pressing for assimilation—both ritual and linguistic—of its diverse membership. Because all masses were said in Latin, the Church hierarchy did not consider Slovenian-speaking priests essential to Slovenian communicants. With the loss of their language and their ethnic-language church, Slovenian young people have come to identify themselves not as Slovenes but, generally, as Catholics and, ethnically, as Slavs. Since their homeland was incorporated into Yugoslavia in 1945, they express affinity with a generalized group of related Slavic peoples rather than with their own language group. They think of American Croatians, for example, as compatriots who speak the "same" language.

Similarly, most third-generation Italian Americans grew up in predominantly English-speaking homes and do not command the mother tongue of their grandparents. But some American Italian communities retain a mixed language which inserts mother-tongue vocabulary into English (unlike "Finglish," which incorporates English vocabulary into the mother tongue). This variety of English, interlarded with Italian words and phrases, functions as a home and family language and as a form of in-group speech for Italian American schoolchildren in ethnically mixed schools.

Italians in Pittsburgh's Panther Hollow section exemplify the "Italo-English" spoken in urban areas throughout the United States (Casciato and Radcliff-Umstead 1975). Although native southern Italian dialects gave way to English as second-generation children attended English-speaking schools, Americans in the third, fourth, or fifth generation continue to enjoy expressing themselves in consciously Italian-influenced English. Panther Hollow "Italo-English" contains nouns, verbs, adjectives, and set expressions derived from the founding dialects. For English *fix*, for example, "Italo-English" speakers substitute the Abruzzese *congia*, adding English tense endings: *I will congia, she congias, he congiad. Woman* is *femmina; women, femminas. Benediga* ("God bless") is used as a greeting and *crisha sanda* ("grow holy") when a child sneezes. Many of the words retained reflect ethnic group values and attitudes. *'Nzacca*, a verb meaning "push oneself into a situation that is not one's own business," takes on a variety of English endings and uses: a *'nzaccer* is a person who visits others without inviting them in return; *'nzaccing* oneself is wearing out one's welcome. And Panther Hollow Italians still employ *merigan* ("dog") as the substitute for the like-sounding *American*, sometimes replacing it with the even more derogatory *merdagan* ("dog excrement"). As a special ethnic dialect, "Italo-English" preserves a sense of linguistic and cultural continuity among Italians in spite of language loss.

PIDGINIZATION AND CREOLIZATION

Under certain circumstances, contact between two or more language communities results not in multilingualism or in the loss of a non-dominant tongue but in the emergence of a new language—a pidgin or a creole. Pidgins and creoles should not be confused with mixed languages like "Italo-English." All mixed languages retain the basic structures of one language as they incorporate elements from another. But pidgins and creoles, although based on the languages in contact, are grammatically and, to some extent, lexically and phonologically distinct from any of their source languages. They seem most likely to evolve when speakers of at least three mutually unintelligible varieties need to communicate with one another on a regular basis.

PIDGINS

Commercial activities most often give birth to these new languages. When members of different language communities wish to bargain repeatedly with one another, they may develop a new language by combining elements of the languages in contact—a process called **pidginization**. Pidgins never serve as anyone's native language, and their use is usually limited to a narrow set of interactions—often business dealings—with members of other language communities. For the whole range of more complex social and intimate exchanges within their own community, pidgin speakers normally use their native language. Functioning as auxiliary, or secondary, languages, pidgins consist of simplified grammatical structures and small vocabularies, which prove perfectly adequate to their restricted purposes. As might be expected, pidgins have tended to develop in coastal and island areas, where the seafaring members of one language community have first made contact with speakers of other languages. In particular, pidgins have arisen along the west coast of Africa, the east coast of Asia, and in the Pacific islands as each of these localities was reached by European ships.

In the United States, some pidgin languages predate European contact. Native peoples, who originally spoke hundreds of distinct languages, first devised pidgins for intertribal communication. Later some of these pidgins were adapted for use with European settlers. Until the mid-nineteenth century, Mobilian pidgin—based on Choctaw and Chickasaw, with some elements from other native American languages as well as from French and English—was used among all the Indians along the Gulf of Mexico and up the Mississippi as far north as the Ohio River. In parts of New Jersey, Delaware, New York, and Pennsylvania, another Amerindian pidgin took its vocabulary from the local Munsee, Unami, and Unalachtigo dialects of Delaware (an Algonkian language) and its word order from English. The native population used this pidgin to communicate with Swedish, Dutch, and English traders during the seventeenth and early eighteenth centuries. In northwest Alaska, the native peoples spoke with visiting sailors in a pidgin which combined elements of Inupik Eskimo, Hawaiian, Spanish, and Danish. A general American Indian Pidgin English may also have been used in many parts of the United States from the beginning of English settlement until about 1900.

The best-documented of these early Amerindian pidgins is Chinook Jargon, which flourished from southern Oregon all the way to Alaska during the nineteenth century. Before the arrival of French and English trappers and traders, the Jargon—incorporating vocabulary from the Chinook and Nootka languages—was probably used among the local tribes. At later stages, words derived from English, French, and Salishan entered Chinook Jargon, bringing its vocabulary to a total of about 500 items (Taylor 1981). Among these, *potlatch* ("a gift or lavish hospitality"), *skookum* ("large or powerful"), and *siwash* ("Indian") gained some currency in mainstream English. For the most part, the syntax of Chinook Jargon reduces the grammars of all its source languages to their common elements. This reduced grammar eliminates such features as the dual-number category of the Chinook language (a marker for two items—absent in English, which marks only singular and plural) and the progressive/nonprogressive categories of English (e.g. *are walking* vs. *walk*—a distinction absent in the Amerindian languages that contribute to Chinook Jargon). After the Civil War, when masses of English speakers began to settle in Oregon, Chinook Jargon quickly faded. Today fewer than a hundred people claim some knowledge of the Jargon.

European Americans have commonly misperceived Amerindian pidgins and pidgins in general as debased or "broken" forms of a European tongue and have often wrongly judged pidgin speakers as unable to master a complex language. In reality, pidgin speakers command a native language, as complex as English, in addition to their pidgin. And the pidgin itself combines elements from two or more languages in regular and systematic ways.

Even the pidginization process—the construction of a pidgin out of its various source languages—follows certain regular linguistic patterns. When one of the communities in contact is politically and/or socially dominant, the language of that group (called the **superstrate language**) tends to provide the pidgin with most of its vocabulary. The languages of the socially subordinate groups (called **substrate languages**) tend to contribute mainly grammatical features. In the numerous contact situations created by European colonialism, the superstrate language was, of course, European; consequently, many of the world's pidgins have European-based vocabularies. A prominent example is the West African Pidgin English spoken on the west coast of Africa as a result of the British and American slave trade (Traugott 1976). In this pidgin a sentence such as the following (given here in English spelling) might occur: *King he talk say you done come* ("The king says you have come"). It is easy to see why English speakers might mistakenly label an utterance with so much English vocabulary and so little English syntax "broken English."

But speakers of West African Pidgin English are not simply failing to learn the rules of English grammar. Rather, pidgin languages obey consistent and logical, if simple, grammatical rules of their own. For example, the typical pidgin lacks inflections, even when they are present in both the superstrate and the substrate languages. That is, pidgins seldom mark such categories as number (*girl/girls*) or possession (*girl's*) in nouns, case (*I/me*) or gender (*he/she/it*) in pronouns, tense (*talk/talked*) in verbs. Actually, in any language most grammatical inflections are redundant since the information they carry can almost always be retrieved from other cues: word order can distinguish subjects from objects and indicate possession; tense can be conveyed by adverbials (such as *long time before* for past tense); number can be clarified by numerals or by pointing to the object or objects in question. Elaborate gesturing can supplement pidgin grammar.

Pidgins not only eliminate the redundant grammatical categories present in their source languages; they also use syntactic devices that exist in their substrate languages but not in European languages. West African Pidgin English, for instance, has serial verb structures, as in *go start begin teach* ("set out to teach"). Similar serial constructions can be found in such West African languages as Ewe and Twi.

Moreover, pidgin speakers make efficient use of their small vocabularies. Most of these contact languages have vocabularies of fewer than 4,000 words—compared with 40,000 in English. Yet pidgin speakers manage to maximize these limited resources by extending word meanings beyond their definitions in the source language. For instance, in West African Pidgin English, *stick* has been extended to mean "tree." Another device for stretching the resources of a small vocabulary is to combine two words in order to express a concept that would otherwise require an additional vocabulary item. In West African Pidgin English, *woman fowl* means "hen," and *house sick* means "hospital."

Because of their limited functions, pidgins may lack the range and complexity of native languages, but it is clearly inaccurate to consider them debased or unstructured. On the contrary, they testify to the ingenuity and adaptability that one language community can display when confronted by a pressing need to communicate with another.

CREOLES

The basic difference between pidgin and creole languages is that creoles have a population of native speakers. Sometimes creoles evolve when two pidgin speakers who do not share each other's primary language marry and start a family. Their children then learn the household pidgin as their first language and, in the natural process of language acquisition, transform it into a creole. As a native language, a creole must serve in every social sphere and is therefore necessarily more complex than a pidgin in both vocabulary and structure; the term **creolization** describes this process of complication and enrichment. Such a process may have occurred, for instance, when a few French trappers and their American Indian wives passed Chinook Jargon down to their children.

The three most significant U.S. creoles, however, grew out of the plantation system: Gullah, spoken today by as many as 300,000 blacks on the Sea Islands off the coast of South Carolina and Georgia and in the neighboring coastal regions; Louisiana French Creole (also called

"Gombo"), spoken by perhaps 80,000 blacks in Louisiana; and Hawaiian Creole, spoken by somewhat less than half the population of Hawaii. Why did the West Africans who were brought to the West Indies and the southern United States, as well as the Asians later brought to Hawaii, develop creoles rather than simply maintaining their original languages and/or adopting a European one?

In the West African case, language maintenance became impossible because slave traders purposely separated members of the same language community in order to lessen the threat of rebellion. Thus on any given plantation, slaves would speak a number of different and often unrelated languages—a situation which made their native tongues useless for communicating with one another, much less with their masters. Unlike any other immigrant group, West Africans had no choice but to abandon their native languages immediately.

Besides preventing the retention of African languages, the plantation system made it difficult for slaves to learn the European language of their overseers. For one thing, the social distance separating blacks from whites was much greater than the distance between native-born Americans and white immigrant groups. Less social contact meant that blacks had less opportunity—and probably less desire—to perfect their English or, in Louisiana, their French. Moreover, within the closed system of plantation societies, blacks greatly outnumbered whites. Their considerable numbers and social isolation guaranteed that many black Americans would speak a language of their own. And circumstances dictated that this language could not replicate that of either their black ancestors or their white masters.

Cut off from their own linguistic roots yet denied sufficient access to the language of their masters, black slaves in the English-speaking colonies developed a **plantation creole**, in which English, as the superstrate language, contributed most of the vocabulary while the substrate West African languages provided numerous grammatical features. It is unclear whether West Africans first learned a pidgin, which was then creolized by their children born in the New World, or whether the extreme conditions of their dislocation caused them to skip the pidgin stage and immediately develop a creole for use in every social interaction. What is clear is that creoles evolved very quickly throughout the Caribbean and in much of the plantation region of the United States.

Plantation creole was preserved longest among the field slaves, who came into the least contact with whites. Because of their greater exposure to white society, house slaves, artisans, and freedmen used fewer creole elements. That is, the speech of these more privileged blacks became more like the standard language—a process called **decreolization**. As contacts between blacks and whites have gradually increased, the speech of almost all Afro-Americans has decreolized to some degree. Those most integrated into the dominant society today speak standard English while those least integrated retain some creole features. The majority of U.S. blacks probably fall somewhere between these two extremes.

Structurally, creole languages resemble the pidgins out of which they often grow. Like pidgins, they inherit their vocabulary mainly from the superstrate language although, as full languages, they include many more vocabulary items than pidgins do. As in pidgins, the substrate influence on creoles remains in several grammatical features. And creoles, too, have few inflections, relying more on word order than on word endings to convey syntactic relationships. Unlike pidgins, however, creoles are complex enough in both vocabulary and grammar to serve the full range of needs for human speech, whether intimate or formal in style, mundane or philosophical in subject matter.

For linguists, then, creole languages are defined by the abrupt circumstances of their emergence and by certain structural tendencies they share. These languages should not be confused with the more popular definitions of creoles as "descendants of Europeans born in the American South or the Caribbean" or "non-Europeans in colonial settings." This confusion is especially likely to arise with respect to Louisiana, where *creole* can refer to the descendant of a French or Spanish colonist, to the regional variety of French spoken by descendants of French or Acadian ("Cajun") settlers, or to the French- and West African-derived language spoken by blacks. Only the last of these is a creole in linguistic terms, and only this sense of the word is intended in this book.

One other trait that creoles share with pidgins is low status. In part, creoles suffer from negative prestige because they are so often spoken by populations that were once enslaved and continue to be undervalued. But creoles also retain low status because, like pidgins, they are frequently—and unjustly—perceived as illiterate versions of superstrate languages. For instance, in the Jamaican Creole sentence (given in English spelling), *Andrew him hear what them de say and him know what de go done* (meaning, "Andrew hears what they are saying and he knows what is going to be done"), the verbs *hear, say,* and *go* lack their standard English inflections (Traugott 1976). Standard English would also omit the first *him* and convert *them* and the second *him* to the subjective case (*they* and *he*). But this comparison with standard English overlooks some distinct and systematic features of Jamaican Creole: present-tense verbs are uninflected (*hear,* not *hears*), the progressive is indicated by the African-derived word *de* (*de say*, not *are saying*), and pronouns take only one case (*them,* not *they* or *their*). Such an analysis suggests that Jamaican Creole is not an inferior version of English but a somewhat different language with rules of its own. It is important to remember that creoles are just as logical and expressive as any other language in the world.

CHAPTER 9

Case Studies in Language Contact

THE PREVIOUS CHAPTER has explained the processes of linguistic change and accommodation at work in our multilingual society. Some languages have coexisted with English for various lengths of time in a bilingual or even trilingual situation. Some tongues have accepted English borrowing and eventually become mixed languages. Many have nearly disappeared. Under the particular exigencies of the plantation system, other languages contributed to pidgins or creoles.

This chapter presents case studies that illustrate these linguistic processes. Southwest Spanish and Pennsylvania German represent the few communities that have managed to preserve a non-English language over many generations. The section on American Indian languages exemplifies the impact of European colonization on indigenous tongues. The case of Serbo-Croatian typifies the comparatively rapid language loss experienced by many immigrant ethnic communities. The final sections on Gullah and Black English Vernacular and on Hawaiian Pidgin and Creole show the creolization and decreolization processes that have operated on the language of plantation workers and their descendants.

SOUTHWEST SPANISH

Spanish speakers not only comprise by far the largest language minority in the United States; they have also resisted assimilation to English monolingualism longer and more successfully than any other language community. As of 1975, 90 percent of Spanish mother-tongue claimants were living in households where Spanish was still spoken at least some of the time. Of these, 49 percent reported that more Spanish than English was used at home. And Spanish shows no signs of losing ground among the younger generation. In 1976, fully 42 percent of U.S. Spanish speakers were under nineteen years old. Thus the Hispanic community offers the best and strongest example of stable bilingualism in the United States.

As Chapter 1 explains, the large Spanish-speaking population in this country, like the English-speaking population, is ethnically and linguistically diverse. Cubans, many of whom settled in the Miami area, speak one variety of Antillean Spanish. Puerto Ricans, located mainly in New York City, speak a slightly different variety of the same dialect. Chicanos (the designation preferred by politically conscious Mexican Americans) speak a Mexican-derived Spanish. They are concentrated in the Southwestern states but present throughout the country. Besides bringing their various Spanish dialects to the United States, Hispanics adapted their language to their new surroundings once they arrived. The Cuban Spanish spoken around Miami shows the impact of Southern regional English; the Puerto Rican Spanish spoken in New York borrows some vocabulary from Black English Vernacular; Chicano Spanish incorporates some native American features.

Although all these varieties of Spanish have been modified by their contact with English, none of them seems in any present danger of extinction. On the contrary, the situation of U.S. Hispanics manifests many of the conditions that favor language maintenance, outlined in Table 18. The Spanish language has high international visibility and was spoken in the Southwest before English. Hispanics exhibit strong loyalty to their families and to the Roman Catholic religion. They have recently come to the United States in large numbers and settled in neighborhood enclaves. They live close enough to their homelands to maintain close ties, and massive immigration continues to replenish their communities. Finally, since most U.S. Hispanics, except some

Cubans, are poor and non-white, they encounter formidable barriers to entering the mainstream society of monolingual English speakers.

Among the several varieties currently flourishing in the United States, Chicano Spanish is the home language of roughly half the Spanish-speaking population. It therefore serves as the focus of this section.

Chicano Spanish stretches across so much of the Southwest that it falls into four major regional dialect areas: 1) Texas, 2) New Mexico and southern Colorado, 3) Arizona, and 4) California (Cárdenas 1975). The New Mexican variety stands apart from the others because it is spoken mainly by descendants of seventeenth-century settlers (see Chapter 1), rather than by recent immigrants, and it experienced little influence from English until the 1930s. Archaic forms distinguish the Spanish of this relic area. One example (Craddock 1981:202) is the outmoded form *onde* ("where"), which in standard Spanish has since become *donde* through contraction of *de + onde* ("from where, whence").

The Texas, Arizona, and California areas are sometimes grouped together as "Border Spanish" since all reveal the strong and continuing influence of Mexican Spanish. Yet they do display noticeable differences. The Texas variety bears the greatest resemblance to Mexican Spanish; the California variety has borrowed most from English; and Arizona Spanish retains some of the archaic flavor of the New Mexico dialect.

Regional dialects of Chicano Spanish, however, vary far less than the social dialects within each region. These include: **Northern Mexican Spanish, Popular Spanish**, an English-influenced variety called **Mixed Spanish** (*Español Mixtureado*, also labeled "Tex-Mex," "Spanglish," or "Pocho"), and a slang known as **caló**. An individual Chicano might speak one or more of these varieties depending on such demographic factors as age and length of residency in the United States and on such sociolinguistic factors as conversation partners and topics. The characteristic features and uses of each variety will be sketched below.

In addition to commanding one or more varieties of Spanish for use in the private domain and with other Hispanics, bilingual Chicanos speak English in the public domain and with Anglos. With other bilinguals, they often opt for code-switching, discussed under "Multilingualism" in Chapter 8. This impressive verbal repertoire should put to rest the common misconception that bilingual Chicanos speak neither Spanish nor English well enough to communicate in a complex social interaction or that they speak only a corrupt mixed language. One young man in East Austin, Texas, explained language use among Chicanos this way (Elías-Olivares 1979:132–33):

> If you're gonna make anything, you know, or do anything you have to know how to communicate and you're never gonna have the same group. You may be talking to an anglo, so you have to learn to speak English. You may be talking to the poor white then you talk the slang or the hippie; then you talk to the mexicano professional *que avienta puras palabras grandes* (who spouts only big words), you have to speak that way, *los viejitos otra manera y de aí a la gente de tu edad, mexicanos, el estilo de nosotros y ai está* (with old people another way and then with people your own age, mexicanos, our way of talking [*caló*] and there it is).

Notice that the informant further demonstrates his sensitivity to these complicated language norms by code-switching when he begins to describe the various kinds of Spanish.

NORTHERN MEXICAN AND POPULAR SPANISH

Among the varieties of Spanish, Northern Mexican Spanish, the language of educated northern Mexicans and many Mexican immigrants, serves Chicanos as a formal or standard dialect. It is spoken by radio and television announcers, as well as by teachers and other prestigious community members. Thus Northern Mexican Spanish commands a certain amount of respect among Chicanos. One teacher's aide remarked about the Spanish spoken by her school principal (Elías-Olivares 1979:131):

> *El español d'ella está tan elevado y tan bonito y tan correcto, que me da vergüenza hablar con ella. Ella pasaría por una mexicana del otro lao.* (Her Spanish is so refined and so pretty and so correct, that it embarrasses me to speak with her. She could pass for a Mexican from the other side [from Mexico].)

But the formality associated with this variety can also alienate those who do not speak it regularly. Children who learn Northern Mexican Spanish in school will be ridiculed if they try to use it with their friends. And recent immigrants from Mexico who speak this variety may find that their Chicano neighbors think them stiff and distant, even though they are simply using their native dialect. To remedy this awkwardness, most immigrants quickly adopt the English-influenced local speech called Mixed Spanish.

Most first-generation Chicanos are fluent in Popular Spanish, the colloquial variety spoken throughout Latin America by the working classes. Popular Spanish functions as a major medium of communication with older community members and in the home. It differs from the more formal variety in a few phonological features, such as the absence of final -s, the deletion of unstressed syllables, and the pronunciation of *ch* sounds (/č/) as *sh* (/š/). The few grammatical differences from the standard often involve a variant use of prepositions.

MIXED SPANISH

Among members of the second and third generation, Mixed Spanish has wide currency, particularly in the barrios of such Southwestern cities as El Paso, San Antonio, and Los Angeles. It is not a random mix of Spanish and English words and structures but rather a variety of Spanish that incorporates many borrowings from English. Its phonology and grammar remain recognizably Spanish. Although despised by many Anglos as a substandard hybrid jargon and by older Chicanos as a corruption of Spanish, the mixed language nevertheless serves as a marker of ethnic awareness and group solidarity among the young.

English borrowings into Mixed Spanish take all the forms outlined in the "Borrowing" section of Chapter 8. Individual English words, adapted to Spanish phonology and grammar, are the most easily and frequently borrowed (Espinosa 1975). Some of these words represent items or activities typically associated with Anglo culture: *mira* ("meter"), *jira* ("heater"), *suera* ("sweater"), *lonchi* ("lunch"), *balún* ("balloon"), *troca* ("truck"), *sangüichi* ("sandwich"), *beisbol* ("baseball"), *boila* ("boiler"), *aiscrím* ("ice cream"), *penquila* ("painkiller"). Borrowed verbs usually acquire the Spanish infinitive ending -*ar*: *batyar* ("to bat"), *espeliar* ("to spell"), *quiquiar* ("to kick"), *cuitar* ("to quit").

Mixed Spanish also incorporates a substantial number of loan translations—literal translations of English expressions into Spanish (Espinosa 1975, Ornstein 1975). Examples include: *tener un bien tiempo* ("to have a good time"), *escuela alta* ("high school"), and *viaje redondo* ("round trip"). In addition, many English modifier + noun combinations have been translated into Mixed Spanish in the form noun + *de* + modifier: *leche de bote* ("canned milk"), *máquina de lavar* ("washing machine"), *trabajo de pinturas* ("paint job").

In some cases the original meaning of a Spanish word has shifted in Mixed Spanish to fit the definition of a related English word (Barker 1975). The meaning of *birria* has changed from "a meat dish" to "beer." *Ganga* has become "gang" rather than "bargain." *Mecha*, originally "wick," has acquired the meaning "match." And *carro* has changed from "cart" to "car."

Mixed Spanish has borrowed far less from English phonology. A few sounds that occur in English but not in Spanish have been introduced into Mixed Spanish, mainly in English loan words (Phillips 1975). The English sounds /š/, /ǰ/, /θ/, /æ/, and /ə/ have all been attested in Mixed Spanish where they would not occur in standard Spanish: /š/*erife* ("sheriff"), /ǰ/*obe* ("job"), /θ/*eorías* ("theories"), /æ/*ccidente* ("accident"), and *n*/ə/*rsi* ("nurse"). Otherwise, Mixed Spanish retains the Spanish sound system intact.

The impact of English grammar on Mixed Spanish has apparently also been slight (Peñalosa 1980). Occasionally, a speaker of this variety will use the English adjective + noun word order instead of the standard Spanish noun + adjective sequence, producing *mi chiquito hermano* ("my little brother") instead of the standard *mi hermano chiquito*. Or, by analogy with English, the gerund (the *-ing* form in English, the *-ndo* form in Spanish) might occur where standard Spanish requires the infinitive: *gasta dinero en tomando* ("he spends money on drinking") rather than standard Spanish *gasta dinero en tomar* (literally, "he spends money on to drink"). Mixed Spanish speakers may also omit Spanish articles where they would be absent in English: *religión es algo muy personal* ("religion is something very personal") instead of standard *la religión es algo muy personal* (literally, "the religion is something very personal"). Most such Anglicized syntactic structures, however, have been attested primarily in the Spanish of young children; bilingual adults borrow little from English grammar.

CALÓ

The dialect called *caló* (formerly *Pachuco*) is essentially Mixed Spanish with a large and rapidly changing slang vocabulary (Elías-Olivares 1979, Peñalosa 1980, Barker 1975). This variety of Spanish now functions as an in-group language for Chicano street gangs and, to an extent, for Chicano youths in general, much as Black English Vernacular does in the black community. It originated in Spain as a blend of the Romany language spoken by gypsies and the *germanía* jargon used by underworld figures. *Caló* probably entered the United States from Mexico in the late nineteenth century. During the 1930s, it was adopted in the El Paso area by drug dealers and other criminals, called *Pachucos* (after a slang term for El Paso) or "Zoot-Suiters" (after their characteristic baggy suits). The slang, then known as *Pachuco*, spread from El Paso through the Southwestern prison system and went with migrating men on the freight trains to Tucson and Los Angeles. Now that *Pachucos* are no longer active, the current street slang is called *caló, tirilí, vato,* or *tarzán.* Its vocabulary constantly passes into the other dialects of Chicano Spanish and is constantly updated by new generations.

Speakers of *caló* preserve its in-group character by using many loans from English, adopting Mexican slang, redefining ordinary Spanish words, inventing new words, and quickly replacing terms that become too well-known to the larger community (Peñalosa 1980). *Espatiar* ("to spot"), for instance, stems from English. *Ramfla* ("automobile") comes from Mexican slang. *Carnal* ("pal") is redefined from standard Mexican Spanish in which it means "related by blood." *Carlongo* ("coat") seems to be an invented word. Heroin has been designated by the Spanish words *la chiva* ("the thing") or *la madre* ("the mother"), but its label changes often so that outsiders will not know what is being discussed. The rapid changes in *caló* vocabulary are also reflected in its many synonyms for "policeman": *cachuchón, camacho, chero, chota, jura, julia, ley, pasta, píldora, placa, tecolote.*

As the language of street-wise males, *caló* is usually considered inappropriate for "decent" women to use. A young Chicana commented (Elías-Olivares 1979:127):

> *Concocí a una señora y usaba esas palabras, se oyían muy feas* (I met a woman and she was using those words, they sounded very ugly), that's not the kind of language . . . coming from *una mujer, no se oye bien* (a woman, it doesn't sound good). It's all right for them [the men] *pero en una mujer se oye feo* (but from a woman it sounds ugly).

Chicanos also consider it disrespectful for young people to use the slang with their elders. But style-shifting to *caló* can be an appropriate means for any Chicano to signal emphasis or anger, show disrepect, or convey humor.

CHICANO ENGLISH

Although many Southwestern Chicanos control one or more of these Spanish dialects, nearly all of them—except some immigrants—also speak English. In fact, the Chicano community actually uses more English than Spanish. English is always the language of choice in interactions with Anglos and is often preferred in formal interactions among Chicanos. As Chicanos advance into mainstream society, they use more and more English, even in the home. Many third-generation Chicanos, especially those who have moved into the middle class, have abandoned Spanish altogether.

The type of English spoken by Southwestern Chicanos depends not only on their social class but also on the extent of their contact with Anglos. Chicanos with high social status in their own community but limited Anglo contacts tend not to speak the regional variety but a standard English derived from national media. A study of bilingual Chicanos from San Antonio, for instance, revealed that none of them used the local Anglo expressions *Christmas Gift, snap beans, corn shuck,* or *pully bone* (Sawyer 1975). Instead, they used the national standard equivalents: *Merry Christmas, string beans, corn husk,* and *wish bone.* In southern California, most Chicanos follow the national standard in distinguishing the vowel sounds of *caught/cot* and *pin/pen* (Peñalosa 1980), although most standard-speaking Anglos in their region do not make these discriminations. Another study of Chicano English in Austin concluded that Chicanos were likely to adopt the regional standard only if they had attended high school and considered the "right" accent essential to getting ahead.

Besides adhering to national rather than local speech norms, some middle-class Chicanos hypercorrect their English, carefully ridding it of Spanish loan words—even those in general use among Anglos (e.g. *patio, bronco, corral*). This excessively "purified" English testifies to the linguistic insecurity of those who still feel uncertain that their speech is acceptable to those in power (Sawyer 1975). By contrast, in their Spanish, Chicanos borrow freely and creatively from English, as noted above.

Many working-class Chicanos raised in the barrio speak a Spanish-influenced variety of English. Even though they are native speakers of English, they may seem to have a "Spanish accent" because they learned their English in a Spanish-speaking community. This inherited influence from Spanish affects mainly intonation and distinctions in English pronunciation that have no counterparts in Spanish.

Table 19 displays the pronunciation and intonation features of Chicano English that are most likely to reveal the underlying influence of Spanish. These features serve as important sociolinguistic markers in both the Anglo and the Chicano communities.

LANGUAGE ATTITUDES

Unfortunately, Spanish-influenced English is more often scorned than any other language variety in the Chicano verbal repertoire (Ryan and Carranza 1977). Neither Chicanos nor Anglos have much respect or affection for it. In one matched guise test, for instance, sixty-three Chicana and non-Chicana high school students evaluated the taped speech of standard and Spanish-influenced English speakers in two contexts (home and school) and with two rating scales (one for such status-related characteristics as success, education, and occupa-

T A B L E 19. Phonological Interference from Spanish in Spanish-Influenced English

FEATURE	EXAMPLE/EXPLANATION
Consonants:	
/v/ = /b/	*vest = best*
/š/ = /č/	*cheap = sheep*
/z/ = /s/	*raise = race*
/θ/ → /t/	*thin* pronounced *tin*
/ð/ → /d/	*then* pronounced *den*
/y/ → /ǰ/	*yes* pronounced *Jess*
Vowels:	
/ɪ/ = /i/	*sit = seat*
/æ/ → /a/ or /ɛ/	*cat* pronounced *cot* or *man* pronounced *men*
/ə/ → /a/ or /o/	*one* pronounced *wan* or *come* pronounced *comb*
Stress and Intonation:	
Syllable timing	All syllables pronounced for same length of time rather than length depending on stress
Full vowels in unstressed syllables	*carton* pronounced *car tone*
Different stress pattern	*níght tráin* pronounced *night tráin*
Statement intonation resembles question intonation	*I'm going now* sounds like *I'm going now?*

tional level; the other for such solidarity-related characteristics as friendliness, kindness, and trustworthiness). As might be expected, the students tended to rate the Spanish-influenced speakers higher in the home context than in the school context and higher on solidarity than on status. But in both contexts and on both scales, the students gave the standard English speakers more positive ratings than the Spanish-influenced English speakers. Even the Chicanas in this study discriminated against the Spanish-influenced variety. Other studies give similar evidence that the dominant culture has bequeathed its negative evaluation of this minority dialect to the minority group itself. Only those with enough ethnic pride to label themselves with the politically conscious term "Chicano" respond favorably to Spanish-influenced English. To judge from these studies, speakers of this dialect must expect to encounter significant obstacles to success in mainstream society.

Some evidence indicates that this prejudice against the language of Hispanics has also led to low esteem for Spanish (Ryan and Carranza 1977). Based on taped speech samples, bilingual Anglo and Chicano high school students rated English speakers higher than Spanish speakers on both status and solidarity scales. And in another study, 51 percent of Anglo college students and 31 percent of Chicano college students considered Southwest Spanish to be just "border slang." Even more negative attitudes toward Spanish are held by older Chicanos and those at the lower end of the economic scale, who associate poverty with Spanish and success with English.

Yet not all of the results of language attitude tests are so discouraging. Many Chicanos seem to value Spanish highly (Ryan and Carranza 1977). The same bilingual high school students who rated English higher than Spanish on the status and solidarity scales also preferred Spanish to English for use in the home. Another survey had even more encouraging results for advocates of Spanish language maintenance. Forty-seven Chicano adults listened to taped speech samples in standard Spanish, standard English, Mixed Spanish, and Spanish-influenced English. Across the whole group, evaluations of standard English and standard Spanish speakers were about the same. Those with Chicano awareness actually rated Mixed Spanish significantly higher than standard English. Those with some college education preferred standard Spanish to standard English. Thus better-educated and politically-conscious Chicanos seem to respect standard Spanish and retain a considerable attachment for the mixed variety they identify with their own culture. These studies suggest that, if Chicanos continue to consolidate their pride in their linguistic and cultural heritage, the Spanish language may have a long and vigorous future in the Southwest.

PENNSYLVANIA GERMAN

One of the oldest unassimilated language communities in the United States is the "Pennsylvania Dutch" speech island in the farming district west and north of Philadelphia. German—*Deutsch* in their own tongue—religious dissenters settled the area three hundred years ago, and separatist, traditionalist sects have maintained cultural and linguistic integrity down to the present day. The linguistic history of Pennsylvania German testifies to the strength of religious belief as a cultural determinant, enabling these communities to resist the vast array of political, economic, and social pressures that have caused the demise of other, far larger German language communities.

The pledge of religious tolerance attracted many dissenters to the Pennsylvania colony—among them Pietists from the Rhine provinces and from Switzerland and southern Germany. Cut off from further immigration during the Revolutionary War period, they evolved a local dialect based on the majority's Rhineland speech and incorporating elements from other regional homelands, the standard German used in their Lutheran Bible, and some English influences. Subsequent German immigrants found the colonial settlers culturally archaic and linguistically distinct.

Nineteenth-century German immigrants were political or economic rather than religious refugees. They were intent on cultural and linguistic maintenance, but for printing and public speaking they chose to adopt the standard German dialect, which the colonial communities used only in religious services. These German activists guided bilingual legislation through state governments: German-speaking elementary and secondary schools were authorized, and public and legal notices were ordered in German as well as English (Kloss 1966). Although more liberal colonial communities, such as the Moravians, joined the German mainstream, the conservative Pietists, such as the Amish and Old Order Mennonites, continued to adhere to social isolation and the colonial dialect.

Those who adopted the language and customs of the later immigrants ultimately suffered the same cultural and linguistic fate. Extreme anti-German sentiment in the early twentieth century encouraged the bulk of the German population in Pennsylvania, as elsewhere in the country, to abandon their language and separate institutions and merge into Anglo-American society. The separatist, traditionalist sects in the core area of southeast Pennsylvania had long been accepted in the region and were regarded as eccentric but certainly not un-American. Thus the conservative "Plain people" and their Pennsylvania German dialect remained largely unaffected by political forces that erased a language community numbering in the millions. In fact, the 1930s witnessed a cultural revival of Pennsylvania German, including expanded literary and religious prose writing, the introduction of regular Pennsylvania German-language columns into regional newspapers, and spelling standardization and a grammar book for the dialect.

Pennsylvania German has been shaped by its isolation from European German and has diverged radically from the codified, standard language (Gilbert 1971). Like many American dialects of European languages, it has been primarily a spoken, not a written form. Grammatical categories that have been kept distinct in the literary language have collapsed in the vernacular. Redundant gender and tense endings have fallen together. The subjective and objective cases have been merged. Recent developments in standard German—such as the "polite" or formal pronoun of address—simply do not appear in the Pennsylvania dialect.

English has had a profound influence on Pennsylvania German. Lexical borrowings are extensive, as Table 20 illustrates. A single sentence may contain several loans, as in *Mein stallion hat ueber den fenz geschumpt und dem nachbar sein whiet gedaemaetscht* ("My *stallion jump*ed over the *fence* and *damaged* my neighbor's *wheat*"); *Ich muss den gaul abharnessen und den boggi griesen befor wir ein ride nehmen* ("I must *harness* up the horse and *grease* the *buggy before* we take a *ride*"). Although the structure of these sentences is German, some English nouns and verb roots have replaced their German equivalents; the verbs show German prefixes and suffixes. The idiom *ein ride nehmen* is a loan translation from English.

Because Pennsylvania German speakers refused to take up new inventions—such as electricity and automobiles—their lives have not been drastically transformed, as the lives of so many other immigrants have been. Thus their language is not inundated with loans for new and foreign objects and processes. And since they carry on contact with the non-Pietist world in English, Pennsylvania Germans can continue speaking their own dialect with a mixed but predominantly German vocabulary.

The uses of native German words have also been affected by the

T A B L E 20.   **English Influences on Pennsylvania German Vocabulary**

PENNSYLVANIA GERMAN	ENGLISH	STANDARD GERMAN
daadi	daddy	Vater
bu	boy	Bube, Junge, Knabe
faektri	factory	Fabrik
schtori, g'schickt	story	Geschichte
humbuk	humbug	—
kaesch	cash, money	Geld, Bargeld
weri	very	sehr
lof-letter	love letter	Liebesbrief
schtaert	start	anfangen
boggi	buggy	Wagen
duh; geduh	do; done	tun; getan
blaum	plum	Pflaume
juscht	just	jetzt
figgeren	figure, do arithmetic	rechnen
waschkessel, waschboiler	wash kettle, wash boiler	Waschkessel
weck; aweck	wake; awake	wecken; wach
gemixte pickles	mixed pickles	gemischte Gurken
eul, aul	owl	Eule
eicharnch, schgwerl	squirrel	Eichhörnchen
as	as	als

presence of English. Pennsylvania German speakers say *Was zeit iss es?*—a literal translation of English "What time is it?"—rather than the standard German *Wieviel Uhr ist es?* (literally, "How much hour is it?"). There is a tendency to substitute prepositional phrases for grammatical relations expressed through case marking in German. This also affects sentence word order: *weg vun deheem* (literally, "away from at-home") has replaced standard German *von zu Hause weg* (literally, "from to house away"). Pennsylvania German *Mer fiedert 's hoi zu de Kieh* ("one feeds hay to cows") contrasts with standard German *Man fuettert Kuehe mit Heu* ("one feeds cows with hay").

As further evidence of language mixing, the word *liverwurscht* combines the English *liver* with the German *wurscht* ("sausage"). Such mixed terms appear in both Pennsylvania German and the Midland dialect of English.

The Amish and Old Order Mennonites practice not only a religion but a way of life. Their farms are economically self-sufficient. Outmoded dress, tools, and vehicles set them visibly apart from English-speaking society. They participate in public life only when required and shun all unnecessary contact. Children attend school for the legal minimum of eight years, then receive German language training in the community. While other European language communities have sacrificed linguistic continuity to social and economic mobility, the Pennsylvania Germans have maintained their unique language as one of the barriers they impose between themselves and outsiders. Both because they wish to remain isolated and because the German language is an intrinsic part of their religious practice, Pennsylvania German will continue in use as long as these communities survive.

AMERICAN INDIANS: THE CASES OF DELAWARE AND CHEROKEE

Many native American languages, especially those originally spoken in the Eastern United States, have suffered decline and even death. Delaware and Cherokee survive today, but their futures are in doubt. Although the two language communities have very different linguistic and cultural histories, no distinctions among tribes approach the effect of the displacement and racial suppression endured by all Eastern Indian tribes as European settlers established themselves on the continent.

DELAWARE

The Delaware language is near extinction. Once the tongue of tribes spread along the Atlantic coast from Connecticut to New Jersey, it is now known only to a handful of elders in two Delaware communities in Oklahoma. The Algonkian *Lenapé*—renamed "Delaware" by the English after the colonial governor of the region they inhabited—fell victim to European diseases and territorial wars with other tribes displaced by white settlers. By the late eighteenth century their numbers had dwindled from 10,000 to 2,300 (Weslager 1972).

In the first stage of a long, arduous forced migration to Oklahoma, the Delaware were pushed back from desirable coastal lands into eastern Pennsylvania. William Penn, who regarded them with great respect, commented (quoted in Weslager 1972:166):

I have made it my business to understand [the Delaware language] that I might not want an interpreter on any occasion. And I must say, that I know not of a language spoken in Europe that hath words of more sweetness in accent or emphasis than theirs.

Yet Europeans and other, powerful Indian tribes were given title to Delaware lands. As a result, the Delawares were dispersed over Ohio, Michigan, Missouri, and southern Ontario by 1800. The Ontario Delawares separated permanently from the main body; they intermarried with other tribes and gave up the Delaware language before the end of the century. Shunted from one Midwestern territory to another, the American Delawares diminished constantly in numbers and in ethnic integrity. Some split off to join other Algonkian peoples in northern Wisconsin, where the language has also died out. By 1870 the surviving Delawares had been removed to Oklahoma "Indian Territory"; one community of perhaps 800 was granted joint ownership—with non-Algonkian Caddo, Wichita, and Kiowa peoples—of lands near Anadarko, and a second community settled near Dewey, where they were incorporated into the Cherokee nation.

Delawares are not literate in their language. The language and culture have been transmitted orally. In the Dewey community the Delawares have maintained a sense of tribal identity, despite their minority status. Until recently many practiced the traditional religion, which requires recitation of songs and prayers in the tribal tongue. Retained in religious and ceremonial settings, the Delaware language at Dewey became diglossic with English. The few remaining speakers are familiar with the traditional oral materials but do not use Delaware for other purposes. At Anadarko, too, the language is spoken only by a few old people, but they make more general conversational use of the mother tongue. The Anadarko Delawares converted early to Christianity and have not maintained a sense of distinct tribal identity. Yet, because they were more numerous and lived in closer proximity, the language continued in use. Now both communities—the traditionalists and the nontraditionalists—are experiencing language death (Cooley 1978a).

Contemporary Delaware has become reduced in structure and vocabulary—indications of obsolescence (Cooley 1978b). Experiences of youth—hunting terms, names of plants, animals, and states of weather—are expressed in native words, but recent or nontraditional experiences are named with English words. The vocabulary is frozen and it is shrinking; as old words are forgotten, they are replaced with non-native words. Grammatical categories have fallen together. Certain verb endings, for example, have become less distinct from one another over the past twenty years. Some Delaware words are pronounced according to English sound rules, especially if the speakers are not taking care to be "accurate." All of these are signs of disuse. No children are learning Delaware; the language is not replenished and will become extinct within the next generation.

CHEROKEE

Unlike the Delaware, the Cherokee embraced European innovations, yet they too have faced great obstacles in their attempts to maintain linguistic and tribal autonomy. The Cherokee made their homes in the highlands of southern Appalachia and thus did not face serious territorial challenges from European settlers until the end of the eighteenth century. One tribal member, Sequoyah, observed that, in their unsuccessful resistance to the whites, coastal tribes had been defeated by not only military but also communicational technology. An illiterate monolingual, Sequoyah created a writing system for Cherokee by drawing symbols for vowels and consonant-vowel sequences from the European documents that came into his hands. Sequoyah's syllabary was so well-suited to the language that within a year the majority of the tribe's adults could read and write in their language (Walker 1981). They established a printing press in 1828 and began publishing a Cherokee language newspaper (see Figure 25). The Cherokee translated American law into their language and attempted to meet the whites on their own terms—through a judicial challenge to President Jackson's 1830 Indian Removal Act. Yet, in spite of favorable rulings from the U.S. Supreme Court, they were removed from their homeland and force-marched on a "Trail of Tears" across the country into Oklahoma.

The Cherokee printing press was confiscated and destroyed by the Georgia government in 1835 on the grounds that it was being used to print material urging resistance to removal. Survivors of the "Trail of Tears" reestablished the press in Oklahoma and used the written medium for tribal government and Christian religious education, as well as for printing newspapers and books. When the U.S. government dissolved the Cherokee nation in 1907, it once again confiscated the press. Cherokee children were forced to attend English-speaking residential schools, tribal records began to be kept in English, and literacy declined (Spolsky 1978). By 1960 only a third of the Cherokees

CHEROKEE ALPHABET.

CHARACTERS AS ARRANGED BY THE INVENTOR.

Ꭱ Ꭰ Ꮃ Ꮵ Ꮐ Ꮽ Ꮺ Ꮅ Ꮑ Ꮌ Ꭹ Ᏹ Ꮟ Ꮲ Ꭳ Ꮇ Ꮄ Ꭽ Ꮼ

Ꮰ Ꮤ Ᏼ Ꮈ Ꭿ Ꮝ Ᏺ Ꮁ Ꭺ Ꮷ Ꮍ Ꮞ Ꮠ Ꮆ Ꮘ Ꮚ Ꮜ Ꮖ Ꮓ Ꭷ

Ꮸ Ꮢ Ꮒ Ꭶ Ꮩ Ꮀ Ꮣ Ꭼ Ꮻ Ꭲ Ꭴ Ᏸ Ꮂ Ꮫ Ꭻ Ꮶ Ꮙ Ꮔ Ꮎ Ꮳ

Ᏻ Ꮴ Ꮧ Ꮾ Ꮪ Ꮥ Ꮯ Ꭵ Ꮕ Ꮦ Ꮉ Ꮡ Ꮱ Ꭾ Ꭸ Ꮋ Ꮭ Ꮿ Ꮹ Ꮨ

Ꮮ Ꮏ Ꮗ Ꮬ Ꮊ Ꮛ

CHARACTERS SYSTEMATICALLY ARRANGED WITH THE SOUNDS.

Ꭰ a	Ꭱ e	Ꭲ i	Ꭳ o	Ꭴ u	Ꭵ v
Ꭶ ga Ꭷ ka	Ꭸ ge	Ꭹ gi	Ꭺ go	Ꭻ gu	Ꭼ gv
Ꭽ ha	Ꭾ he	Ꭿ hi	Ꮀ ho	Ꮁ hu	Ꮂ hv
Ꮃ la	Ꮄ le	Ꮅ li	Ꮆ lo	Ꮇ lu	Ꮈ lv
Ꮉ ma	Ꮊ me	Ꮋ mi	Ꮌ mo	Ꮍ mu	
Ꮎ na Ꮏ hna Ꮐ nah	Ꮑ ne	Ꮒ ni	Ꮓ no	Ꮔ nu	Ꮕ nv
Ꮖ qua	Ꮗ que	Ꮘ qui	Ꮙ quo	Ꮚ quu	Ꮛ quv
Ꮝ s Ꮜ sa	Ꮞ se	Ꮟ si	Ꮠ so	Ꮡ su	Ꮢ sv
Ꮣ da Ꮤ ta	Ꮥ de Ꮦ te	Ꮧ di Ꮨ tih	Ꮩ do	Ꮪ du	Ꮫ dv
Ꮬ dla Ꮭ tla	Ꮮ tle	Ꮯ tli	Ꮰ tlo	Ꮱ tlu	Ꮲ tlv
Ꮳ tsa	Ꮴ tse	Ꮵ tsi	Ꮶ tso	Ꮷ tsu	Ꮸ tsv
Ꮹ wa	Ꮺ we	Ꮻ wi	Ꮼ wo	Ꮽ wu	Ꮾ wv
Ꮿ ya	Ᏸ ye	Ᏹ yi	Ᏺ yo	Ᏻ yu	Ᏼ yv

SOUNDS REPRESENTED BY VOWELS.

a as *a* in *father*, or short as *a* in *rival*.
e as *a* in *hate*, or short as *e* in *met*,
i as *i* in *pique*, or short as *i* in *pit*,
o as *aw* in *law*, or short as *o* in *not*,
u as *oo* in *fool*, or short as *u* in *pull*,
v as *u* in *but* nasalized.

CONSONANT SOUNDS.

g nearly as in English, but approaching to k. d nearly as in English, but approaching to t. h, k, l, m, n, q, s, t, w, y, as in English.

Syllables beginning with g, except Ꭶ, have sometimes the power of k; Ꭿ, Ꮪ, Ꮫ, are sometimes sounded to, tu, tv; and syllables written with tl, except Ꮭ, sometimes vary to dl.

FIGURE 25. Cherokee Syllabary as Printed by Elias Boudinot, First Editor of *The Cherokee Phoenix,* 1828–1832

could read and write in the language. Only one typewriter with the syllabary characters remained in the state. The language was written primarily by practitioners of traditional medicine and read primarily during religious services, when the congregation reads aloud from the Cherokee Bible.

When the tribe renewed its struggle for ethnic identity in the 1960s, one of its first actions was once again to cast the syllabary into type and reinstitute a tribal press. The press has produced educational materials aimed toward child and adult literacy and a newsletter. Some Cherokee language courses are taught in area schools. A recent survey of speaking ability (Pulte 1979) found that half of the children under eighteen have some knowledge of the language, but their actual use of Cherokee is far more restricted. The tribal tongue is limited primarily to two settings. Cherokee is required for ceremonial and official occasions, although enough English is incorporated that all participants can follow the events. The only other significant use of Cherokee is within nuclear families in which both parents are full-blood Cherokees. In Pulte's sample of Oklahoma communities, all mixed-blood children are monolingual English speakers. But 80 percent of the adults in all-Cherokee households converse with each other in the tribal language. Of these adults, 56 percent speak to their children in Cherokee as well. Over half of these children who regularly hear Cherokee at home are also active Cherokee speakers: 60 percent regularly respond to adults in Cherokee and 63 percent use Cherokee with siblings and playmates. Thus it appears that slightly less than half the young people in all-Cherokee families have a passive knowledge of the language (i.e. 56% of the 80% in Cherokee-speaking households) and about two-thirds of these are active speakers.

But even full-blood Cherokees may have limited opportunities for speaking the language. Many members of the tribe have married non-Cherokees, so that conversation among extended families is always in English. Since most time is spent outside the nuclear household, Cherokee may actually be used in only a small percentage of day-to-day interaction. Outside the primary Oklahoma communities, the language is nearly obsolete. A few speakers remain in North Carolina, descendants of the Cherokees who escaped removal from the tribal homeland in the 1830s. The language should persist for some time to come, although its utility will become more and more restricted.

The many Cherokees who have left the Oklahoma and North Carolina communities are generally monolingual English speakers. In Los Angeles alone, there are 1,500, living in mixed neighborhoods with Indians from other tribes and Hispanics (Fuchs and Havighurst 1972). If their young people speak a second language, it is Spanish, not Cherokee. Like other English-speaking Indians, the urban Cherokees employ a variety of English unique to their tribe. Even those who have no knowledge of the tribal language use nonstandard phonology and grammatical structures which derive from the ancestral tongue.

These two languages, Delaware and Cherokee, illustrate the fate of most native language communities from the Eastern states. In the Great Plains and the Southwest, where Indians have retained at least a portion of their traditional lands, large tribal language communities continue to thrive. Languages such as Navajo, Hopi, Siouan (or Lakota), and Apache are not only actively spoken but consciously maintained by their communities through native language or bilingual schools and training in tribal ritual and culture. Although many native American languages have died away, others have survived four hundred years of European hegemony and governmental policies specifically designed to drive them out of existence. Indians must be considered among the most linguistically and culturally retentive Americans.

SERBO-CROATIAN

Serbo-Croatian, the majority language of Yugoslavia, is a single tongue shared by two distinct cultures that were once a single people. Croatians live in the Adriatic coastal provinces and Serbians in the neighboring highlands. Serbs, like Russians and other eastern Europeans, practice a form of Orthodox Christianity specific to their nationality and language. And, like other Orthodox peoples, they employ the Cyrillic alphabet derived from monastic writings. Croats, converted to Roman Catholicism in the ninth century, have developed a culture that is oriented toward western Europe. They transcribe this same language using Latin characters.

Although Serbs and Croats have long histories of cultural and literary achievement and have come to this country in considerable numbers, few Americans are conscious of them as a unique people. Since they lacked national political autonomy during the period of mass immigration to the United States, they tend to be lumped with other Slavic and with non-Slavic southeast Europeans. At the turn of the twentieth century, when emigration from the Balkan region reached its height, Serbia had just achieved a tenuous national political autonomy, and Croatia, like many other Slavic language communities, lay under the hegemony of the Austro-Hungarian and Ottoman Empires.

These political facts had direct impact on the future of Serbo-

Croatian language communities in the United States. Admitted as "Austrians" or under some other misnomer, the Croats were shuffled among other subject Slavic peoples by immigration authorities and by the Roman Catholic Church. The political partitioning of the Croatian homeland had limited movement within the speech community, thus encouraging diverse regional dialects. As a result, some American Croatian dialects are so distinct as to be unintelligible to other American Croatian speakers. Different citizenship and religious affiliation obscured the essential unity of Serbs and Croats as a language group, and, consequently, the size and significance of their linguistic community. In addition, ethnic mixing across shifting political borders in the region had led to widespread bilingualism; many Serbs and Croats commanded German or neighboring Slavic languages such as Slovenian or Macedonian. Their linguistic abilities enabled Serbo-Croatians to merge into other language communities. Because of this multilingual environment, Serbo-Croatians had a history of relatively free use of loan words. So they readily accepted English loans, which contributed to language shift.

The American political climate also presented a challenge to ethnic and linguistic autonomy. Nativists in the United States regarded eastern European immigrants as interchangeable objects for scorn and discrimination. In response, the targeted communities solidified across ethnic and religious lines. As the most numerous of the Yugoslavian peoples in this country and the leaders of the independent, multi-ethnic Yugoslav nation created after World War I, the Serbo-Croatians have tended to absorb other Balkan Slavic ethnic and linguistic communities. Though a few Slovenes and Macedonians adopted Serbo-Croatian, the effect has been to encourage use of English, as the need for a common language increased.

The oldest Serbo-Croatian-speaking community in the United States is a cluster of early nineteenth-century settlements of Croatian oystermen in remote areas of southeastern Louisiana. In the late 1960s, after seven generations in residence, families still maintained Croatian-speaking homes and some Croatian children enrolling in public schools had no knowledge of another language (Ward 1976).

Other Serbo-Croatian language communities have a history different from this Louisiana speech island, as the section on "Slavic and Other Eastern European Languages" in Chapter 2 indicates. The Serbian and Croatian communities in Milwaukee, Wisconsin, typify those throughout the industrial Northeast. The somewhat differing linguistic histories of Serbs and Croats in that city also illustrate how cultural and demographic factors can affect language change and ethnic maintenance (Ward 1976).

The Milwaukee Serbian community grew up after 1900, reaching a population of 2,500 by 1912, when they established a local Serbian Orthodox parish and Serbo-Croatian-language singing and theatre groups. Originally, Serbs were almost exclusively factory laborers, but some eventually acquired small businesses which served the community and helped to maintain the language in public use.

During the immigration hiatus between 1924 and 1948, English encroached on Serbian life, coming into use even in the church. But renewed immigration since the War has led to revival and expansion of mother-tongue institutions. The recent arrivals, now making up 50 percent of the Serbian community, include many educated and professional people who are especially intent on retaining Serbian language and culture. They have established a Serbo-Croatian-speaking parish and a school that teaches Serbian history and culture and the Serbo-Croatian language. Today Milwaukee Serbs support a social and cultural center, Serbian press, and Serbo-Croatian-language broadcasting.

Yet the community is dispersing geographically, and the young people are growing up in English-speaking neighborhoods. Serbs can be expected to make active use of their language only through the end of this century. Thereafter, unless new immigrants replenish the community, the need for the language will be reduced to cultural and ritual functions.

Although Milwaukee Croats are equally active culturally, their use of Serbo-Croatian has declined dramatically and is now restricted primarily to the home. The Croats, too, established themselves in the city around the turn of the century, consecrating a Roman Catholic Church in 1917 and founding a second parish in 1928. But these churches did not remain exclusive centers for Croatian culture. Poles, Slovenes, Italians, and other Catholics diluted the ethnic composition to one-half and one-third Croatian. Unlike the Serbian Orthodox school, the parish school curriculum includes no Serbo-Croatian language courses.

Nor did the Croatian community experience a large influx from the homeland after World War II. Without the reinforcement of continuing immigration and without a strong ethnic institution tied directly to the mother tongue, the language will soon cease as a regular means of communication among Croats. But the lodges, fraternal organizations, soccer clubs, and singing and dancing societies, even the Croatian music broadcasts will remain as expressions of Croatian ethnic identity.

In most stable Serbo-Croatian language communities, whether ethnically Serb or Croat, English has become the primary language by the third generation (Jutronić 1974, 1976). In one very active community—Steelton, Pennsylvania—just 53 percent of third-generation Croats claimed any knowledge of Serbo-Croatian, and all of these reported only limited speaking ability. Eighteen percent could read and 12 percent could write in Serbo-Croatian, largely because of church school rather than family training.

By contrast, most of the first, immigrant generation had acquired a command of English: three-fourths reported good English speaking ability; the remaining minority rated their English as fair. The Steelton Serbo-Croatians came mainly from uneducated, peasant backgrounds. The men found employment as unskilled steelworkers, and the women worked in the home. Yet 88 percent taught themselves not only to speak but also to read in English.

Their emphasis on linguistic maintenance is reflected in the language practices of their children, the first generation born in the United States and educated in English-speaking schools. Since they grew up with Serbo-Croatian-speaking parents, it is not surprising that 95 percent of the second generation reported Serbo-Croatian speaking ability—two-thirds rating themselves as good speakers. But significantly, almost one-half indicated that they read Serbo-Croatian newspapers, and over one-third wrote letters in Serbo-Croatian. Although 21 percent make use of the ethnic language with their own families, only 2 percent of the second generation maintain monolingual Serbo-Croatian-speaking homes.

For their children, the third generation, use of Serbo-Croatian is highly restricted, functioning in large part as a special style for humor, emphasis, and in-group solidarity, rather than for ordinary communication. It is especially used for swearing: although only 6 percent of their parents reported swearing in Serbo-Croatian, 59 percent of the third generation make use of the ethnic language in this way. One young person noted, "Most students [in his ethnically mixed school] who do not even know what Croatian is swear in our language" (Jutronić 1976:177). Still, most of the third generation agreed with their parents and grandparents that Croatian Americans should continue to learn the language of their forebears. But, while their parents stated educational value as the primary reason for language maintenance, the younger people stressed ethnic tradition and family heritage. For these basically monolingual Croatian Americans, the Serbo-Croatian language has become an historical and cultural artifact, an aspect of ethnic identity—like music, dance, and religious ritual—rather than a functioning part of their everyday lives.

GULLAH AND BLACK ENGLISH VERNACULAR

The most significant creole language in the United States is Gullah (also called "Geechee" or "Sea Island Creole"). Although now spoken only in coastal and island regions of South Carolina and Georgia, this creole provides crucial insights into the language history of the United States: linguists believe that Gullah is the last surviving vestige in this country of the plantation creole which was once the general language of black slaves. Today the language of most black Americans has been decreolized by contact with standard English. But Gullah has remained in the creole stage because its speakers live in an isolated relic area (compare the situation of Appalachia, discussed in Chapter 4). Slaves continued to be imported to the Gullah region directly from Africa until 1858, and the ratio of blacks to whites in this area was sometimes twenty to one (Turner 1974). Thus, just as in Appalachia, contact with standard English speakers has been minimal in the Gullah region, and, consequently, both language and culture have been slow to change. Gullah speakers have preserved African influences not only in their language but also in such cultural expressions as cooking, herbal medicine, basketmaking, and music.

To some extent, decreolization in the direction of standard English has now taken place within the Gullah community. As with the types of linguistic variation outlined in Chapter 7, variation among Gullah speakers correlates with demographic factors, particularly age, gender, and occupation (Nichols 1978, 1981). Predictably, those who have interacted least with standard English speakers use creole forms most frequently. They include older women, whose traditional roles have kept them entirely within the Gullah community; young children, who have not yet been exposed to standard English at school; and adolescent males, who gain prestige with their peers for verbal skills associated with the creole. Among young and middle-aged adults, men use more creole forms than women, partly because the clerical and teaching jobs open to women require competence in standard English, while the construction work available to men requires no language-related skills. Thus young and middle-aged women seem to be leading the Gullah-speaking community in the decreolization process.

In the black community throughout the rest of the United States, decreolization is more pervasive. One partially decreolized dialect that linguists have studied is the casual speech of urban black youths who participate fully in the vernacular street culture. This variety has been called **Black English Vernacular (BEV)**. Although the language these young men typically use with one another has assimilated somewhat to standard English, it still has more nonstandard features—and is thus closer to its creole origins—than most other decreolized varieties used by black Americans. As with Gullah speakers, blacks throughout the country will probably speak an even more decreolized variety if they are adult, upwardly mobile, female, or isolated from their peer group. In addition, Northern blacks tend to approximate standard English more than Southern blacks. And in formal situations all blacks style-shift toward standard English. Black English Vernacular, then, in no sense represents the language of all black Americans—a few of whom speak a creole, many of whom speak standard English at least some of the time. Rather, the speech of black Americans should be seen as a composite of dialects along the **post-creole continuum** illustrated in Figure 26. Demographic variables such as region, class, age, and gender—along with sociolinguistic processes such as style-shifting—determine where any individual speaker will fall on the continuum at any given time.

Creole/Gullah —————— BEV ————— Standard English

FIGURE 26.   Post-Creole Continuum

Nor should BEV be understood as in any way a product of racial characteristics; like every other language variety, it is strictly a product of culture. Thus blacks who are completely assimilated into mainstream society may never exhibit any traces of BEV, while whites or Hispanics who have grown up in black neighborhoods may speak it almost perfectly. The many BEV features that characterize the speech of Southern whites (see Chapter 4) further testify to the strength and influence of black culture in the United States.

The case study below focuses on continuity and change along the post-creole continuum between Gullah, as a surviving plantation creole, and BEV. One of its purposes is to display the evidence for the creole origins of BEV and to exemplify the decreolization process. A further purpose is to dispel the deeply ingrained and completely unfounded prejudice that many Americans harbor toward BEV. The following detailed examination of Gullah and BEV vocabulary, phonology, and grammar will demonstrate that, far from being "sloppy," "substandard," or "illogical," the language of Afro-Americans is just as complicated, subtle, and systematic as standard English—though its different history has made it a different variety. Because of racist attitudes toward its speakers, this minority dialect continues to be considered socially inferior to standard English. But there are no valid arguments for considering the language of Afro-Americans linguistically inferior to standard English.

VOCABULARY AND PHONOLOGY

In the area of vocabulary, both Gullah and BEV largely conform to standard English. But in Gullah about 250 items survive from West African languages (Turner 1974), and a number of these still occur in BEV (see Figure 27 to locate the West African languages mentioned in parentheses): *buckra* "white man" (compare Ibibio and Efik /mbakara/, "he who governs or surrounds"); *chigger* (compare Wolof /jiga/, "insect"); *goober* (compare Kimbundu /ŋguba/, "peanut"); *gumbo* (compare Tshiluba /tšiŋgɔmbɔ/, "okra"); *samba* (compare Hausa /sambale/, "a dance"); *tote* (compare Kimbundu and Umbundu /tuta/, "to carry"); *voodoo* (compare Ewe /vodu/, "a tutelary deity or demon"); *yam* (compare Mende /yam/, "sweet potato"). As evidence of the deep imprint Afro-Americans have left on American culture, some of these words have entered the general vocabulary of American English.

The phonology, or sound system, of Gullah deviates markedly from standard English and often renders it unintelligible to standard English speakers. Because of the influence of West African phonology, long vowels and such consonant sounds as *j, ch, sh, f,* and *v* differ in Gullah from their standard English counterparts. Through decreolization, BEV has approximated standard English pronunciation for most of these sounds. But BEV still retains the Gullah pronunciation and, behind that, the West African influence in the features described below.

Like many varieties of English (see Chapter 4), Gullah and BEV are *r*-less. This feature might derive from Southern white regional speech or from the British dialects of early slave dealers. But it is equally possible to trace the *r*-lessness of Gullah and BEV to the many

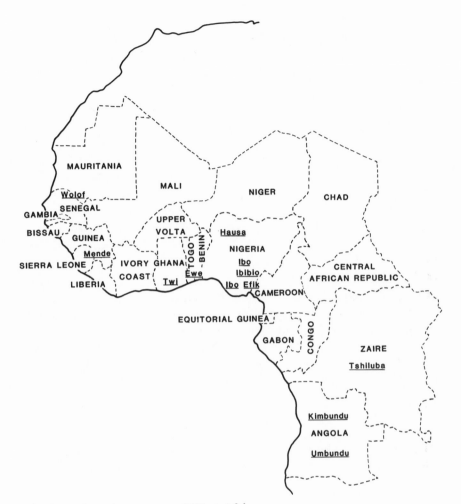

FIGURE 27. Languages of West Africa

r-less languages of West Africa. The treatment of *th* sounds in Gullah and BEV has a similar explanation. The *th* sounds of *thin* /θ/ and *then* /ð/ are absent in most world languages, including those of West Africa. As a result, Gullah and BEV speakers substitute other closely related sounds for *th*—most often the voiceless /t/ for the voiceless /θ/ and the voiced /d/ for the voiced /ð/, producing *tin* for *thin* and *den* for *then*.

Two other phonological tendencies of Gullah correspond to important pronunciation features of BEV. First, just as standard English speakers contract *you are* to *you're* and *he has* to *he's*, so speakers of

Gullah and related Caribbean creoles sometimes contract auxiliary verbs beginning with the voiced stops /b/, /d/, or /g/ (Rickford 1974, 1977). Thus the verb *does* can be reduced to *'oes* /əz/, and *go* can become *'o*. In BEV, this loss of voiced stops affects the /g/ in the phrase *I'm going to*. In standard English this phrase can be reduced to *'mgonna* /mgənə/, but in BEV loss of the /g/ can create *'m'onna* /mənə/ or even *'m'a*, resulting in such utterances as *'m'a tell you* for *I'm going to tell you*. Similarly, contraction of initial /d/ may explain the distinctive use of *ain't* by speakers of Gullah and BEV. Many nonstandard speakers—black and white—substitute *ain't* for *isn't/ aren't* or *hasn't/haven't*, as in *we ain't leaving now* or *we ain't left yet*; but speakers of Gullah and BEV also substitute *ain't* for *didn't*, producing *we ain't leave*. The latter use of *ain't* may result from contraction of the initial /d/ in *didn't*, which yields a word sounding very much like *ain't*.

The other phonological trait of Gullah retained in BEV is **consonant cluster simplification**—that is, dropping one member of a group of two or more consonants. To some extent, consonant cluster simplification occurs in all varieties of English. The spellings of *lamb* and *gnat* indicate that the final *-mb* and initial *gn-* clusters were once pronounced but have since been simplified by all English speakers. And in casual speech, most standard English speakers would say, *That was the las' straw*. Yet—perhaps because certain consonant clusters do not occur in West African languages—speakers of Gullah and BEV simplify consonant clusters more consistently than do standard English speakers; some BEV speakers never pronounce them in their full form. So *ol'* for *old, groun'* for *ground, twis'* for *twist* are regular pronunciations in Gullah and BEV. Although consonant clusters are most often simplified at the ends of words, sometimes word-initial clusters are reduced: Gullah can have *'tay* for *stay*, or *'trap* for *strap*, and BEV can produce *'pecific* for *specific* or *'poon* for *spoon*.

GRAMMAR

Certain grammatical features of Gullah and BEV offer even better illustrations of decreolization in progress. BEV shares with Gullah a number of creole grammatical features but has replaced others with either the standard form or a form intermediate between Gullah and standard English.

As in most other creoles, Gullah nouns and pronouns have few inflections. Normally, nouns have no *-s* or *-'s* ending to signal plural or possessive. Instead, plurality is marked by numerals or pronouns, as in *five day* or *dem book,* and possessive is indicated by word order, as in *Mary coat.* Pronouns are marked for person (*me* vs. *him*) and number (*me* vs. *we*) but often not for case or gender, producing such sentences as *me not going there* or *he name Liza.* The Ibo word *una* ("you") is preserved in the Gullah second person pronoun.

In the process of decreolizing, BEV speakers have added standard English inflections to most nouns. Plurals are usually marked, except by some young children, who learn from one another creole forms that they will discard when they grow up. BEV possessives, however, are more variable, alternating between the uninflected creole form (*Sue dress*) and the inflected standard form (*Sue's dress*), sometimes even within a single utterance.

As for pronouns, once again preschool speakers of BEV sometimes exhibit the creole forms, unmarked for case or gender: *me got juice* (Labov 1972a:205) and *he a nice girl* (Dillard 1972:56) have been attested, although either one could simply represent a common developmental error in any child's acquisition of English. For other BEV speakers, most personal pronouns are inflected according to standard English rules. In the course of decreolization, pronouns were probably first marked for subjective/possessive versus objective case (*he* vs. *him*), then for gender (*he* vs. *she*), and only later for the possessive case (*his/her*), as illustrated in Figure 28. Many BEV speakers still do not mark the possessive in second person or third person plural pronouns, resulting in *you house, they house.* Since the standard English possessives for *you* and *they* (*your* and *their*) both end in *r*, it seems likely that *r*-lessness in BEV phonology has reinforced the retention of this creole grammatical feature.

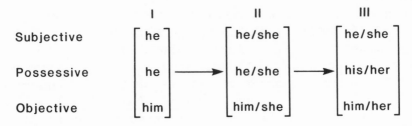

FIGURE 28. Decreolization of Gullah Pronouns
Source: Nichols 1981.

The verb systems of Gullah and BEV differ from standard English in more fundamental ways than nouns and pronouns do. In West African languages and the creoles that descend from them, the **tense** of verbs (whether they represent past, present, or future action) is less often marked than their **aspect** (whether they represent ongoing or completed action). Standard English has inflectional endings for present tense, signaled by an *-s* in third person singular (e.g. *she works*), and for past tense, typically marked by an *-ed* suffix (e.g. *she worked*). Consistent with its general lack of inflections, Gullah almost never shows the third person singular *-s* for present tense and seldom has the *-ed* past tense marker. So *Liza work hard* could mean either "Liza works hard" or "Liza worked hard," depending on the context. Speakers of BEV also leave the present tense uninflected, producing *she go* or *he don't*. As they learn standard English, BEV speakers sometimes hypercorrect by adding the *-s* suffix to present tense verbs where it does not belong: *we walks, you thinks*. In the BEV past tense the *-ed* ending is often eliminated through consonant cluster simplification; thus *roped* /ropt/ can be realized as *rope,* or *rolled* /rold/ as *roll*. Where consonant cluster simplification does not apply, however, BEV usually conforms to standard English by marking the past tense, as in *coated* or *broke*.

It is in their sophisticated aspect system that Gullah and BEV depart most radically from standard English. Although its aspect system is relatively weak, standard English does distinguish continuing action with the progressive aspect (*Molly is/was arriving*) and completed action with the perfective aspect (*Molly has/had arrived*). By contrast, West African languages, Gullah, and BEV have elaborated aspect systems. In Gullah, the African-derived word *duh* /də/ marks not only progressive but also **habitual** aspect, which refers to regular and repeated, rather than momentary, action. Thus *duh* often occurs in constructions where standard English requires an adverb like *sometimes* or *usually*, as in *he duh cut wood* ("he cuts/cut wood sometimes") or *now the children duh fret* ("now the children are usually fretting"). During the decreolization process, Gullah speakers began to replace *duh* with the similar-sounding English word *does*, still using it to mark habitual aspect: *he does work* ("he is usually working") or *he does quiet* ("he is usually quiet"). As the creole assimilated further to standard English, *he does quiet* changed to *he does be quiet*, then *he does work* became *he does be working*. At this stage, the habitual aspect marker was *does be*, and many older Gullah speakers still use this form today. But *does be*, too, has undergone duh ⟶ does ⟶ does be ⟶ 'z be ⟶ be

FIGURE 29. Development of Invariant *be*

modification. By the phonological rule allowing African-based creoles to lose initial voiced stops (described above), *does be* was reduced to *'z be* and eventually to *be* (Rickford 1974, 1977). In BEV this *be* continues to mark habitual aspect; since it is never conjugated, linguists have called it **invariant be**. Examples of this usage in BEV include: *she be working* ("she is usually working"), *I be happy* ("I am habitually happy"), *he be at school* ("he is regularly at school"), but not *I be leaving right now*, which cannot occur since it represents momentary action. Although its form has changed, the habitual aspect marker remains, having passed from African languages to Gullah and from there to BEV. Figure 29 charts its history.

In addition to invariant *be*, two other aspect markers have carried over from Gullah into BEV. *Done* indicates recently completed action (roughly equivalent to standard English *have*) in such Gullah utterances as *I done tell them*. BEV retains this **completive done** but usually inflects the main verb for past tense: *I done forgot my hat*. This creole feature has not only been preserved by many black speakers but has also been adopted for emphasis by numerous Southern whites. The other aspect marker in Gullah and BEV is **remote-time been**, which refers to a process begun in the distant past that in standard English can only be represented by adverbials like *for a long time* or *a long time ago*. Constructions such as *he been tell me that* ("he told me that a long time ago") and *I been know you* ("I have known you for a long time") occur in both Gullah and BEV. Through its aspect system the language of black Americans thus efficiently conveys subtleties about process that are unavailable in standard English except by circumlocutions and adverbial phrases.

Gullah and BEV also differ from standard English with respect to use of the main verb *to be* (called the **copula**). Before adjectives, the copula is regularly absent in Gullah and BEV, as it is in numerous West African and other world languages; sentences like *he tall* or *me sick* can thus occur. Before nouns, Gullah and BEV occasionally omit the copula (e.g. *dat* [*was*] *slavery trouble*) but more often have some form of *to be*, as in *you is a fool*. In clauses that begin with *it is* in standard English, Gullah substitutes the habitual marker *duh* (Turner 1974): *when duh daylight* ("when it is daylight") and *duh God wo'k* ("it is God's work"). In BEV *duh* has been replaced by standard English *it is* or *it's*.

At the level of sentence structure, too, some vestiges of West African languages survive in Gullah and BEV. Gullah, for instance, inherited the use of serial or two-part verbs from West African languages. In these constructions, verbs fulfill the function usually assumed by prepositions or subordinating conjunctions in standard English. Hence Gullah can have *then they take 'em go Charleston* for "then they take them to Charleston." Similarly, Gullah speakers often use the Twi word *say* /se/, meaning roughly "say," as part of a serial construction after verbs of saying, thinking, or wishing, probably because it coincidentally sounds exactly like the English word *say: they tell me after say they catch bird* or *they 'low say we too old*. In standard English the Gullah *say* is usually best translated as the subordinating conjunction *that*: "they told me afterwards that they caught birds" or "they allowed that we were too old." Occasionally, *say*, meaning "that," can be heard in a BEV utterance, but only after the verb *tell*: *they told me say they couldn't get it*.

West African syntax has also left its imprint on the word order of questions in Gullah and BEV. In standard English, questions are distinguished from statements in part by their inverted word order: *Jennifer can bring tomatoes* corresponds to the question *what can Jennifer bring*? In Gullah and BEV, however, as in some West African languages, word order can be the same in questions as in statements, producing questions like *why she ain't over here*?

As the above description of Gullah and BEV indicates, there is considerable evidence that many elements of BEV can be traced to creoles based on West African languages. Thus the ways in which this variety diverges from standard English result not from random errors but from systematic linguistic and historical processes. The evidence presented in this case study is summarized in Table 21.

HAWAIIAN PIDGIN AND CREOLE ENGLISH

Anyone who has traveled to Hawaii or even watched any of the popular television series set in Hawaii realizes that Hawaiian English has its own distinct flavor, if only in vocabulary. Most mainland speakers recognize such words from the Hawaiian language as *aloha, hula, luau, lei,* and *ukulele*. About seventy-five to a hundred other Hawaiian words occur regularly in the English spoken in Hawaii (Carr 1972). Here are a few of them: *haole* ("white person, usually from the mainland"), *pau* ("finished"), *mauka* ("toward the mountains"), *makai* ("toward the sea"), *pilikia* ("trouble"), *pupule* ("crazy"), *ono* ("delicious"), *wahine* ("Hawaiian woman").

But English in Hawaii differs from mainland English in more ways than a few vocabulary items, for the plantation system shaped language history there just as it did in the South. Whereas Southern whites imported slaves from many different West African language communities, Hawaiian planters engaged contract laborers who spoke a number of different Asian languages. Plantation workers in both the South and Hawaii had to create a new language immediately in order to communicate with co-workers and overseers. In both cases they developed first an English-based pidgin, then a creole.

Apart from their early encounters with British and American trading ships, native Hawaiians first felt the pervasive influence of English when New England missionaries settled on the island of Hawaii in 1820. During the next sixty years, these missionaries learned the Hawaiian language, devised a Hawaiian alphabet, translated the Christian scriptures into Hawaiian, and established schools for native Hawaiians. So efficiently did the American settlers work that by 1850 nearly the entire Hawaiian population was literate in either Hawaiian or English (Reinecke 1969). As the century wore on, however, English became increasingly predominant as the language of instruction and public life.

Sugar cane plantations, employing native Hawaiian labor, began to appear about a decade after the arrival of the American missionaries. But disease and intermarriage with non-Hawaiians reduced the indigenous Hawaiian population, making it necessary in 1852 to start importing Chinese laborers to work the cane fields. By the turn of the century, planters were augmenting their work force with Japanese, Filipino, Korean, and Samoan contract laborers as well. After 1880, speakers of Cantonese and Hakku (Chinese languages), Ilocano and Cebuano (Philippine languages), Japanese, Korean, Samoan, and Hawaiian thus came together on sugar cane and later on pineapple plantations. Pidginization was the natural outcome.

Since the Hawaiian plantation system arose relatively recently, linguists have been able to interview first-generation pidgin speakers, who use Pidgin English to supplement their native Asian language. The pidgin spoken by this immigrant generation shows the clear influence of their first language, so that Chinese Pidgin English, for instance, differs from Japanese Pidgin English.

TABLE 21. Black English Vernacular and the Decreolization Process

CREOLE FEATURE	GULLAH EXAMPLE	BEV USAGE SAME AS GULLAH	BEV USAGE PARTLY DECREOLIZED	BEV USAGE SAME AS STANDARD	STANDARD ENGLISH USAGE
Phonology:					
Absence of post-vocalic *r*	*matte', bi'd*	x			*matter, bird*
th sounds altered	*tin, den*	x			*thin, then*
Loss of initial *b, d, g* in auxiliaries	*'m'a, ain't*	x			*I'm gonna, didn't*
Consonant cluster simplification	*ol', twis', 'pecific*	x			*old, twist, specific*
Grammar:					
Nouns					
Absence of plural marking	*five day*			x	*five days*
Absence of possessive marking	*Mary coat*		*Mary coat or Mary's coat*		*Mary's coat*
Pronouns					
Absence of case marking	*me not going*			x	*I'm not going*
Absence of gender marking	*he name Liza*			x	*her name's Liza*

Verbs

Feature			
Absence of present tense marking	he work hard	x	he works hard
Absence of past tense marking	Liza catch 'em; Henry rope cows	x	Liza caught 'em; Henry roped cows
Habitual marker	he duh/does cut wood, he does be cutting wood	he be cutting wood	he usually cuts wood
Completive marker	I done tell you	I done told you	I have told you
Remote-time marker	he been tell me dat	x	he told me that a long time ago
Copula absent before adjectives and nouns	he tall, dat slavery trouble	x	he is tall, that was slavery trouble
duh in it is clauses	when duh daylight	x	when it's daylight

Sentence Structure

Feature			
say as subordinating conjunction	dey 'low say we too ol'	they tell me say they couldn't get it	they allowed that we were too old, they told me that they couldn't get it
Inverted word order in questions	why she ain't over here?	x	why isn't she over here?

Despite differing influences from the substrate languages, however, all the variants of Hawaiian Pidgin share a large number of features (Tsuzaki 1971). They all lack plural and possessive inflections on nouns, resulting in such constructions as *some mountain* ("some mountains") and *my husband house* ("my husband's house"). The generalized form *'em* substitutes for objective pronouns *him, her, it,* and *them,* as in *no can fool 'em.* Copulas are absent before adjectives (*me too much happy* for "I am very happy"), as they are in Hawaiian and Cantonese. Verbs are negated with *no* or *never* but are not marked for tense or aspect; *me see* could mean "I see," "I saw," "I will see," "I am/was seeing," depending on the context.

Hawaiian Pidgin English was creolized—that is, transformed into a native language—by the children of Pidgin speakers, often because their parents did not share a native language and used Pidgin in the home. The verb system of Hawaiian Creole illustrates how the Pidgin took on additional complexity in the process of creolization. Unlike Hawaiian Pidgin, the Creole has markers for past tense (*been, went,* or *had*), for future tense (*go* or *gon*), and for progressive and habitual aspect (*stay*). Thus *I been come Honolulu* means "I had come to Honolulu," and *I no go stay eat* means "I will not be eating" (Tsuzaki 1971). Confusingly, Hawaiians commonly call this variety "Pidgin English" or "Pidgin," but it is technically a creole language, so linguists call it Hawaiian Creole.

Today, English in Hawaii is ranged along a pidgin–creole–standard continuum. An entirely English-speaking system of education and extensive migration from the mainland have accelerated the decreolization process so that few Hawaiians speak a pure pidgin or creole. Pidgin is spoken by less than 5 percent of the population—mainly older immigrants who came originally to work on plantations (Nichols 1981:82). About half the population are descendants of plantation workers and speak Hawaiian Creole, usually in combination with more decreolized varieties of English. As with Black English Vernacular, region, age, and socioeconomic status largely determine who speaks Hawaiian Creole. Speech on the less accessible islands of Kauai and Hawaii tends to show more Pidgin or Creole features than the English on the densely populated and cosmopolitan island of Oahu, where more standard English is heard. Creole also serves as a sign of ethnic and peer-group solidarity among teenagers, particularly young men. The Creole used by these young people includes the most recent slang. Of course, those with higher socioeconomic status speak more standard varieties of English.

One interesting characteristic of pidgins and creoles should by now be apparent: all such languages share many grammatical traits even when their substrate languages are unrelated. Among English-related creoles, Gullah has a West African substrate while various Asian languages underlie Hawaiian Creole; yet the two creoles exhibit a number of similar features which do not seem to derive from English. In both, for example, nouns are not marked for plural or possessive, the copula is absent before adjectives, and tense and aspect are marked by auxiliary verbs (e.g. *been, go*) rather than inflections (e.g. *-ed, -ing*). Linguists have not yet agreed on a single explanation for these striking similarities among pidgins and creoles throughout the world. But it seems likely that, confronted by the urgent need to communicate, all people simplify their speech in similar ways, regardless of their language background. This explanation implies that, despite the enormous diversity in the languages of the world, some linguistic processes may be common to all humanity. Or, as linguists would say, they may be **universal**.

FURTHER STUDY IN LANGUAGE CONTACT

READINGS

BOWEN, J. DONALD and JACOB ORNSTEIN, eds. *Studies in Southwest Spanish*. Rowley, Mass.: Newbury House Publishers, 1976.

DILLARD, J. L. *Black English: Its History and Usage in the United States*. New York: Random House, 1972.
Popular account of the creole origin and features of Black English Vernacular.

DREYFUSS, GAIL RAIMI. "Pidgin and Creole Languages in the United States," *A Pluralistic Nation: Language Issues in the United States*, edited by Margaret A. Lourie and Nancy Faires Conklin, pp. 61–77. Rowley, Mass.: Newbury House Publishers, 1978.
On Gullah, Louisiana French Creole, and Hawaiian Creole.

FERGUSON, CHARLES A., and SHIRLEY BRICE HEATH, eds. *Language in the USA*. Cambridge: Cambridge University Press, 1981.
Collection of survey essays about American language communities; extensive bibliography.

HAUGEN, EINAR. "The Analysis of Linguistic Borrowing," *English Linguistics: An Introductory Reader*, edited by Harold Hungerford, Jay

Robinson, and James Sledd, pp. 429–56. Glenview, Ill.: Scott, Foresman, 1970.
Defines key terms.

——. *The Norwegian Language in America: A Study in Bilingual Behavior*. Bloomington: Indiana University Press, 1969.
Most detailed study of an immigrant language community.

HYMES, DELL, ed. *Pidginization and Creolization of Languages*. Cambridge: Cambridge University Press, 1971.
Major collection on pidgins and creoles worldwide; descriptions of languages and theoretical articles.

LABOV, WILLIAM. *Language in the Inner City: Studies in the Black English Vernacular*. Philadelphia: University of Pennsylvania Press, 1972.
Collection of influential studies, some technical, some for the general reader.

LIEBERSON, STANLEY. "The Causes of Bilingualism Differ from the Causes of Mother-Tongue Shift" and "Language Shift in the United States: Some Demographic Clues," *Language Diversity and Language Contact*, edited by Anwar S. Dil, pp. 126–30 and 158–72. Stanford, Cal.: Stanford University Press, 1981.

PEÑALOSA, FERNANDO. *Chicano Sociolinguistics: A Brief Introduction*. Rowley, Mass.: Newbury House Publishers, 1980.

REINECKE, JOHN E. *Language and Dialect in Hawaii: A Sociolinguistic History to 1935*, edited by Stanley M. Tsuzaki. Honolulu: University of Hawaii Press, 1969.
Nontechnical description with an emphasis on history.

SEAMAN, P. DAVID. *Modern Greek and American English in Contact*. The Hague: Mouton, 1972.

ST. CLAIR, ROBERT, and WILLIAM LEAP, eds. *Language Renewal among American Indians*. Rosslyn, Va.: National Clearinghouse for Bilingual Education, 1982.

TURNER, LORENZO DOW. *Africanisms in the Gullah Dialect*. Ann Arbor: University of Michigan Press, 1974.
Classic work on this subject, first published in 1949.

WEINREICH, URIEL. *Languages in Contact: Findings and Problems*. The Hague: Mouton, 1974.
Reprint of the 1953 essay which laid the groundwork for contemporary understanding of language contact.

WOLFRAM, WALT. "Objective and Subjective Parameters of Language Assimilation Among Second-Generation Puerto Ricans in East Harlem," *Language Attitudes: Current Trends and Prospects*, edited by Roger W. Shuy and Ralph W. Fasold, pp. 148–73. Washington, D.C.: Georgetown University Press, 1973.
Describes the influence of Black English Vernacular on Puerto Rican English.

ACTIVITIES

1. Is there any evidence of multilingualism in your community? Do your local bookstores, newsstands, or libraries carry non-English publications? Do any local radio or television stations have non-English broadcasts? Are interpreters available in public institutions such as banks, government offices, schools? Are there mother-tongue churches or social organizations? Are there ethnic stores or restaurants where other languages are spoken? You might be able to draw a map of ethnic neighborhoods similar to Figure 9.

2. Look for English influences on the pronunciation, vocabulary, and grammar of the Pennsylvania German text given in the Appendix. You should be able to determine these dialect features by contrasting the sample with the English and standard German translations.

3. Study the Gullah text and its interlinear translation given in the Appendix. Table 21 will help you recognize salient features of Gullah pronunciation and grammar. Based on what you have learned about the continuum between Gullah and Black English Vernacular, try translating the Gullah text into BEV.

4. Examine the Hawaiian Creole texts in the Appendix and on page 273 for features of pronunciation, vocabulary, and grammar not found in standard English. You may wish to organize a formal list of Hawaiian Creole features similar to those presented for other varieties in Tables 7 and 21.

5. If you live in a bilingual community, you can develop your own matched guise test. First, tape record several bilinguals reading the same passage in the non-English language and in English. Intersperse these samples so that it will not be obvious that each voice was recorded twice. Then, play the tape for other community members with a fairly good knowledge of both languages. Solicit their subjective reactions to the two languages by asking them to rate each voice on personal characteristics and socioeconomic status.

6. Interview speakers who can report on the use of a non-English language in their family. Who used the ethnic mother tongue and who used English? When and with whom? Did they use the mother tongue outside the home as well? How did family members feel about each language? In what language were they literate? How many of their friends and associates spoke the mother tongue? Were there any special sets of terms especially important to learn in the mother tongue (e.g. food words, kinship names, prayers, or religious terms)? Use Table 18 to develop other questions and to analyze this family's language retention or loss.

PART V

Implications of Linguistic Pluralism

You took our language away. Now give it back!

—native Alaskan woman
to a Bureau of Indian Affairs official

CHAPTER 10

Policy and Education in a Multilingual Society

T HE SURPRISING MULTIPLICITY of U.S. languages described in the previous chapters has direct ramifications for public policy. Employers, public schools, and agents of government have behaved during most of this century as if we were a nation of monolingual English speakers. Only recently have attempts been made to bring our major institutions into line with our actual linguistic situation. Since the 1960s—as the section on "Minority Language Rights" explains—the major direction of U.S. language policy has been toward ensuring equal civil and educational opportunity for all Americans. However, legislative and judicial actions have not swept away long-standing mistrust of linguistic pluralism. The section "Attitudes as Policy" describes the ways in which self-appointed linguistic arbiters such as dictionary makers, media spokesmen, and literary critics have imposed their personal views on a linguistically insecure public whose very diversity creates a demand for clear standards of social behavior and rules of correctness.

As the institution that most embodies and perpetuates our language attitudes and policies, public education requires particular attention. What happens in this nation's schoolrooms will largely determine whether we continue our futile efforts to homogenize

American speech or begin to value our rich linguistic reserves. The sections "Education for Non-English Speakers" and "Education for Nonstandard Speakers" outline some current issues and strategies for educating speakers of minority languages and dialects.

MINORITY LANGUAGE RIGHTS

Throughout its first century, the United States was an openly multilingual nation. There were treaties, public notices, and education in a variety of indigenous and immigrant languages. Subsequently, in the latter half of the nineteenth and first half of the twentieth centuries, the rights of non-English speakers were eroded by anti-foreigner and racist sentiment and action. In recent years, however, federal court rulings and legislation have reinstated many minority language rights. In the 1980s we are witnessing large-scale legal and illegal immigration from Mexico, resettlement of Southeast Asian refugees, and an influx of refugees from various Caribbean and Central American countries. The U.S. government may react by restricting minority civil and language rights, just as it did after the earlier periods of massive population shift described in Chapter 2.

In the past quarter century of struggle for their civil rights, non-English- and nonstandard-speaking groups throughout the country have strongly demanded redress of grievances against federal, state, and municipal policies. Federal policy has shifted to reflect these renewed demands but not without opposition. Language issues such as bilingual education, non-English ballots, and the status of nonstandard varieties of English have become the focus of heated public debate that will determine not just the linguistic future of this country but our commitment to maintaining a multicultural society.

Regulations and legislation governing immigration, naturalization, voting procedures, education, employment, and public documents and publications all embody policy on language use. Governmental policy even affects the extent and choice of foreign language study. In many of these areas, significant changes are pending judicial decisions and legislative action, but general trends can be discerned.

Civil Rights

Since 1965, U.S. immigration law has been neutral with respect to racial, national, and linguistic background. These revised codes nullified language requirements imposed in the early years of this century. Yet English language ability still plays a part in deciding whom to admit. Immigration officials take skills and employability into account when ranking applicants—a policy that clearly favors speakers of English. A disproportionately large number of entrants from western Europe now come from the United Kingdom. However, because most visas are granted on the basis of blood or conjugal relation to U.S. residents, the majority of newly arrived immigrants—and almost all of the large numbers of refugees admitted—do not command English.

Historically, and in some states until 1926, all residents were eligible to vote regardless of foreign or domestic birth. U.S. birth or naturalized citizenship was not a prerequisite. Thus immigrants might participate in state and municipal elections immediately upon taking up residence. Uninformed about candidates or issues, they were sometimes recruited to vote *en masse* by unscrupulous political machines. In the 1850s Connecticut and Massachusetts passed the first literacy requirements for voters in order to limit the political influence of the English-speaking, but largely illiterate, Irish immigrant population. As mass immigration continued, other states adopted restrictive language legislation in order to disenfranchise non-English-speaking and illiterate newcomers.

Although the distinction between permission to immigrate and granting of citizenship evolved early in the nineteenth century, until 1906 immigrants could gain access to citizenship without any knowledge of English. In the course of the nineteenth century, as the United States expanded territorially, non-English-speaking populations—French in the Louisiana Territory, Hispanics in the Southwest—were immediately declared citizens. But in 1906, naturalization law began to require the ability to speak English, and thousands of immigrants enrolled in English language training programs, much as today. In 1950 the language requirement was expanded to include the ability to read and write English. For the first time, foreign-born voters could be expected to be literate in English and thus presumably meet the standards for suffrage in those states that maintained literacy requirements. Previously, some naturalized citizens had not been eligible to vote; they had met the federal standards for citizenship but not those of their local election board.

The trend to restrict the vote to American citizens had the effect of limiting the franchise in many Northeast, Midwest, Mountain, and West Coast states, but it did not affect the large numbers of freed blacks in the post-Civil War South. Legislatures in that region therefore followed the lead of Northern states and adopted literacy requirements directed against native-born, rather than foreign-born, citizens. Since education of slaves had been strictly forbidden, almost all blacks were illiterate and thus ineligible to vote. Although the federal courts have not found literacy requirements unconstitutional in principle, the Supreme Court disallowed language tests in certain Southern states because they were specifically enacted with discriminatory intent. The Voting Rights Act of 1965 forbade education and literacy provisions where less than half the population was registered to vote—in effect, the heavily black Southern states. The Voting Rights Act and its extensions have enabled thousands of citizens to register to vote in that region and opened the question of language requirements and restrictions in other areas as well.

Using the Voting Rights Act as a precedent, indigenous minority language groups, especially Hispanics and native American tribes, have pressed their own claims—in many cases proving the discriminatory intent of federal, state, and local language-related laws. Indians, for instance, sued the Bureau of Indian Affairs to regain the right to use tribal languages in Indian schools—a privilege denied since the first years of this century. In some Southwest states, Hispanics have successfully lobbied for bilingual public announcements in train, bus, and air terminals and general postings of safety and informational notices. Champions of minority rights have also requested multilingual versions of military placement and federal and state employment qualifying examinations.

Multilingual government publications have proliferated. In 1960 the Social Security Administration was the sole agency in the Department of Health, Education, and Welfare to publish non-English information for American readers; now federal agencies issue many documents in Spanish and some in other languages as well. Non-English speakers base their demands on the principles of equal protection and equal delivery of government services. If information about services and opportunities is not printed and announced in the language they command, how, these advocates ask, can citizens avail themselves of them?

Federal law now authorizes minority language election ballots where 5 percent or more of the voters are literate in a language other than English. Local election boards in various areas have printed ballots in Spanish, Japanese, Filipino, and other languages. Some states and municipalities have enacted statutes assuring minority speakers' rights. For example, a New York City consumer protection law requires that contracts such as leases, warranties on products, and installment payment plans be written in the same language in which the oral transaction with the landlord or salesclerk was conducted.

Still, many Americans—whether native-born or foreign-born—face discrimination on the basis of language. The Equal Employment Opportunity Commission recently found it necessary to promulgate guidelines that limit the right of employers to forbid their workers' use of minority languages at the workplace. Where security, safety, or damage to the employers' businesses are not factors, employees should retain the right to converse in the language of their choice.

EDUCATIONAL RIGHTS

But the bellwether of attitudes and policies concerning non-English languages in the United States has been bilingual education. Until the late nineteenth century, school laws either made no mention of the language of instruction or permitted instruction in non-English languages; Ohio and Pennsylvania, for instance, had legislation that authorized teaching in German in the public schools. But by 1903, in response to massive immigration and growing antipathy to foreigners, fourteen states had passed laws requiring English as the medium of instruction. By 1923, the number of states requiring English had soared to thirty-four.

This prohibition against non-English languages in the schools continued until the 1960s, when minority groups began to insist that their languages and cultures be validated in the classroom. Their agitation led to the federal Bilingual Education Act of 1968, which appropriated funds for the development of bilingual education programs directed at low-income children of limited English-speaking ability—primarily Hispanics and native Americans. The programs were to provide these children with subject matter instruction (in science, math, etc.) in the home language, as well as English instruction, for the first few years of school. Their goal was to smooth the transition from the home language to the school language by offering two or three years of instruction in both tongues before progressing to instruction in English.

The Bilingual Education Act was refined and expanded in the 1970s. In 1974 Congress amended the Act by requiring evaluation of bilingual education programs and enlarging the limited-English-speaking constituency and range of programs to which the Act applied. Also in 1974, the Supreme Court, in the landmark *Lau v. Nichols* case, held that school districts must devise programs to ensure equality of educational opportunity to students of non-English-speaking backgrounds. To implement this decision, the Office of Civil Rights in 1975 issued a set of guidelines called the "Lau Remedies," which specified that, whenever a school district had twenty or more students from one language group, subject matter instruction in that language—not just instruction in English as a second language—was required at both the elementary and intermediate levels. The 1978 reauthorization of the 1968 Act allocated additional research funds to determine the effectiveness of bilingual education.

In compliance with federal legislation and regulations, many state governments have adopted measures to fund and otherwise encourage bilingual education. By 1981, twelve states had stipulated conditions under which bilingual education was mandatory: Alaska, California, Connecticut, Illinois, Indiana, Iowa, Massachusetts, Michigan, New Jersey, Texas, Washington, and Wisconsin. Eleven other states had laws permitting bilingual education, and twenty-six had no provisions regarding language of instruction. Only one state, West Virginia, still required instruction to be exclusively in English.

In the late 1970s, the Carter Administration paid increasing attention to the education of those with limited English-speaking ability. Within the Department of Education, the Office of Bilingual Education and Minority Language Affairs began to offer services not only in bilingual education for schoolchildren but also in bilingual vocational training and refugee education. In the 1979–80 school year, for example, Congress budgeted 150 million dollars for bilingual education and funded programs in some 540 school districts in forty-two states. About 65 percent of these districts offered Spanish/English programs only, but the other 35 percent together provided education in nearly seventy different languages. Special legislative measures were passed to help teach English to the large numbers of Southeast Asian and Caribbean refugees who arrived in the late 1970s and early 1980s. Yet, even with state and federal governments spending substantial amounts on bilingual education, only one out of ten children with limited English was receiving any bilingual services in 1980. And budget cuts in the 1980s will probably reduce that proportion.

In the 1960s language policy in the United States began to address the issue of education not only for students with a non-English language background but also for children who speak a nonstandard variety of English—particularly Black English Vernacular. Educators and legislators became concerned over statistics indicating that public schools have failed their nonstandard-speaking constituents: 46 percent of blacks were completing high school, compared with 67 percent of whites. Thus, beginning in the mid-1960s, the federal government funded research on the linguistic features of Black English Vernacular, supported the development of experimental primary readers written in BEV, and sponsored Head Start programs to teach standard English to preschool BEV speakers.

One recent court decision has also affected the teaching of nonstandard speakers. In 1979 a U.S. District Court mandated that the Ann Arbor, Michigan, School Board devise a plan for helping teachers to identify Black English Vernacular speakers and to use that knowledge in teaching BEV speakers to read standard English. This precedent-setting decision implies that, to offer equal educational opportunity to nonstandard-speaking children, schools must take active steps to ensure that teachers understand the children's home dialect and use that knowledge in the teaching of standard English. Presumably, similar orders could be applied to those who teach speakers of any nonstandard variety, such as Appalachian English or Spanish-influenced English. The sections below on "Education for Non-English Speakers" and "Education for Nonstandard Speakers" show how language policies are realized in the classroom and outline some of the controversies these policies have generated.

The fate of bilingual education for non-English-speaking Americans may affect the related issue of second language learning for English speakers. The study of foreign languages has declined precipitously in American schools and colleges. As few as 15 percent of high school students—including English-speaking students in bilingual education programs—study a second language. Only 8 percent of colleges and universities require study of a second language as a prerequisite to admission, compared with 34 percent in the mid-1960s. The federal government has officially acknowledged the importance of reversing this decline in foreign language training. In the 1975 Helsinki Accords on East-West trade and security, all signing nations agreed to encourage the study of foreign languages and cultures as a necessary step toward international peace and understanding.

Critics in Congress, business, and education regard this trend away from foreign language study as a threat to our economy and national security, as well as a contributing factor to ethnic and cultural intolerance within the United States. A 1980 Presidential Commission on Foreign Language and International Studies found that, while

10,000 English-speaking Japanese were actively engaged in business activities in this country, American industry fielded fewer than 900 representatives in Japan—most of whom lacked a working knowledge of the Japanese language or culture. This despite the existence of a sizable ethnically Japanese and Japanese-speaking segment within the American population. Unfortunately, these indigenous language talents, rather than being enhanced through multicultural education, are discouraged and thus lost to American business, industry, and diplomacy.

A definition of American nationality that encompasses the reality of dual identity—American and ethnic—would enable the United States to make direct use of the resource its citizenry represents. Any narrower definition makes our multiculturalism a liability rather than an asset.

ATTITUDES AS POLICY

Attempts at linguistic homogenization have a long history in Western societies. From European critics and classicists Americans inherited the notion of linguistic change as language decay. Just as Classical Latin devolved into Vulgate and, eventually, into the Romance vernaculars, so, the argument went, had English declined from a state of grace and clarity—from the age of Shakespeare, King James, Samuel Johnson, Jane Austen, Matthew Arnold, or Winston Churchill, depending on the time and temperament of the critic. Scholars, oriented to classical and canonical texts, took older forms of language as models for expression and argument, coming to regard contemporary speech as sadly deficient by comparison. This academic bias is reflected among a general public educated to enshrine the usage of their forebears as precise and lofty while decrying their successors' speech as barbaric.

Discussions of "correctness" thus often center on Anglicization of forms from literary European languages. Reanalysis of *criteria* and *phenomena* as singulars, for example, is highly stigmatized because this particular linguistic innovation reveals the user's ignorance of Greek derivational patterns. Similarly, speakers and writers are urged to maintain *appendices* and *indices* as plurals for Latin-derived *appendix* and *index*. Yet following such a rule would lead a speaker to *cervices* for *cervix*, a form few listeners could comprehend although it is considered acceptable.

As languages change they constantly incorporate new forms and abandon old ones. These processes are rarely so complete that regular rules can be established for any grammatical subset. The merger of *lie* and *lay* regretted by today's stylists is only a fragmentary relic of a once important verbal distinction. Verb pairs like *lie/lay*, meaning "to lie" and "to make lie," were common in earlier forms of English, but speakers gradually fused them or altered their meanings to some other distinction. *Drench*, for example, once meant, "to make drink," an idea for which no simple verb now remains. Contemporary American English speakers are no more at a loss to express themselves without the *lie/lay* distinction than they are without the *drink/drench* contrast. In fact a merger of *lie/lay* would constitute a regularization of the grammar.

Such irregularities are a natural part of language, the reflexes of ongoing change and innovation. Confusions that took place centuries ago may still be evidenced in the language today. In the thirteenth century, for example, English speakers merged two verbs, *to awaken* and *to keep awake,* conjugated *awake/awoke/awoken* and *awake/awakened/awakened*, respectively. Today the two forms compete as synonyms: *I awoke him* versus *I awakened him.* Neither is more "correct," although individual speakers may prefer one to the other, even varying their choice in different contexts. No rule could be formulated to differentiate between them in either meaning or stylistic correctness.

Yet grammatical usage is such a prominent social indicator in the United States that Americans remain convinced that there must be a single best answer to every stylistic dilemma. The diversity that characterizes American speech exacerbates this desire to assure social acceptance by conforming to some illusive standard. Thus a people who pride themselves on individuality and self-determination in personal and public life acquiesce readily to language rules from a host of self-appointed arbiters of linguistic etiquette.

Dictionary makers have long been chief among the authorities, setting standards for acceptability, spelling, and pronunciation based simply on their editors' observations or personal preferences, and they have traditionally drawn upon scholarly and literary texts for their descriptions and judgments. Dictionaries, then, have tended to represent a form of English that is not spoken by any contemporary users. And these books are vested with more authority than any speaker, no matter how educated or articulate. Decontextualized dictionary definitions become the "meaning" of words. Alternative pronunciations become "better" or "worse" according to their order in the dictionary entry. Words not found in the dictionary simply cannot be used.

Recently even dictionary makers have begun to abandon the "decline-and-decay" theory of language change. Some have added information derived from contemporary spoken and written English to their canonical sources. *The American Heritage Dictionary* introduced a review panel of the "cultivated elite"—selected public officials, writers, and professors—whose usage it presents as an appropriate standard of reference for American speakers. Controversial entries include the differing opinions of panel members. Even this elite, of course, is simply rendering its own subjective judgments on acceptable usage.

Some exponents of set standards continue to insist that language change can and must be stopped. John Simon—one of the most prominent contemporary spokesmen of this school—advocates a national language academy with authority to police public officials and employees, educators, writers and publishers, and the print and broadcast media. Such preservationists focus much of their scorn on jargon, slang, neologisms, and Anglicizations of foreign words. But they are most disturbed by any recognition that competing varieties are inherent in English, particularly in a multicultural society such as the United States. Simon (1980:148) writes that

> Black English, for example, has a perfect right to exist; it just hasn't the right to change Standard English. . . . Either BE is something different from Standard English, in which case it is no more entitled to interfere with it than Portuguese is, or it is—or means to be—part of Standard English, in which case it has to espouse the latter's rules.

The illogic of Simon's assumption that any interaction—whether between individuals or speech communities—can take place without mutual influence and change should be obvious to anyone who has read Parts III and IV of this book.

Such attempts to control and direct language use and language change have been initiated primarily by a few individuals whose prominence derives from press or public relations work, not the study of the English language or linguistics. Simon, for example, is a drama critic. Edwin Newman, writer of several "authoritative" books on English usage, is a broadcast journalist. William Safire, who contributes a regular column on usage to the *New York Times*, is a former Presidential speech writer. Yet the attitudes of such self-appointed language watchdogs have had the force of policy, shaping teacher training, school curricula, and public opinion. Although they seek to change the way language is used, their effect has been far more profound on linguistic self-concept than on actual practice. Because they preach the dangers of decay and vulgarity in every linguistic innovation, they have heightened linguistic controversy and insecurity, without offering any substantive advice on the pressing language questions facing the nation.

Because American law and social custom grant a maximum of autonomy, privacy, and self-determination to individual citizens, the United States, unlike many other countries, has never formulated a comprehensive national language policy. Most restrictive legislation—prohibitions against non-English schools, censorship of the minority language press—has been ruled unconstitutional. Turn-of-the-century immigration precipitated fears of "dilution" of English as the common tongue and "corruption" from foreign influences. The recent massive influx of legal and illegal immigrants has rekindled this hysteria. Then American minority language presses, published to inform their language communities about U.S. affairs, were decried as divisive and even seditious. Now media critics wrongly represent bilingual education programs, designed to aid in extending English-speaking ability and literacy, as threats to national unity.

Advocates of forced assimilation recently put forward a proposal for a constitutional amendment which would make English the official national language, severely limiting the public uses to which other languages could be put. The so-called Hayakawa Amendment would have prohibited use of public funds for any communication in a language other than English, including public notices, voter information, air traffic control, and educational instruction—except for foreign language study by English speakers and certain limited programs in English as a second language.

Although this proposal met with no supportive action in Congress, it received extensive media coverage which has added to the growing body of misinformation about American linguistics. On the one hand, it fueled the misconception that the dominance of English and the linguistic unity of the United States are endangered, when in fact only a small minority of Americans do not command English and their proportions in the immigrant populations are not increasing. On the other hand, minority language citizens responded with strongly worded defenses of their linguistic civil rights, calling for protective language legislation.

Misunderstandings about the nature of language evolution and negative attitudes toward linguistic diversity make rational debate of such matters extremely difficult. So long as attitudes of any minority of speakers—the "cultivated elite" or maintenance advocates—are the unexamined basis for policy making, it will remain impossible to discover the most effective means of enhancing communication among Americans.

EDUCATION FOR NON-ENGLISH SPEAKERS

During most of this century, public schools were the strictest enforcers of English monolingualism in our society. Rather than nurturing our linguistic diversity, schools tried to eradicate it by insisting on English as the only legitimate medium of communication. To this end, speakers of minority languages were submerged in the regular curriculum, taught entirely in English. Often the use of non-English languages on school premises was forbidden and severely punished; immigrant parents were instructed to speak only English to their children. For newcomers who were highly motivated to prosper in mainstream society, this approach frequently succeeded—though almost always at the expense of the home language and culture. The speech communities for which the submersion policy least often succeeded were those that were less eager and less able to assimilate, those that had not immigrated willingly or had not immigrated at all, those whose path to upward mobility was already barred by racism—particularly Hispanics and native American peoples.

Members of these minority groups often did not speak, read, or write well in standard English even after generations of schooling in this language. But it was not until the 1960s that lawmakers and educators began to pay serious attention to the school failure of these American children. Since then, many public schools with large minority enrollments have implemented new programs and methods to help improve their students' proficiency in English.

ENGLISH AS A SECOND LANGUAGE

One approach to remedying the school problems of minority language speakers has been instruction in **English as a second language (ESL)**. Training in ESL is the only special attention that some non-English-speaking youngsters receive. Under this plan, students with limited English proficiency are typically "pulled out" of regular classes such as physical education, art, or music for several hours a week. Apart from this modicum of special instruction, however, they must try to keep up with native English speakers in their subject matter classes, which are taught entirely in English. Predictably, the limited-English students fall behind—often irrecoverably—in these subject areas, at least partly because they know too little English to understand their teachers completely.

A few intensive ESL programs have been implemented and seem to offer slightly better results than "pull out" classes. In these programs, school-aged non-English speakers can spend all summer learning English, often through the "submersion" technique, whereby only English is spoken in the classroom. Then they participate in "pull out" classes during the school year. Preschool children receive similar intensive ESL instruction before entering regular public school classes.

With regard to methods, ESL classes and curricular materials have in the past stressed repetition of set phrases and sentences, imitation of the teacher's utterances, and memorization of vocabulary. Most linguists now believe, however, that language acquisition, whether first or second, occurs not through imitation but through the learner's gradual "creative construction" of how a language operates, based on repeated exposure to it. For the ESL classroom, this newer theory of language acquisition implies that situations of natural communication aid students substantially more than formal drill or memorization. That is, the communication should emerge from a genuine need and desire for interaction in English and should emphasize content, not form, just as in exchanges with young children learning their first language. Non-English speakers probably learn more English from an engaging and spontaneous conversation than from anything they memorize.

The ESL-only model for educating students with limited English is an attractive remedy for several reasons. It is less expensive than a full bilingual education program and requires fewer specially trained teachers. It can accommodate students from a large number of language backgrounds in a single class. It allows minority language students substantial opportunity to improve their English skills by interacting with native-English-speaking teachers and peers in regular classes. And it can optimize the innate predisposition of preadolescents to learn a second language more easily and more fully than older students.

Unfortunately, the disadvantages of the ESL-only model seem to outweigh its advantages. Several hours a week of ESL instruction usually fail to teach minority language students enough English to keep up in other classes—unless they are also getting ample practice in using English at home and in their communities. In addition, the "pull out" method segregates children with limited English in a way that invites their English-speaking classmates to stigmatize them, particularly if the non-English speakers are also economically and socially disadvantaged. Such negative attitudes can further alienate a segment of the student population that already suffers discrimination because of its minority status. And there is mounting evidence that children who feel alienated from school are highly prone to academic failure.

TRANSITIONAL MODEL

ESL-only programs do not qualify as bilingual education under current federal laws, which require that ESL classes be complemented by subject matter instruction in the home language. Most government-sponsored bilingual education programs are structured on the **transitional model**: after two or three years of bilingual instruction in the early primary grades, minority language children presumably develop enough English and subject matter skills to make a successful transition to a monolingual English curriculum. In a typical transitional program, students first learn math, science, social studies, and reading in their home language while they study ESL. It may seem detrimental to their later English literacy to teach students to read in a non-English language. Yet minority language speakers eventually do better with English literacy if they first learn to read in their home language and later transfer this skill to English. As their knowledge of English improves, some subject matter is presented in English while some continues to be presented in the home language.
Bilingual subject matter classes may be structured in a number of ways. With the **preview-review method**, a lesson is introduced in one language, developed in the other language, then reviewed in the language used for the introduction. With the **concurrent method**, both languages are used throughout the class session; some portions of the lesson are presented in one language, some in the other. Both these approaches lend themselves to team-taught classes in which one instructor models English and the other—often a community member working as a teacher's aide—models the home language. A fully bi-

lingual instructor can, of course, teach such a class alone by code-switching for the various segments of the lesson.

More prevalent than either the preview-review or the concurrent approach is the **alternate language method** for bilingual subject matter instruction. Under this system, students receive instruction on one day or at one time through one language and on another day or at another time through the other language. Sometimes the same lesson is presented first in one language, then in the other.

In adapting, combining, or selecting among these methods, educators should keep in mind some current research findings on second language acquisition in children. One research finding is that students of a second language filter out utterances in that language that they do not feel motivated to understand. So they are less likely to listen to subject matter instruction in English if they have already heard or will soon hear the same content in their home language. A more effective way of motivating students to learn in English is to give them interesting but comprehensible new information in the target language—information that supplements what they are learning in the home language.

In view of these findings, some proponents of the transitional model propose bilingual programs consisting of these elements: 1) basic skills such as math, science, and reading taught entirely in the home language; 2) ESL classes in which students learn fundamental communication skills and vocabulary items necessary to pursue subject matter courses in English; 3) classes less dependent on verbal skills—such as art, music, and physical education—taken in English along with English-speaking students; and 4) substantial involvement of adult members of the minority language community in the educational process. After two or three years of such a program—and perhaps a gradual transition away from the home language—advocates of the transitional model argue that students who started school with little or no English should have enough competence in both English and basic subject matter areas to be able to transfer to a monolingual English curriculum.

Although all government policy concerning bilingual education is based on transitional models similar to those sketched above, many leaders of the bilingual education movement strongly criticize this approach. They point out that two or three years of bilingual instruction may not be enough to allow minority language children to perform as well as their English-speaking peers in monolingual classes. Only after five or six years of bilingual education do minority language children achieve national grade-level norms in tests of English reading (Cummins 1980). In fact, children with five or six years of bilingual education actually tend to outperform their monolingual peers on both verbal and nonverbal intelligence measures (Cummins 1980, Kessler and Quinn 1980). Thus bilinguals apparently have a cognitive edge over monolinguals if their bilingualism is well enough developed. By transferring bilingual education students into mainstream English-only classes in about the third grade, educators may be depriving them of the potential advantages of their bilingualism.

Critics of the transitional model also argue that it encourages language shift, rather than language maintenance, and thus undermines this nation's valuable linguistic diversity. Bilingual education laws at both the federal and state levels specify that the primary goal of teaching in non-English languages is to facilitate the learning of English, not to promote the maintenance of the minority language. For instance, in the California Bilingual Education Improvement and Reform Act of 1980, "The Legislature finds and declares that the primary goal of all programs under this article is, as effectively and efficiently as possible, to develop in each child fluency in English." Critics of the transitional model and its explicit goal of language shift maintain that, even in programs that celebrate ethnic history and culture, minority language students cannot help but get the message that English is more highly valued for all purposes than their home language. Thus, as they learn to speak more English, they tend to speak less of their other language, even at home. One study of the Spanish/English bilingual program in Redwood City, California, indicated that bilingually schooled Hispanic children spoke more Spanish than those educated in English only. But the data also showed that the children spoke less Spanish after two years in the bilingual program than when they first enrolled (Cohen 1975).

In addition, proponents of language maintenance find an irony in transitional programs: if they succeed in improving the school performance of minority language students, they may in some ways be failing the ethnic speech community. The price of individual success in the dominant society—whether in school or in later careers—is almost always rejection of the home language and culture, a weakening of ethnic ties. So, whereas transitional programs seem in the short run to promote ethnic diversity, they may in the long run prove one of this nation's most effective tools of assimilation. This is precisely the intent of many lawmakers, but it meets strong resistance from ethnic community leaders.

MAINTENANCE MODEL

Those who hope to sustain the vigorous and long-term use of a minority language—whether as a valuable national resource or as a vehicle of ethnic solidarity—urge the adoption of a **maintenance model** of bilingual education. A few federally funded programs actually follow this model, and many more at least claim language maintenance as a secondary goal. That is, they aim to improve students' skills in their home language as well as in English. In general, maintenance programs differ from transitional programs in three major respects.

First, according to the maintenance model, a two or three year bilingual education program may be sufficient to teach English to minority language students but is inadequate to develop the full range of communicative skills in the home language. Ideally, classes should be taught in the home language and in English through grade twelve.

Second, students must become not only fluent but also literate in their home language. Typically, they read and write about the history, literature, and mores of the ethnic community in the ethnic language. The goal of this emphasis on ethnic culture is to make students both bilingual and **bicultural**—that is, able to participate in both the home and mainstream cultures. Only if they learn actively to value the ethnic community and culture are students likely to continue priding themselves on their ethnic identity and speaking their home language, even after they have become completely competent in English.

Third, if a maintenance program is to succeed, it must centrally involve parents and other ethnic community members in its planning and implementation. Although schools can promote and reinforce language maintenance, they cannot prevent language loss unless the ethnic tongue continues to play a vital role in home and community interactions—in such settings as churches, social organizations, ethnic media, neighborhood conversation, local commerce. But some communities may be more interested in assimilation than in linguistic or cultural maintenance. Parents may fear that education in the home language will come at the expense of the English and subject matter proficiency they know is crucial for their children's upward mobility. Or they may view these programs as a form of tracking or segregation designed to keep ethnic group members out of mainstream classes and eventually out of mainstream society—a concern shared by some bilingual education experts. If these fears are not alleviated through constant consultation, careful program design, and entirely voluntary participation, the maintenance model will probably polarize the com-munity it was meant to support. It can only succeed if the ethnic com-munity wants and helps it to.

One extremely successful maintenance-oriented program for Navajos has been developed in the Rock Point Community School at Chinle, Arizona. The school began as a Bureau of Indian Affairs (BIA) boarding school where Navajo children were totally submerged in English and mainstream culture. But since the 1960s the school has gradually been brought under tribal control. Because this native American community values the retention of Navajo language and customs, its locally elected school board began in 1971 to develop an impressive bilingual program which now extends through senior high school. Nearly all children enter Rock Point speaking only Navajo. Through the third grade, they are taught mainly in Navajo, including Navajo reading skills, while they learn English as a second language. Each class up to the sixth grade is staffed by an English-speaking teacher and a Navajo-speaking teacher. In grades three through six, students learn Navajo literacy and Navajo social studies in the Navajo language, science and social studies in both languages, and math, reading, and oral ESL in English. As a testimonial to this school's suc-cess, its fourth and fifth graders score significantly higher on tests of English reading than students in monolingual BIA schools. Junior and senior high school students continue to develop their skills in Navajo literacy by helping to generate Navajo curricular materials for the lower grades (Templin 1980).

In spite of their apparent benefits to minority language students, maintenance programs engender more controversy than any other model of bilingual education. The most alarmist of their critics draw unfounded parallels with the secessionist movement in Quebec. Former U.S. Ambassador to El Salvador Henry E. Catto, Jr. warns that, because of bilingual education, "By the end of the next decade it is entirely possible that the United States will once again confront the fateful choice it faced in 1860: schism or civil war" (*Newsweek*, 1 December 1980). Assimilationists like Catto ignore the fact that nowhere in the United States does the Spanish-speaking population approach the 81 percent majority that French speakers can claim in Quebec. Nor are U.S. Hispanics as unified, either ethnically or geographically, as French Canadians. Moreover, in Canada critical matters of policy such as language choice can be decided by provincial governments, whereas in the United States state regulations cannot contradict federal policy. And, except for a minority in the

Southwest, most U.S. Hispanics—unlike French Canadians, who co-founded Canada—are in the economically and politically marginal position of being relative newcomers.

Other objections, though less extreme, also focus on the potential divisiveness of maintenance programs. Some adversaries resent the use of public funds to support minority languages. And they fear that, in cities like New York and Miami with huge Spanish-speaking populations, maintenance programs may exacerbate the considerable tension that already exists between Hispanics and Anglos. They believe that strong ethnic and language loyalties will cause dissension and that only linguistic and cultural assimilation can bring harmony. Other critics allege that Hispanic leaders are using maintenance programs as a political power base. They point out that about 80 percent of federal bilingual education funding goes into Hispanic communities, not only to educate children but also to train and employ Hispanic teachers, thus threatening the job security of teachers who speak only English.

Defenders of maintenance programs point out that, contrary to popular belief, nearly all U.S. bilingual programs are transitional rather than maintenance-oriented. Thus most public money is not being spent to promote minority languages but to help students learn English as efficiently as possible. They argue that assimilationists should applaud, not excoriate, these programs. Furthermore, even the few maintenance-oriented programs that do exist are unlikely to increase dissension between the minority and the dominant communities. Ideally, a successful maintenance program would graduate fully bilingual, biliterate, bicultural citizens who would find their capabilities highly marketable in mainstream society. Far from feeling alienated from the mainstream culture, many of these bilinguals would be willing and able to join it. Thus even maintenance programs might ultimately form a bridge to assimilation. Ethnic strife is surely more apt to erupt if community members find public education inaccessible, unresponsive, or irrelevant than if they can help develop well-planned maintenance programs.

OTHER MODELS

Bilingual education need not, of course, be restricted to minority language children. It can also greatly benefit English speakers who wish to regain a lost ethnic tongue or simply add a second language to their repertoire. Indeed, business and political leaders are becoming increasingly aware that Americans will have to improve their command of non-English languages if the United States is to retain a position of world prominence. To some extent, these goals for English speakers can be met by placing them in bilingual education classes with students from non-English-speaking backgrounds. And this approach has the further advantage of helping minority language speakers learn English through interaction with English-speaking peers.

A few bilingual education programs have been designed especially for native-English-speaking children on what might be called an **enrichment model**. These programs differ from regular foreign language classes in that they also use the non-English language as a medium for subject matter instruction, thereby increasing the students' exposure to it. Some of these programs employ the **immersion method**, first developed to teach French to English speakers in suburban Montreal. By this method, English-speaking children follow a curriculum completely in another language for their first two years of school. Then English is gradually introduced until about half the day is spent learning in English, half in the other language. By the end of the fourth grade, immersion students perform as well in English and in subject matter areas as those educated in English only. And in their non-English language, they far surpass students who have only studied it in regular foreign language classes. In fact, in second language reading and listening skills, they approach native speaker proficiency (Swain 1978). Apparently, the immersion method succeeds best with children who already speak the dominant language (English) and consider it a privilege to be learning another language rather than with children who speak a stigmatized tongue and are being compelled to learn a more valued one. The success of dominant culture children in second language learning can be attributed both to their enthusiasm about learning a new language and to teachers' confidence in the abilities of middle-class white students. And these children's English—as the majority language—has plenty of reinforcement and respect outside the school to compensate for its de-emphasis in the classroom.

Not all of those who need to learn English in this country are children. Cuban, Haitian, Central American, and Indochinese adults, as well as children, continue to arrive on U.S. soil with no English skills. Florida, particularly Dade County, has become the chief haven of Caribbean refugees while the Indochinese have spread out throughout the country. The problems are perhaps most acute for the Indochinese since their languages and cultures differ so radically from ours, and about 66 percent of them do not speak enough English for daily survival and minimum employment. These uprooted peoples must learn basic English communication skills in the shortest possible time. That is, they must learn enough English to shop, write checks, apply for jobs, use the telephone, order restaurant food, negotiate public transportation. Their education must be intensive and practical. And ESL instructors must teach not just a new language but often a completely new and alien culture. With the help of federal funds, adult education centers and community colleges have assumed much of the responsibility for this challenging educational task.

As recent developments, government-sponsored ESL and bilingual education programs still suffer from uncertainty about their effectiveness and widespread confusion about their differing aims and implications. Clearly, however, they represent the largest legal, moral, and financial commitment this country has ever made to minority languages and their speakers.

EDUCATION FOR NONSTANDARD SPEAKERS

The situation of those who enter school speaking a nonstandard dialect in some ways resembles the plight of students who speak a non-English language. Both groups come to understand very quickly that their language is not the language of the classroom. And both learn that the standard English used in the classroom is essential to school success. Traditionally, this discovery has posed the same dilemma for both kinds of students: they could choose to sacrifice their home language or dialect in order to succeed in school, or they could reject school language and values and retain those of their own speech community. If they took the first option, they might perform well in school and later in mainstream life; if they took the second, they would inevitably perform poorly.

These similarities between the problems of nonstandard- and non-English-speaking students have led some educators, beginning in the 1960s, to propose similar solutions for the two groups. These policy makers decided that, just as the goal for non-English speakers was bilingualism, so the goal for nonstandard speakers should be **bidialectalism**—full fluency both in their home dialect and in standard English and the ability to shift between the two varieties as appropriate.

Elegant as this proposal sounds, however, it encounters even more serious obstacles than bilingual education.

One of the obstacles to teaching bidialectalism has to do with the way English grammar has usually been taught in public schools. In the conventional English class, it has been assumed that, as with Latin, English grammar can be learned by memorizing certain rules (e.g. use *who* for subjects, *whom* for objects) and that any departure from those rules constituted "bad grammar." Linguists call this kind of grammar **prescriptive** because it prescribes "proper" language use rather than describing actual language behavior. And what this kind of grammar prescribes is a conservative version of standard English. So firmly entrenched in American education is prescriptive grammar that educators and public alike continue to feel that all nonstandard varieties of English are based on "bad grammar" because they fail to conform to prescriptive rules learned in school. Nonstandard speakers, for instance, often break the rules that prescribe one negative per clause (*Don't come here anymore* vs. nonstandard *Don't come here no more*) and subject-verb agreement (*she talks* vs. nonstandard *she talk*). Moreover, teachers and grammarians have persuaded generations of pupils that "bad grammar" signals faulty logic, ignorance, and general incompetence as well as linguistic—and perhaps even moral—corruption. For all these reasons, the traditional approach to nonstandard dialects has been the misguided and unsuccessful attempt to eradicate them.

As the previous chapters of this book explain, sociolinguists have now demonstrated that language variation is inevitable and that all varieties are equally valid, logical, expressive, and coherent. But this new perspective has been slow to gain a foothold in either public education or folk wisdom. As a result, teachers and other standard English speakers—and often nonstandard speakers themselves—continue to stigmatize nonstandard English more than they do other languages. These long-standing prejudices seriously impair efforts to encourage bidialectalism, for teachers are more reluctant to dignify nonstandard English as an acceptable language, especially in the classroom, than they are, say, Spanish. And, just as many non-English-speaking parents resist bilingual programs, many black parents claim that tolerating Black English Vernacular in the classroom is covertly racist. They suspect that their children are being denied the kinds of language training that will allow them to prosper in mainstream life. Unless nonstandard dialects gain more acceptance in society at large, it will remain nearly impossible to foster them in the classroom.

In contrast to this position, some educators question whether it is ethical to require nonstandard speakers to learn standard English at all. Unlike non-English speakers, nonstandard speakers can always understand and make themselves understood. They can learn to read and function in American society without mastering standard English. And we now know that nonstandard dialects are not linguistically inferior. Hence, these educators argue, it is presumptuous to thrust standard English on nonstandard speakers unless they want to learn it. In 1974 the influential Conference on College Composition and Communication committed itself to this view in a resolution called "Students' Right to Their Own Language." Thus the goal of bidialectalism has been assailed from both sides—by those who wish to eradicate nonstandard varieties and by those who prefer to leave them alone.

The other obstacle to bidialectalism is not pedagogical or social but linguistic. To become bilingual, non-English-speaking children must learn a new and separate set of language habits, and adults who speak the two languages can be counted upon to help distinguish between them. But sociolinguistic research suggests that nonstandard-speaking children actually have almost all the features of standard English in their nonstandard verbal repertoire. As Chapter 6 documents, nonstandard speakers shift styles by using more standard English features in formal situations. Their problem is that—apart from a few highly stigmatized forms such as *ain't*—they cannot always differentiate between standard and nonstandard features and often mix them within a single utterance: *She has a morning class and a afternoon class, and she have their name taped down on a piece of cardboard* or *They seen the birds, saw the ducks*. Even adults, who can identify more of the stigmatized forms, may be uncertain about which of their variants is standard English. Witness the following exchange (cited in Ervin-Tripp 1979:41):

SIX-YEAR-OLD: She done ate up all of my potato chips.
MOTHER: Done ate! She has . . . have ate up all my potato chips.

Becoming bidialectal, then, is a matter of learning which features in the nonstandard repertoire to use when. So subtle and difficult a process is this that some linguists suspect that no one can become truly bidialectal: those who command standard English will lose their fine sense of the complex variation between standard and nonstandard features that comprises the nonstandard dialect. Whether or not bidialectalism is a realistic goal, many educators at least agree that standard English can be more successfully taught to nonstandard speakers if their home dialects are taken into account. The following pages sketch some of their strategies for teaching nonstandard speakers to speak, read, and write in standard English.

SPEAKING

In teaching nonstandard-speaking children to speak standard English, some teachers have managed to use their students' home dialects to advantage. By studying the salient phonological and grammatical contrasts between standard and nonstandard varieties (see, for example, Table 7 for contrasts with Appalachian English and Table 21 for contrasts with Black English Vernacular), teachers can determine which of their students' dialect features to select for special attention. Some instructors have tried to teach standard English as a second dialect by adapting methods developed to teach English as a second language. They ask students to memorize and repeat the standard English equivalents of their nonstandard features. As noted in the previous subsection, however, memorization and drill are now considered inadequate techniques by many ESL teachers. And it is clearly even less appropriate to ask nonstandard speakers to memorize and repeat features that already exist in their verbal repertoire.

Instead, nonstandard speakers need help in consistently choosing standard forms. They need to learn how to carry on a conversation using exclusively standard features when the appropriate occasion—such as a job interview—arises. One effective means of teaching students to select either standard or nonstandard forms consistently is to ask them to play roles or tell stories using voices other than their own. By pretending to be doctors, judges, social workers, or English teachers in spontaneous skits or narratives, students can try out standard English speech patterns without embarrassment or threat to their own identity. Teachers who wish to encourage bidialectalism can also ask students to play characters from the ethnic culture that epitomize nonstandard speech norms. Classmates can help perfect the appropriate language variety. This technique draws on and improves the knowledge of style-shifting that students already possess. And it allows them to gain skill at conducting entire interactions in either the standard or the nonstandard variety.

For the most part, however, any attempt to teach nonstandard speakers to control a consistently standard speech will only succeed if the students want to learn how to speak that variety. If they respect and identify with nonstandard speakers exclusively, they will feel little incentive to separate themselves from their reference group by adopting standard speech (see the section on "Pressures against Standardization" in Chapter 5). If, on the other hand, students know and admire some standard speakers and desire to enter mainstream life, they will feel more highly motivated to master standard speech—especially if they have been taught to perceive it as simply a tool for upward mobility rather than as an embodiment of "good grammar" that puts their home dialect to shame. Often these students will learn to speak standard English just by unconsciously patterning their speech on that of a standard speaker they know and respect.

READING

With regard to teaching nonstandard-speaking children to read, educators agree that this important task should not and need not be delayed until the children have learned standard English. Some of the advocates of this ordering of priorities point out that written English includes spelling and grammatical conventions that differ from every spoken dialect. If these conventions of writing differ somewhat more from nonstandard than from standard speech, the distinction is relatively small and should pose few reading problems—particularly since, as already mentioned, most nonstandard speakers have all the standard features in their repertoire. One technique suggested by this faction is to allow nonstandard-speaking children to translate into their own dialect when they read aloud. For example, a speaker of Black English Vernacular might render the following reading (Wolfram et al. 1979:3):

> Text: John missed a game, and Ruth's brother doesn't like it.
> Reading: John miss' a game, an' Ruf brovuh don't like it.

A teacher who knows the features of BEV described in Chapter 9 will recognize this rendition as a competent translation into BEV. Since the child has obviously understood this sentence well enough to translate it, there is no reading problem and no need for "correction" to standard English. Indeed, students who are told to say *Ruth*, not *Ruf*, may not be able to hear the difference any more than could a Midwesterner who is told by a New Yorker to say *merry*, not *Mary*. Constant confusing corrections of this kind might cause the beginning reader more problems than any interference from the home dialect.

Teachers who wish to adopt this method, however, must acquire a good knowledge of their students' home dialects so that they can distinguish between an accurate translation and a real misreading. A BEV-speaking student who offers the following reading is misconstruing the text and should be corrected (Wolfram et al. 1979:8):

> Text: He's done trying to please everyone.
> Reading: He done tried to please everyone.

Only by understanding the use of completive *done* in BEV could a teacher appreciate this student's mistake.

Other educators have experimented with primary readers written in nonstandard varieties. This group feels that, just as non-English speakers succeed best by first learning to read in their home language, so nonstandard speakers should learn to read in their home dialect. Several sets of dialect readers have been published. Most attempt to move children from reading in nonstandard to reading in standard English. For instance, *Bridge: A Cross-Culture Reading Program*, published in 1977, presents stories in three versions for junior and senior high school BEV speakers. One story (cited in Cazden and Dickinson 1981:460) begins:

Black English Vernacular

No matter what neighborhood you be in—Black, White, or whatever—young dudes gonna be having they wheels. . . . You know how Brothers be with they wheels. They definitely be keeping them looking clean, clean, clean.

Transition Form

No matter what neighborhood you look at—Black, White, rich or poor—if you find teenagers, you find old cars. . . . They love they cars. They spend most of their time taking care of them.

Standard English

Young guys, Black or White, love their cars. They must have a car, no matter how old it is. James Russell. . . spent a great deal of time keeping his car clean. He was always washing and waxing it.

Such dialect readers, however, have not proved popular. Those parents and teachers who want to keep nonstandard varieties out of the classroom consider them patronizing. Moreover, no research shows that dialect readers work any better than other techniques to improve the literacy of nonstandard speakers.

A third technique, called the **language experience method**, has the enthusiastic support of some investigators. To use this approach, instructors transcribe stories told by one or more children in the class. Sometimes they record the stories just as they are told, faithfully rendering dialect features and sentence fragments, though in standard spelling. Alternatively, the teacher may wish to help students develop their stories or even to use more standardized forms. Here is one such session, in which the teacher is trying to increase the pupils' verbal range as they construct their story together (Whatley 1980:72):

CHILD 1: It was real big.
TEACHER: How big, as big as what?
CHILD 1: As big as that desk over there.
TEACHER: What desk; over there where?
CHILD 1: Sitting in the corner.
TEACHER: So (*reads what has been written*) "It was as big as that desk over there, sitting in the corner."
Who can tell me something else about it?
CHILD 2: It made a lot of noise.
TEACHER: What kind of noise? What did it sound like?
CHILD 2: It sounded like (*noise*)
TEACHER: I don't know if I can write that. Let's see (*writes* yee-ow-o) OK, (*reads*) "It made a lot of noise that sounded like yee-ow-o." Right?
CHILD 2: Yep. Yee-ow-o!

Advocates of the language experience method point out that students are bound to be more interested in reading materials they themselves have generated than in those created out of an alien linguistic and cultural experience (e.g. "The boy has a boat. The boy likes the boat. The boat is red."). Also, unless the teacher chooses to change them, the reading materials will be written in the students' home dialect and thus optimally accessible. Finally, this method can solve the problem of how to cope with students from various dialect backgrounds in the same classroom: children can invent separate stories in their own dialects, thereby creating individually tailored reading materials.

WRITING

When teaching nonstandard speakers to write, instructors also find it useful to know the salient features of students' home dialects. Such knowledge helps to distinguish errors caused by dialect interference from more general problems with the conventions of writing. In the area of spelling, speakers of any dialect can be expected to encounter some problems since English orthography so little resembles pronunciation. Thus everyone must memorize the distinct spellings of *wright, write, right,* and *rite; to, too,* and *two; there, their,* and *they're.* But, as Table 21 implies, BEV speakers may have even more homophones to cope with than standard speakers: *bole, bowl,* but also *bold; for, four,* but also *foe; tin* and *thin.* Besides confusing the spellings of these additional sets of homophones, nonstandard speakers may spell words as they sound in their home dialects: BEV speakers may write *tes* for *test* and Appalachian English speakers may write *tobaccer* for *tobacco,* just as standard English speakers may write *lim* for *limb.* In an effort to be especially careful with their spelling, these students may also hypercorrect (see Chapter 6)—producing *speciment* for *specimen* or *lorn* for *lawn.* Such areas of phonological interference can be pinpointed for special attention during spelling lessons.

At the sentence level, students who write *they don't have no crime* or *the Boogie-man came around to my mother side* are creating grammatical constructions in their home dialects. In certain contexts—such as personal letters, autobiographies, or stories—the use of dialect features can be completely appropriate and effective. Thus some writing teachers—especially those who wish to support and sustain home dialects—often capitalize on the verbal skills of their nonstandard-speaking pupils by making a number of such assignments. As a transition away from writing in their home dialects, students can translate some of these assignments into standard English. (It would be interesting, incidentally, to discuss with them what is lost in the translation.) They can then begin writing business letters, job applications, or news reports in standard English. Like the role-playing recommended above, writing assignments with clearly differentiated contexts and purposes help students to distinguish among standard and nonstandard features in their repertoire.

Hypercorrection can affect written grammar as well as spelling—particularly when students try to adopt a formal written style that they have little experience with. For instance, nonstandard speakers, who commonly use *was* after *we, you,* and *they,* might have been told to use *were* instead. By generalizing this rule to *I* as well, they could produce a sentence like *I were like the young man in the story we read in class.* Such an occurrence should not be mistaken for random usage. Rather, it should be seen as systematically related to the students' spoken dialect.

Like standard speakers, nonstandard speakers also confront other obstacles in coming to terms with standard written English. Some of these simply result from a lack of familiarity with the written medium and should not be confused with dialect interference. Two non-dialect-related difficulties appear in the following sentence from a student essay:

> In the article that, "Robert Isabella, wrote called The Gunfighter" shows Mr. Isabella personally feeling toward the so called, hero of the early west.

First, this sentence would be grammatically ill-formed in any dialect and probably reflects the author's discomfort with formal writing. Note that the "bad grammar" in this sentence (no one would ever be likely to utter it) contrasts with such supposedly "bad grammar" as *they don't have no crime*, which is actually "good" nonstandard grammar (a nonstandard speaker could readily utter it). Second, the author of this sentence is clearly unfamiliar with the conventions of punctuation, misplacing the first quotation mark and all the commas in the sentence. Other non-dialect-related issues in writing include organization (e.g. *We left at dawn. Susan is my best friend. She left with us.* would be better organized for written narrative as *We left at dawn. Susan, my best friend, left with us.*) and level of formality (*They sure screwed it up* is less acceptable in formal writing than *They certainly bungled it*). All the problems mentioned in this paragraph stem from unpracticed attempts to translate speech into writing and can afflict speakers of any dialect.

TESTING

The long-range goal of teaching nonstandard speakers to speak, read, and write in standard English can only be to enhance their opportunities in a society that expects and rewards this dialect. But competence in standard English may also determine what opportunities students have before they leave school. Increasingly, the public school careers of young Americans are being decided by standardized tests, which currently serve as a basis for both tracking and promotion. In fact, as of 1978, forty-six states responding to a survey were either already requiring competency tests for high school graduation or were planning to (Chall 1978). And investigators have repeatedly demonstrated that standardized tests—which are almost invariably normed on a white middle-class population—unfairly discriminate against nonstandard speakers. What they too often test is knowledge of the

TABLE 22. ITPA Grammatical Closure Subtest with Comparison of "Correct" Responses to Appalachian and Black English Vernacular Alternant Forms

Stimulus with "Correct" Item According to ITPA Test Manual	Appalachian English Alternant	Black English Vernacular Alternant
(Items considered to be "correct" according to the procedures for scoring are italicized.)		
1. Here is a dog. Here are two *dogs/doggies*.		dog
2. This cat is under the chair. Where is the cat? She is *on*/(any preposition—other than "under"—indicating location.)		
3. Each *child* has a ball. This is hers, and this is *his*.	his'n	
4. This dog likes to bark. Here he is *barking*.		
5. Here is a dress. Here are two *dresses*.		dress
6. The boy is opening the gate. Here the gate has been *opened*.		open
7. There is milk in this glass. It is a glass *of/with/for/o' milk*.		
8. This bicycle belongs to John. Whose bicycle is it? It is *John's*.		John
9. This boy is writing something. This is what he *wrote/has written/did write*.	writed/writ has wrote	writed/has wrote
10. This is the man's home, and this is where he works. Here he is going to work, and here he is going *home/back home/to his home*.	at home	
11. Here it is night, and here it is morning. He goes to work first thing in the morning, and he goes home first thing *at night*.	of the night a-paintin'	
12. This man is painting. He is a *painter/fence painter*.		
13. The boy is going to eat all the cookies. Now all the cookies have been *eaten*.	eat/ate/eated/et	ate

No.	Sentence		
14.	He wanted another cookie, but there weren't *any/any more*.	none/no more	none/no more
15.	This horse is not big. This horse is big. This horse is even *bigger*.	more bigger	more bigger
16.	And this horse is the very *biggest*.	most biggest	most biggest
17.	Here is a man. Here are two *men/gentlemen*.	mans/mens	mans/mens
18.	This man is planting a tree. Here the tree has been *planted*.		
19.	This is soap, and these are *soap/bars of soap/more soap*.	soaps	soaps
20.	This child has lots of blocks. This child has even *more*.	mostest	mostest
21.	And this child has the *most*.		
22.	Here is a foot. Here are two *feet*.	foots/feets	foots/feets
23.	Here is a sheep. Here are lots of *sheep*.	sheeps	sheeps
24.	This cookie is not very good. This cookie is good. This cookie is even *better*.	gooder	gooder
25.	And this cookie is the very *best*.	bestest	bestest
26.	This man is hanging the picture. Here the picture has been *hung*.	hanged	hanged
27.	The thief is stealing the jewels. These are the jewels that he *stole*.	stoled/stealed	stoled/stealed
28.	Here is a woman. Here are two *women*.	womans/womens	womans/womens
29.	The boy had two bananas. He gave one away and he kept one for *himself*.	hisself	hisself
30.	Here is a leaf. Here are two *leaves*.	leafs	leafs
31.	Here is a child. Here are three *children*.	childrens	childrens
32.	Here is a mouse. Here are two *mice*.	mouses	mouses
33.	These children all fell down. He hurt himself, and she hurt herself. They all hurt *themselves*.	theirselves/ theirself	theirselves/ theyselves/ theirself/theyself

SOURCE: Walt Wolfram, "Beyond Black English: Implications of the Ann Arbor Decision for Other Non-Mainstream Varieties," in *Reactions to Ann Arbor: Vernacular Black English and Education*, edited by Marcia Farr Whiteman (Arlington, Va.: Center for Applied Linguistics, 1980), p. 21. Reprinted with permission of the publisher.

dominant language and culture rather than the mental capacities they are supposed to measure. One result of relying on these tests has been that three times more blacks and four times more Chicanos have been labeled mentally retarded than would be expected from their percentage in the general population (Mercer and Brown 1973).

The clearest way standardized tests discriminate against nonstandard speakers is in assessing so-called "verbal aptitude"—which turns out to mean proficiency in standard English. For example, in the grammatical closure subtest of the Illinois Test of Psycholinguistic Abilities—often used to establish reading readiness—children are asked to supply a missing word as the tester points to a picture. But only standard English responses are considered correct. By responding to each of the items appropriately in their home dialects, speakers of Black English Vernacular or Appalachian English could "miss" twenty-four out of the thirty-three questions on this subtest, as Table 22 illustrates. Simply because they speak their home dialects correctly, then, ten-year-old BEV or AE speakers might be diagnosed as having a psycholinguistic age of less than five years (Wolfram 1980).

Somewhat more subtly, cultural differences can also handicap nonstandard speakers taking standardized tests. Narratives designed to test reading skills or story problems intended to test math aptitude may depend on knowledge or attitudes not shared by members of non-mainstream cultures. One standardized reading test presents the following vignette (cited in Wolfram et al. 1979:17):

"Good afternoon, little girl," said the policeman. "May I help you?"
"I want to go to the park. I cannot find my way," said Nancy. "Please help me."

The child is then asked to choose the "right" ending for the story from among these possibilities:

The policeman said,
   a. Call your mother to take you.
   b. I am in a hurry.
   c. I will take you to the park.

Obviously, this test question assesses attitudes toward policemen—which for minority children may vary widely from the dominant culture norm—at least as much as it tests reading ability. To appreciate how culturally distinct knowledge can be built into tests of vocabulary and "general knowledge," read through the tests in

Tables 23 and 24, which discriminate against members of the dominant culture.

Besides encoding these linguistic and cultural biases, standardized tests can favor the interactive styles of standard English speakers. As the following chapter on "Intercultural Communication" explains, white middle-class parents encourage their children to expand and repeat questions, while ethnic working-class parents expect their children to answer with minimal responses. Thus it is not surprising that, when shown a picture of a car in a garage and asked to repeat the question, "Is this car in the garage?" many black working-class children "wrongly" say "yes" rather than responding with an imitation (Wolfram and Christian 1976). This problem suggests that the entire testing situation must be taken into account when interpreting test results for nonstandard speakers. It also suggests that norms for interaction, as well as nonstandard phonological and grammatical features, may influence the school performance of minority children. Such differing communicative norms will be the focus of the next chapter.

TABLE 23. A Culturally Biased Test Favoring BEV Speakers

1. If a "brother" is said to have a "do," he has: a. fast-moving cars, b. a flunky, c. a long jail record, d. a process
2. A "clock" to a black means: a. a time device, b. a dummy, c. a rooster, d. a place to stash dope
3. Which word "don't" belong? a. Splib, b. Blood, c. Jive, d. Spook
4. What does it mean when it's said to "pimp"? a. to sweet talk a woman, b. to walk cool, c. to break out in the face, d. to work
5. The phrase "I ain't studin' you" means: a. I don't care what you think, b. I am not studying about you, c. I am not looking for nothing to go right, d. I've never had sex with her
6. Your "Ace-Boon Coon" is: a. a card playin' friend, b. your best huntin' dog, c. your cute buddy, d. an outfit of clothing
7. If Bobbie Jo's head's bad, a. she needs her hair fixed, b. she has a headache, c. she has been drinking, d. she's in love
8. When a black says, "to be or not to be," he: a. means that in order to be somebody, you've got to be white, b. is speaking from Shakespeare, c. means that you are either black or you're not, d. is in love
9. "Henry broke Gary's face." What happened? a. Henry hit Gary in his face, b. Henry out-talked Gary, c. Gary hit Henry in the face, d. They hit each other
10. When Mama doesn't want me to talk back at her, she says, a. "Don't give me no lip!" b. "Button your lip!" c. "Don't talk to me!" d. "Give me a lip-lock!"

11. "What's hapnin!" means: a. Hello, b. What do you want? c. What is occurring here? d. I can't see for looking
12. If Larry's arms are "talking" he needs: a. to stop taking dope, b. someone who understands sign language, c. to stop using his hands to talk, d. Right Guard (deodorant)
13. "To make a hussle" means: a. to play hard, b. to work, c. to win praise, d. to make a lady
14. A "gig" is: a. something to ride in, b. a job, c. an ugly girl, d. your pad or house
15. If a black is agitating a fight between two other blacks, he is: a. mean, b. bambooseling, c. coppin' a plea, d. signifying
16. A "Deuce-and-a-quarter" is a brother's: a. paycheck, b. good hand in a card game, c. half-brother, d. ride
17. To "lean" means: a. to come to me with your problems, b. to lean over while one drives, c. to lean over while one walks, d. to walk humped back
18. To "cop-a-plea" means: a. that one is pleading for something, b. to find something, c. to make an excuse, d. to tell on someone
19. A "mack": a. is a pimp, b. fights a lot, c. is anyone that you don't know, d. is a common person
20. A "blue-eyed soul brother or sister" is: a. a child who has one parent who is black and another parent who is white, b. a child with blue eyes that has two black parents, c. a white person with "soul," d. a black person who thinks that he is white
21. Something that "holds papers" is a: a. sissy bag, b. Whitey's judgment case, c. brief relief, d. folder
22. When a brother says "the Dozens," he means: a. someone is talking about someone else's parents, b. his family, c. that his gang has twelve members, d. that having children is cheaper by the dozen
23. A "Gas-Head" is a person who has a: a. fast moving car, b. stole of "lace," c. "process," d. habit of stealing cars, e. long jail record for arson
24. A "hype" is a person who: a. always says they feel sickly, b. has water on the brain, c. uses heroin, d. is always sick, e. is always ripping and running
25. A "handkerchief head" is: a. a cool cat, b. a porter, c. an Uncle Tom, d. a hoddi, e. a preacher

Answers: 1d, 2a, 3c, 4b, 5a, 6c, 7c, 8b, 9b, 10a, 11a, 12d, 13b, 14b, 15d, 16b, 17d, 18a, 19c, 20a, 21a, 22a, 23c, 24c, 25c

SOURCE: Sol Adler, *Poverty Children and Their Language: Implications for Teaching and Treating* (New York: Grune & Stratton, 1979), pp. 247–57. Excerpted by permission of the publisher and author.

TABLE 24. A Culturally Biased Test Favoring AE Speakers

1. Ginseng or "sang" is: a. a leaf of a tree, b. a square dance, c. an herb used by the Chinese, d. a drink made from the ginger leaf
2. Red-eye gravy is: a. gravy with red food coloring in it, b. gravy made with ham grease (and water or coffee), c. unaged moonshine, d. fish sauce
3. Cracklin's are: a. made from beef, b. pork rind and fat, c. fireworks, d. chicken feed
4. Bee gum is: a. made from honey comb, b. tree sap used for chewing, c. an early American bee hive, d. a sweetgum tree that attracts bees to its fruit
5. A barrel rim or goop, and a piece of wire, "A click and a wheel" is: a. a child's toy, b. a singing frame, c. used part of a bike wheel
6. Sour mash is: a. a fertilizer, b. an ingredient for moonshine, c. a woven fence, d. a home remedy for rheumatism
7. "Annie Over" is a: a. neighbor, b. game played with a rubber ball, c. folk tale, d. song
8. Carbide is: a. added to water to make acetylene gas, b. used to make baking powder, c. used to make extra copies of a newspaper
9. A pounding is: a. driving a nail, b. gifts to a new neighbor, c. a one-pound chicken
10. Leather britches are: a. threaded dried green beans, b. britches worn by mountaineers, c. part of a harness
11. Flying ginny is: a. a name of an early airplane, b. a children's game, c. a title of a children's story, d. a slow mule
12. A tow sack is: a. a foot covering, b. a burlap bag, c. a foot bandage
13. Kiverlid is: a. a bed cover, b. a hat, c. a kitchen utensil
14. Light bread is: a. hot bread, b. store bread, c. corn bread, d. cream puffs
15. Mole beans are: a. a variety of shellout beans, b. for poisoning moles, c. molded beans
16. An Appalachian asking for a "plug" would most likely mean: a. a broken down mule, b. chewing tobacco, c. a stopper for a sink drain
17. A dotey person is: a. crippled, b. fat, c. in love, d. lazy, e. senile
18. The word "blinky" refers to: a. a child's toy, b. an early frost, c. an eccentric woman, d. soured milk, e. spoiled canned goods
19. A bealed head refers to: a. a bloated cow, b. a festering pimple, c. a hairless condition, d. a rotten cabbage, e. a swollen face
20. A man who has granny trouble can look forward to: a. abstaining from sex, b. the birth of his child, c. having only daughters, d. his mother-in-law moving in, e. a stomach condition
21. Jumping jig refers to a: a. dance, b. escaped convict, c. groom, d. racial slur, e. toy
22. To back an envelope is to: a. address it, b. apply a return address, c. mail it, d. put postage on it, e. seal it
23. A back set is a (an): a. brace, b. farm tool, c. ignorant person, d. low chair, e. relapse

24. Which of the following belongs least with the others? a. dodger, b. grits, c. hush puppy, d. pone, e. scrapple
25. An anxious bench might be found in: a. church, b. county jail, c. grocery store, d. hospital, e. one room school

---

Answers: 1c, 2b, 3b, 4c, 5a, 6b, 7b, 8a, 9b, 10a, 11a, 12b, 13a, 14b, 15b, 16b, 17e, 18d, 19e, 20b, 21e, 22a, 23e, 24e, 25a

SOURCE: Sol Adler, *Poverty Children and Their Language: Implications for Teaching and Treating* (New York: Grune & Stratton, 1979), pp. 257–63. Excerpted by permission of the publisher and author.

CHAPTER 11
Intercultural Communication

LIKE OUR PUBLIC POLICY, our personal behavior has often demonstrated our ignorance about the implications of linguistic diversity. Even when we acknowledge the variety of languages spoken in the United States, we all too often fail to realize that different language communities have differing norms for self-presentation, politeness, making requests and queries, telling stories, and just making informal conversation. While we readily admit that many difficulties arise between speakers of distinct languages, intercultural communication—especially among American English speakers—remains an unrecognized problem in our nation, schools, and neighborhoods.

Although most Americans have given up everyday use of their ethnic family tongue, aspects of interactional style derived from the former language may be retained and introduced as a special style of English. Interaction involving speakers of different regional, ethnic, or class dialects is a form of intercultural communication, though less obviously so than conversation between speakers from distinct language communities. In both cases, differing cultural assumptions about appropriate expressions of interest, deference, forcefulness, sincerity, humor, friendliness can lead to serious misunderstanding of the attitude and intent of the speakers and, at times, the very content of the conversation.

Approaches to language education have been shaped by pedagogy developed for foreign language instruction, which of necessity focuses on the profound phonological, lexical, and grammatical contrasts between languages. But, as any traveler would agree, knowledge of formal structures is not sufficient for communication in a foreign culture. Critical aspects of communication—such as the meanings of gestures, when and how long to speak, whom to address, how to tell a story or a joke—are left largely to experience. Educators, like the general public, have little conscious insight into how interaction is structured and contextualized in their own or other languages. Thus none of us is trained to interpret or manipulate such factors, or even to recognize them when they occur in conversation.

Within American English, regional or ethnic vocabulary and contrasting grammatical structures function as overt indicators of distinct language varieties. Often they are superficial differences, easily recognized and overcome in conversation. For instance, no one fails to understand that double negation in nonstandard black and white English is parallel to single negation in standard English. *I didn't recognize none of them* would not be construed by any English speaker as indicating that some or all were recognized. Still, a structure such as invariant *be*, which forms the habitual aspect in Black English Vernacular (see Chapter 9), might lead to misunderstanding in some cases. Asked about Easter Sunday, a black restaurant owner replied, "I don't be open Sunday." His standard-speaking customer planned a fruitless mission for the Sunday following.

Similarly, the "meaning" of double negation is known to users and nonusers, yet the following dialogue points to an emphatic function which nonusers fail to comprehend (Gumperz and Hernández-Chavez 1972:102):

> STUDENT (*reading from an autobiographical essay*): This lady didn't have no sense.
> TEACHER: What would be a standard English alternate for this sentence?
> STUDENT: She didn't have any sense. But not this lady: *she didn't have no sense.*

Many aspects of word choice and grammatical structure that are potentially troublesome are the very dialect differences of which speakers are consciously aware. Thus these sorts of communicational breakdowns are sometimes restored by attributing the difficulty directly to language variation. This may even occur as an overt reference to dialect differences. A Northerner's embarrassing misuse of singular *you* for plural reference was repaired by a Southerner's comment on the speaker's ignorance of the local Deep South dialect. The Northerner addressed a colleague and her student teacher:

> NORTHERNER: Would you come into my office for a minute? There's an issue relating to your course I'd like some advice on.
> COLLEAGUE (*entering office*): OK; sure.
> STUDENT TEACHER (*timidly, hesitating outside office door*): Am I supposed to come too?
> NORTHERNER (*surprised*): Of course!
> COLLEAGUE: Oh, come on, J. She meant *you-all*. You know she can't speak the language!

Unfortunately, lapses in effective communication are rarely so easily detected by the participants. Rather, they come away from the interaction with vague feelings of discomfort that, over repeated instances, may become active antipathy. Those from other speech communities "don't pay attention to what I say," "don't do what they say they're going to," or "are so rude." Subtle interactional failures contribute directly to stereotyping and intergroup strife. In the above example, the student teacher might have gone off believing the Northerner did not like her or did not feel she was competent to participate in policy decisions, or even that the Northerner embodied the regional stereotype of coldness and aloofness.

To compound communicational problems, research has shown that the linguistic practices that create the most serious intercultural misunderstanding are also those about which speakers have least awareness. For instance, community standards for interpersonal distance vary crossculturally. So an outsider who stands closer to community members than their norms allow will be perceived as an aggressive or intrusive personality, not as a member of a different dialect group.

Recent interdisciplinary study of communicative behavior reveals differing speech community norms for interactional style, conversational structure, and spoken and written genres such as arguments and stories. These are as closely and uniquely patterned as the features of accent, vocabulary, grammar, and style-shifting that have been traced in the preceding chapters.

INTERACTIONAL STYLE

Differences in verbal and nonverbal behavior profoundly influence our assessments of other speakers, affecting our interpretations of the intent of a message and thus our understanding of its content. Different cultures have distinct conventions for occupation of physical space, gestures with head and body, touching, and seeking or averting gaze. Rules for eye contact in white middle-class society, for instance, are opposite of those employed by blacks. Among standard-speaking whites, as in northwestern Europe, listeners watch the person speaking, thereby communicating attentiveness and interest; speakers do not themselves initiate eye contact with individual listeners. Interaction in Black English Vernacular, on the other hand, requires listeners to avert their gaze and speakers to watch the audience—a practice found among the West African language communities from which American blacks stem. To blacks, white listening behavior implies impatience or impertinence; to white speakers, blacks appear bored or disrespectful.

When black children whose parents have admonished *Don't cut eye with me*! and whites ordered to *Look at me when I'm talking to you*! come together in a schoolroom, miscommunication is an inevitable result. And the school setting is not a culturally neutral meeting ground; the most critical interaction will not take place among the pupils but between them and their teacher. The children whose cultural background differs from the teacher will be misunderstood, while those sharing the teacher's interactional style will be reinforced in their behavior.

Children who command their teacher's cultural code are better able to win attention and make their needs known. Filmed interaction between a white elementary teacher and a group of pupils demonstrated that a white child was able to solicit the teacher's attention by anticipating the very times she would look away from the child she was interacting with. An equally active black child consistently missed getting the teacher's attention by failing to gauge correctly when she would look around at the group. The white child also watched the pupil the teacher was speaking with—a cue to the teacher that she wanted the next turn at interaction with the teacher. But the teacher failed to observe the black child's mistimed, repeated, but guarded, glance toward her (Byers and Byers 1972).

Other ethnic minorities share the black, rather than the white, rules for eye contact. Among Hispanics, Asians, and American Indians, lowered gaze and even lowered head indicate respect for an older or higher status speaker. This nonverbal behavior is carried over into English language interaction, whether English is used alternately with the family tongue or as its replacement. In a school system dominated by white personnel, such children come to be seen as uninterested, unintelligent, even willfully disrespectful; they have been judged on behavior intended to convey the reverse.

Not just eye contact but other nonverbal and verbal listening behaviors vary crossculturally. Following their community's standards, black listeners move about and make gestures of encouragement or disagreement as signs they are attending to a speaker's talk. Spontaneous verbal expression by listeners is acceptable even in the most formal settings, such as religious services. The length and outcome of competition in young black boys' verbal games depend largely on the listeners' ongoing evaluations of the contestants' remarks.

Each speech community has its own conventions regarding how to initiate talk and who may begin; how long a speaker may continue in the absence of reinforcing remarks or gestures from listeners; when, how, and by whom a speaker may be interrupted; how to close an interaction. Gender and relative age of the participants often profoundly affect the structure of communication. In Arab and many Asian societies, for example, women are expected to display deference and modesty in mixed company. American girls from such ethnic backgrounds might be reluctant to perform verbally before their male classmates.

Even reactions to interactional stress vary according to cultural background. In the face of embarrassment, Anglo-American children often respond with raised voice and hostile words or gestures; native American children may draw a veil of silence and impassivity or quietly withdraw from the situation; Japanese Americans tend to giggle nervously; Afro-Americans often respond by coolly one-upping their opponent with a telling verbal remark. Intercultural communication is rife with learned behaviors which may cause misunderstanding or offense, and many of them arise regularly in classroom interactions.

CONVERSATIONAL STRUCTURES

The structure of dialogue commonly used in school is foreign to many children. Educational interaction tests children by asking questions to which they obviously know the answer; for example, "What did you eat for breakfast?'' This strategy demands that individual children perform for their teacher and the class, demonstrating their knowledge as succinctly or as expansively as possible. This type of interaction requires that the children be willing, in fact eager, to display their talents before others and that they be prepared to risk failure before their peers as an acceptable route to learning. It also requires that the children understand known-answer questioning as a rhetorical device, not as a way of tricking them or making them look foolish.

Some children are trained from infancy in this sort of interaction. Conversation that expands and repeats children's sentence fragments is a common expression of caring and language teaching device in white middle-class homes. Even pre-language infants are addressed in this manner, as in the following pseudo-dialogue between a mother and her sixteen-month-old (Keenan et al. 1978:50):

MOTHER: You know what Mommy has?
MOTHER: I have something you've never seen before.
MOTHER: We have some bubbles.
MOTHER: Would you like to have some bubbles?
MOTHER: Remember bubbles in the bath?

In many working-class and ethnic minority speech communities, however, mothers' speech to infants does not take this question-answer format. Children learn to speak when they have something substantial to say, rather than using statements, questions, and repetitions to gain adult attention. The following two mother-child dialogues contrast white middle-class and black working-class speech norms. The first is the middle-class family (cited in Ward 1970:100):

CHILD: See truck, Mommy.
MOTHER: Did you see the truck?
CHILD: See truck.
MOTHER: No, you didn't see it. There goes one.
CHILD: No I see truck.
MOTHER: Yes, there goes one.
CHILD: There go one. See a truck. See truck, Mommy. See truck. Truck. Put truck, Mommy.
MOTHER: Put the truck where?
CHILD: Put truck window.
MOTHER: I think that one's too large to go in the window.

The child's utterances are regarded by the mother as a performance; he is permitted to repeat his statements; in fact, she encourages this practice by repeating and expanding his sentence fragments. The black child attempts to gain his mother's attention in the same fashion but learns that this is not an appropriate use of language (Ward 1970:101):

> CHILD: Mama, look, a train.
> MOTHER: Yeah, Kenneth, I see it.

This same mother, asking a known-answer question, does not expect a verbal response from her child. He speaks only when he is asked something she herself does not know and then his response is minimal (Ward 1970:101):

> MOTHER (*fondly*): You pissy?
> CHILD: (*silence*)
> MOTHER: You piss in you pant.
> CHILD: (*silence, smiling*)
> MOTHER: You shame you piss in your pant?
> CHILD: No.
> MOTHER: You should be.

Placed in the artificial interaction of test dialogue, young speakers of Black English Vernacular typically offer only minimal responses or refuse to speak. They view known-answer questions as an attempt to trick them or open them to reprimand or ridicule. For example, one child's response to the question, "Where do you live?" was a minimal, reluctant, "Oh, over there," to a woman who had picked her up at her home, but a long, detailed explanation of how to get there when someone else asked the question out of genuine ignorance (Ervin-Tripp 1979).

Afro-American speech communities are highly verbal cultures. Status frequently is determined by verbal acuity in formalized, often competitive speech events, such as **signifying** and **sounding**. These linguistic performances, however, take place among peers, not between children and adults. In sounding, or **playing the dozens**, boys exchange ritual insults, each one attempting to top the last. A good sounder is more highly respected than a boy who has to resort to physical means of defeating his competitors. A good one-liner insults the target or his family: *You so square you shit bricked shit* or *You mama sent her picture to the lonely hearts club, and they sent it back and said, "We ain't that lonely!"* (Kochman 1972a:259, 261). One remark suggests a retort that heightens the insult (Labov 1972a: 316):

A: Hey! I went up Money house and I walked in Money house, I say, I wanted to sit down, and then, you know a roach jumped up and said, "Sorry, this seat is taken."

B: I went to David house, I saw the roaches walkin' round in *combat boots*.

Sounds commonly appear in rhymed form (Labov 1972a:308):

Iron is iron, and steel don't rust,
But your momma got a pussy like a Greyhound Bus.

Signifying, a verbal exchange used by women as well as men, requires getting a point across without ever stating it directly. In the following conversation, a young man attempts to strike up with a somewhat older woman, much to the amusement of his companions (Mitchell-Kernan 1972:323):

A: Mama, you sho is fine.
B: That ain't no way to talk to your mother.
A: You married?
B: Um hm.
A: Is your husband married?
B: Very.

Both participants in this interaction come away amused and highly respectful of the other's verbal ability.

The imaginative use of language that characterizes adolescent Afro-American discourse is not found in all American speech communities. Working-class black males prize skill at verbal repartee, while working-class white boys are far less eager to trust themselves to expression through language (Philipsen 1975). Among Chicago "white ethnics," men who advocate verbal before physical means of settling arguments lose, rather than gain, status with young men and boys. Verbal interchange with officials and other adults causes so much stress that boys making a request or presentation bring an older brother or friend to argue their case for them. Recourse to verbal argument in one's own behalf is a desperate, embarrassing last resort. Children who go to great lengths to avoid verbal disputation cannot be expected to enter eagerly into linguistic examinations in the classroom.

LEARNING STRUCTURES

Parental standards for polite behavior serve as children's models for interactional success. Black parents tend to censure severely their children's attempts at obfuscation and prefer a simple "yes" or "no" or silence in the face of questioning. As long as they remain silent, children are privy to adult conversation; it is understood that they will not attempt to speak on matters about which they have incomplete knowledge (Bauman 1972). In white middle-class homes, children are more often encouraged to participate actively in some adult talk, with adults responding to, correcting, and expanding their efforts at interaction. Thus a black child answering a teacher's query or request with a simple "no" has not intended to be confrontative any more than a white child who responds "why?" But a teacher whose cultural experience equates circumlocution or evasion with politeness will be more offended by the former than by the latter.

Known-answer questioning has proved even less successful with American Indian children. In fact, teachers working with many different tribes report that any form of classroom interaction that singles out one pupil to act as performer seems doomed to failure. Children are reluctant to read aloud and, if forced to, will be accompanied by the whispered recitation of classmates, who supply the text, should the speaker stumble over an unknown word. Rather than vying with one another for the teacher's attention and praise, Indian pupils more often tend to function solidly as a group, aiding fellow students by providing difficult answers or distracting the teacher's attention from an individual in danger of reprimand. Given choice, Indian pupils prefer group projects and less supervised, cooperative work. They are more comfortable with a less directive learning structure, and tests show they learn more in less structured classrooms.

Study of the structure of informal learning within native American communities has provided some explanation of classroom behavior and suggests models that have proved more conducive to these students' success than traditional classroom dialogue. (Data for native American school performance from Philips 1972, Dumont and Wax 1969, John 1972, Cazden et al. 1980.) Indian children tend to be raised by their entire community, not by their immediate families alone. From an early age they move freely among whichever households of kinfolk they choose. They are expected to assume adult responsibility as soon as they are able, and young children strive hard to achieve competence and thereby independence. Even more frequently than in Afro-American communities, children can be found silently attending to adult conversation or observing adults at their work. At some point, an adult or older child invites participation in the tasks, giving the child opportunity for asking questions but offering little explicit direction. When the child feels competent, he or she attempts the task privately; success will be displayed in the resulting accomplishment, and failure will not be seen. These nondirective and largely nonverbal learning strategies recall traditional religious practices, which required young people to retreat into isolation and reemerge as possessors of knowledge and skills suiting them for an adult role in the community.

Schoolroom learning structures are thus extremely alien to native American culture. Testing is public and occurs whenever the teacher chooses, not when the pupils present themselves. Public humiliation is an inevitable result for at least some of the children. A child trained in the tribal practice of private learning and demonstration of skills is placed in severe conflict, and silent refusal to participate in verbal question-answer dialogue commonly results.

Public school instruction is traditionally conducted almost entirely verbally. The teacher directs children's task assignments, turns at talk, and movement in the classroom. This type of interaction parallels the verbal structure of Anglo-American public events, at which preappointed leaders orchestrate a highly structured, often predictable sequence of events, and other participants act as largely passive observers. If audience members take any active part, this, too, is prearranged by common knowledge or announced or noted on the program. Indian meetings and ceremonies are radically unlike these structured affairs. Length is not determined beforehand; participants may arrive, leave, and return at their wish; no single action is the center of everyone's attention; matters of importance are addressed by anyone who wishes to speak rather than by a set of designated experts; music and dancing are group activities in which everyone may join. Small wonder, then, that Indian children are unhappy when required to sit impassively for hours on end; that they call out in a chorus when one pupil is called upon; that they direct remarks to one another as well as to the teacher. Formally directed, question-answer rhetoric has no place in their home culture.

Native Americans place great weight on the manner in which a speaker conveys information or perspectives and measure the value of the knowledge according to the interactional skill of the speaker. Tribal leadership is bestowed on those who possess these talents. Traditionally, tribal decisions are made by consensus, which requires leaders to have not only good ideas but also the linguistic ability to harmonize opposing viewpoints. The Cherokee, for example, abhor open conflict and resolve it, whenever possible, by joking. Public display of anger, hostility, or scorn can lead to loss of status.

Cherokee children are highly respectful pupils, respecting one another as well as their teacher. An instructor who employs individualized question-answer rhetoric to demonstrate a pupil's failings, however, is diminished in students' eyes for being unable to teach without evoking conflict and humiliation. Repeated degradation of fellow students leads Cherokee children to believe that the teacher, as a weak person, has no valuable knowledge to impart. Teachers who respect their pupils' notions of privacy and decorum and who attempt to maintain egalitarian relationships and a sense of common purpose in learning the material are far more successful in training and retaining Cherokee students.

Among other American Indians, as well, school instruction that is less formal and, especially, less separated from everyday life has evoked favorable response from formerly bored, resistant students. One tribally-controlled Navajo school, for example, conducts classes in the open or in community buildings rather than in structures set aside for a single purpose. Pupils spanning a range of ages cluster at group tables to work on projects with classmates rather than sitting at isolated, rowed desks facing the teacher. Parents are integrated into the program; traditional lore and skills taught by them in the home are a recognized part of the curriculum. A successful college-preparatory boarding school for Alaskan Eskimos is staffed by teacher-priests, who recreate the students' village social life by making themselves available in and out of the classroom. They work as classroom teachers, as private tutors, and as friends who share their personal experience with students. This open-ended egalitarian interaction places these students in a communal, cooperative network whose educational goals they can respect and adopt.

Education of Hispanic children is also enhanced by knowledge of the home culture and customs. One successful Hispanic elementary teacher began each day with a series of individual and highly personalized interactions with each student. For these exchanges, she adopted the *cariño* style—a special form of talk used with loved ones and small children and characterized by diminuitives added to names and nouns. The schoolchildren reacted positively to her use of these forms, even employing them in response, as they would with their mothers. She called each pupil to her for a private talk on his or her progress with the classwork, after which the group discussed the children's home lives—sick parents, arguments at home, and the like. After this initial period, the directed work of the day began. This teacher modeled her first contact with the children after Hispanic norms for visits and meetings. In the children's home culture it is considered rude to come to the point of a conversation without first establishing rapport and mutual respect and concern through a preliminary interchange about more personal matters. In this classroom, the children's expectations of a strong personal interest were met by the teacher's structure of the class time and her choice of speech style (Cazden et al. 1980).

NARRATIVE AND ORATORICAL STRUCTURES

A very different approach has been developed to accommodate the native conversational structure of Hawaiian children. (Data on Hawaiian from Boggs 1972 and Watson-Gegeo and Boggs 1977.) Like the children of the speech communities discussed above, Hawaiian pupils have not responded positively to direct question interaction. However, when questions are asked of the group, many pupils will respond simultaneously, overlapping and interrupting one another. Children who raise a hand to volunteer, then shout out the answer may, when recognized by the teacher, say they don't know the answer they have just given. Even in small groups, Hawaiian students are reluctant to discuss their reading assignments when individually queried by teachers. Yet these same pupils vie with one another to tell stories when they are not individually directed to do so. Drawing a lesson from traditional Polynesian story-telling style, teachers have begun to encourage co-narration of stories and co-discussion of readings, with far greater success in reading achievement.

Polynesian narration is not one-to-many but an interaction among many speakers. In parent-child interchanges, the child must often respond to the parent's rapid-fire challenges, which are intended to ferret out misinformation and evasion in the child's talk. Among groups of children, this rhetoric has developed into verbal dueling, in which children interrupt to counter, substantiate, or expand one another's texts. The children are avid and skilled story-tellers, using the co-narrative mode of discourse, in which they play off one another for details of the story and for narrative effect.

In the following example, two six-year-old girls are telling a story to an adult and a seven-year-old boy. The children's speech shows evidence of Hawaiian Creole phonology, vocabulary, and syntax. Simultaneous speech is bracketed together (Watson-Gegeo and Boggs 1977:67–68):

GIRL A: ⌈ An da de-, an da devil, dey get knife, you know. ⌉
GIRL B: ⌊ An he, he get down den—if you ⌋ stayed
a-walk da beach, he stab you. ⌈ You go die from you. ⌉
BOY: ⌊ I go all night, I like go some . . . ⌋
ADULT: Mmmm.
GIRL A: Den he go, you, he going . . .
GIRL B: [O]keh, you go, you going die, [boy's name].
GIRL A: Den he really.
GIRL B: I not lie. ⌈ I telling da truth. ⌉
BOY: ⌊ Mmmm. ⌋
GIRL A: ⌈ Somebody else lying. ⌉
GIRL B: ⌊ He go kill somebody else. ⌋ So he get, dey wen eat guys,
Yeah?
GIRL A: ⌈ Yeah, da guys . . . ⌉
GIRL B: ⌊ Dey, dey . . . ⌋
GIRL A: ⌈ Dey . . . ⌉
GIRL B: ⌊ Chop em up . . . ⌋
GIRL A: ⌈ Devil . . . ⌉
GIRL B: ⌊ Fight for da *kine* [it] and dey suck da blood. ⌋ Dey suck
da blood.
GIRL A: Dey . . . wen . . . eat . . . all . . . da . . . bones, boy.
GIRL B: Yeah.
GIRL A: Dey eat da *na'au* [intestines] an everyting.

The overlaps and interruptions are not random. The girls use repeated unfinished utterances to heighten the tension in the "eating guys" section. In the conclusion, dramatic elongation and sequential reinforcement, rather than interruption, create clarity and finality.

If Hawaiian narrative sounds like a verbal free-for-all to listeners trained in the western European narrative tradition, public speeches by American Indians may appear rambling and lacking in argument. Although structured in the familiar one-at-a-time sequence, Indian oratory, like Polynesian narrative, presumes a relationship between speaker and audience that differs markedly from Anglo-American public talk.

The oratorical tradition upon which American government, education, and enterprise are based judges speakers—and leaders—by their persuasiveness. Thus a good speech has a well-articulated point of view. It presents a selected series of substantiating points—informative or illustrative—and demonstrates how they are related and how they constitute evidence for the speaker's position. Ideas or facts that lend support to an opposing viewpoint are disregarded, unless the speaker feels it is necessary to refute them. It is the speaker's responsibility to provide clear connections between the topics and to present an integrated argument for the audience. The speaker's analysis of the topics, as much as the points themselves, convince the listeners that the espoused view is the correct one.

Among American Indians, such persuasive style would be regarded as an attempt to mislead or manipulate the audience (Cooley 1979, Cooley and Ballenger 1982). Speakers are not expected to interpret information but to offer all known facts, regardless of how they apply to their own personal opinions. The listeners, having been presented with all pertinent information, form their own analysis. Presenting a single viewpoint or only selected facts would be an imposition on the autonomy of one's listeners. Thus topics are simply strung one after the other, with at most an announcement that a new topic is beginning; speeches lack previews and reviews, summaries, and evaluative statements, such as are found in Anglo-American oratory. The interactional goals of Anglo-Americans and American Indians—the one to convince the listeners, the other to submit information for their private deliberation—lead to two radically different oratorical structures.

Narratives by black American children appear to share the structure of American Indian public speaking far more than that of their Anglo-American counterparts. "Sharing time" talk by children in a mixed-race first grade classroom illustrates two distinct forms of discourse (Michaels and Cook-Gumperz 1979). While both black and white pupils were eager to report their personal experiences to the class, the teacher perceived the blacks as failing to conceive properly the task of relating some particular, interesting occurrence. The white pupils tended to produce rather tightly structured narratives, with all their comments explicitly related to a single topic (Michaels and Cook-Gumperz 1979:654–55):

> CHILD: Yesterday my mom and my whole family went with me, um, to a party and it was a Thanksgiving party ⌈ where and we, um . . ⌉
> TEACHER: ⌊ Mmmm . . .   ⌋
> CHILD: My mom, we had to, um, get dress up as pilgrims and my mom made me this hat for a pilgrim.
> TEACHER: Oh great.

The black children's talk, however, was characterized by **topic chaining**, similar to native American discourse. They shifted from one topic to the next without any overt transition to indicate the relatedness between the remarks (Michaels and Cook-Gumperz 1979:656–57):

CHILD: Um, I went to the beach Sunday and to McDonalds and to the park and I got this for my birthday. My mother bought it for me and, um, I had, um, two dollars for my birthday and I put it in here and I went to where my friend named Gigi, I went over to my grandmother's house with her and, um, she was walking around on my back by my house and, um, she was heavy. She
TEACHER: [was in the sixth or seventh grade...]
[OK. I'm going to stop you. I want you] to talk about things that are really really very important.... And tell us what beach you went to over the weekend.

In the first example, with the white child, the teacher is able to identify the central point in the story and amplify and validate it. In the second, she has no idea where the child is headed and, in fact, cuts her off just as she reaches her "point," which was that she was able to carry her older, heavier friend on her back.

ORAL AND LITERATE FRAMEWORKS

All these differences in communicational structure have recently been characterized as evoking an oral, rather than a literate, conceptual framework (Gumperz 1977, Ong 1979, Tannen 1980, Tannen 1982). That is, the primary model on which orally-oriented speakers draw is spoken, face-to-face interaction, not written, impersonal communication. Discourse in an oral framework relies on shared context between speakers and listeners—expectations of common knowledge, values, and world view. It presumes that conversations will mainly occur between members of the same speech community.

Among orally-oriented speakers, context is not explicitly outlined. Connections between topics are not made overt but instead are implied by the speaker's behavior and the listeners' knowledge of his or her attitudes. Native American public speakers, for example, assume their listeners are capable of seeing how topics are related and are confident in their fellow tribe members' ability to draw appropriate, indeed similar, conclusions.

All American speech communities employ orally-oriented discourse styles but to greatly differing degrees—some only occasionally and others regularly. Examples above have illustrated how black Americans rely on active audience response as part of formal, as well as informal, talk. Respected black orators employ recurring phrases, not syntactic cohesion, to structure their speeches. Martin Luther

King's famous "I Have a Dream" speech is an excellent example; the key phrase is used as a refrain at the beginning and end of each topic. Afro-Americans also value allusions to their oral heritage, especially when they are used innovatively and indirectly. For instance, many young boys draw on the well-known fable of a monkey who signified himself into trouble with a lion by ridiculing the lion "till his ass was grass," that is, until he was beaten up. One boy's well-received version of a verbal threat became, *Nigger, it was a monkey one time wasn't satisfied till his ass was grass*—a remark that effectively squelched his opponent (Mitchell-Kernan 1972:327).

White Americans of many ethnicities make use of expressions that incorporate in-group cultural knowledge. Eastern European Jews have retained Yiddish words and phrases in their English and have translated other traditional expressions to create a form of English with a distinct cultural flavor. References to Jewish religion, law, history, and custom occur in everyday speech; features such as intonation and gesture are so well known that they serve as ethnic identity markers. For example, anyone who has celebrated the Jewish holiday Purim will recall the Biblical story of Haman, who nearly succeeded in his plan to exterminate all the Jews of Persia. Such a person will immediately recognize the implications of calling a political leader "a veritable Haman."

Jews, Turks, Middle Easterners, Chinese, and other Americans who have a strong sense of cultural tradition frequently use proverbs and old sayings to express a common view of the world. Rather than being dismissed as clichés, appropriately applied proverbs have the force of strong arguments, because they distil respected wisdom. A whole philosophy about parental responsibility is summed up in the phrase, "The apple never falls far from the tree"—a proverb shared by Americans descended from central European Jews and Germans, especially the tradition-minded Pennsylvania Germans. Anglo-Americans, on the other hand, have lost this respect for proverbs. "Wise Ben" Franklin's much-quoted "A penny saved is a penny earned" and "A stitch in time saves nine" no longer have the force of serious arguments.

Although ethnic language background is the most important determinant of preference among discourse styles, other demographic variables—such as class and gender—also affect orientation toward oral or literate style. Working-class speakers are more firmly within the oral tradition than their middle-class counterparts. Their social mobility is more restricted so they often need to communicate less outside their speech community. Their exposure to formal education is also shorter. Within any speech community, women tend to maintain orally-oriented styles of talk to a greater degree than men. Gossip, in particular, calls upon extensive shared knowledge, interests, and values (including the trustworthiness of the gossip partner). Gossip is characterized by extensive use of direct quotations rather than descriptions of the subject's behavior and thus recreates the face-to-face interaction. Sometimes actual mimickry is used. A successful exchange also involves affective features such as exaggerated intonation, laughing, and verbal and nonverbal expressions of encouragement by the listener, as well as formulaic openings and responses, such as *Have you heard the latest?, You don't say, Not really*, and *Well, I never.*

Speech communities which rely heavily on written communication have developed discourse strategies that depend far less on interaction between speaker and listener. Literacy not only removes the face-to-face component of communication; it creates the potential of a far wider, more diverse audience. Literacy-oriented speakers, therefore, are compelled to encode more information into their talk—by contextualizing their statements; by uttering them in a more obvious, often chronological sequence; by constructing overt connections between their topics; and by coming to a clear conclusion or summation. Rather than directly presenting feelings, they must make their attitudes toward a topic explicit in other ways—specifically, in evaluative statements. Among middle-class Americans, particularly those of Anglo-American background, even conversation within the family and the community has taken on a literacy-oriented style. Thus, as the two above examples of "sharing time" narratives illustrate, children may begin their schooling with very different discourse styles.

It is a literacy-oriented style of discourse that the schools attempt to teach. Analytic, abstract language is the goal; expository, not imaginative, writing is taught. At school, children become audience, not conversation partners. Verbal and nonverbal affective behavior is minimized. Known-answer questioning removes even the context of naturalness from interaction; no actual new information about the subject at hand is exchanged.

Indeed, literacy is the primary purpose of American education. Established teaching methods, however, demand that children enter into an entire culture of literacy in order to receive reading and writing skills. While it is crucial that all members of our complex, multicultural society be trained for context-independent, analytic communication, other forms of discourse remain highly effective in most everyday interchanges. An understanding of the situational and cultural appropriateness of the various styles of communication would better enable the schools to teach orally-oriented students and, simultaneously, to enrich the verbal repertoires of pupils whose speech communities prepare them primarily in literate modes of discourse.

LANGUAGE AS A SOCIAL ISSUE

In the decade of the 1980s, Americans find themselves engaged in major controversy over the nature and future of their society. As the language community histories in the preceding chapters illustrate, such debate is not new. The public sense of urgency concerning linguistic issues has waxed and waned at various times throughout the past two hundred years. Yet, in each era of redefinition of national identity and purpose, the language question has reemerged. And now, once again, fundamental differences of opinion about American society have come to be couched in terms of the dangers or benefits of multilingualism, bilingual education, and standardization of American English usage.

Thus language policy plays a critical role in American life and social policy. Yet, while Americans have debated these issues hotly and long, there has never been an attempt to formulate a national language policy, nor has systematic investigation into the nature of American language problems been authorized. Unlike most nations, the United States has no language planning body. There is no national consensus about the importance of language in social identity and behavior. Nor, indeed, is there sufficient research upon which to base informed discussion.

The material in this volume suggests several critical contexts for American language planning and for thoughtful consideration of contemporary linguistic concerns. First, policy must reflect the facts of American social and cultural history. What factors have forced some Americans to give up their native tongues, and what factors have prevented others from entering the linguistic mainstream? How are claims to language autonomy legitimated? Has linguistic separatism in fact ever led to political separatism in this country? Second, it cannot disregard the personal values of the communities that make up the American nation. Does language maintenance contribute to community and family integrity? Why do monolingual English-speaking third-generation Americans establish ethnic schools in which they and their children study the language of their forebears? What cultural or religious values are lost in the translation to standard English? Third, specifically American language issues cannot be understood separate from the general processes of linguistic change and language contact.

The linguistic research represented here, and especially in this chapter, demonstrates that, for many Americans, speech is an indicator of cultural identity second in importance only to physical appearance. Further, accent, language choice, verbal style, choice of words, phrases, and gestures act as a primary vehicle for creative expression by individuals and by groups.

Still, prevailing mainstream attitudes deny any relationship between language and culture, arguing that revocation of language rights in no way compromises the integrity of cultural freedoms upon which our nation was constituted. Paradoxically, while language is generally viewed as nothing but a means of communication, standard English is held up as the only appropriate embodiment of the national character. Similarly, opinions about the status of American language vacillate between two poles: "[We are] half convinced that the country is going to the dogs linguistically and half dubious that we really do have language problems" (Fishman 1981:35).

As with other questions of social and cultural import, the truth will lie somewhere between the extremes. The United States is not in danger of dissolution into linguistic factions. Yet there are pressing national concerns in the areas of education, equality of opportunity, and personal and community self-determination. If we are to resolve these conflicts in the best national interest, we must all be prepared to educate ourselves about American language history and the nature of linguistic change.

FURTHER STUDY IN MULTICULTURALISM AND PUBLIC POLICY

READINGS

ALATIS, JAMES E., ed. *Current Issues in Bilingual Education. Georgetown University Round Table on Languages and Linguistics 1980.* Washington, D.C.: Georgetown University Press, 1980.
Theoretical and practical articles on bilingual education.

ALATIS, JAMES E., ed. *International Dimensions of Bilingual Education.*

Georgetown University Round Table on Languages and Linguistics 1978. Washington, D.C.: Georgetown University Press, 1978.
More than half these articles focus on the United States.

ANDERSON, THEODORE, and MILDRED BOYER, eds. *Bilingual Schooling in the United States*, 2 vols. Washington, D.C.: U.S. Government Printing Office, 1970.
A good general account.

BURLING, ROBBINS. *English in Black and White*. New York: Holt, Rinehart and Winston, 1973.
Nontechnical description of Black English Vernacular with thoughtful comments on educational implications.

CAZDEN, COURTNEY B., VERA P. JOHN, and DELL HYMES, eds. *Functions of Language in the Classroom*. New York: Teachers College Press, 1972.
Articles on intercultural communication in the classroom.

CHRISTIAN, DONNA. *Language Arts and Dialect Differences*. Arlington, Va.: Center for Applied Linguistics, 1979.
Short, nontechnical pamphlet for teachers.

EPSTEIN, NOEL. *Language, Ethnicity, and the Schools: Policy Alternatives for Bilingual-Bicultural Education*. Washington, D.C.: The George Washington University Institute for Educational Leadership, 1977.

KOCHMAN, THOMAS, ed. *Rappin' and Stylin' Out: Communication in Urban Black America*. Urbana: University of Illinois Press, 1972.
Readable articles on communicational strategies and speech events in the black community.

LOURIE, MARGARET A., and NANCY FAIRES CONKLIN, eds. *A Pluralistic Nation: The Language Issue in the United States*. Rowley, Mass.: Newbury House Publishers, 1978.
See "Part III: Educational Implications" for articles on classroom issues for blacks, Appalachians, American Indians, non-English speakers.

WHITEMAN, MARCIA FARR, ed. *Reactions to Ann Arbor: Vernacular Black English and Education*. Arlington, Va.: Center for Applied Linguistics, 1980.
Articles on evaluating and teaching speakers of Black English Vernacular.

WOLFRAM, WALT, LANCE POTTER, NANCY M. YANOFSKY, and ROGER W. SHUY. *Reading and Dialect Differences*. Arlington, Va.: Center for Applied Linguistics, 1979.
Short, nontechnical pamphlet for teachers.

ACTIVITIES

1. Investigate state and local policies pertaining to minority languages in your area. These might include local ordinances mandating bilingual

ballots, street signs, and public postings. What is the status of bilingual education legislation in your state?

2. If there are bilingual education programs in your area, find out what pedagogical models are followed, what curricular materials are used, and which students are served. Try to interview teachers, parents, students, and school administrators about the goals of their programs (e.g. are they assimilationist or maintenance-oriented?). Also ask about their attitudes toward bilingual education. Do they all agree with one another? The same kinds of questions can be asked about bidialectal education.

3. Look carefully at the student essay reprinted in the Appendix. Use Table 21 to determine which of this student's writing problems derive from the interference of Black English Vernacular. Which other problems can you attribute to his inexperience with the written medium? If you were the teacher who had received this paper, how would you help this student improve his writing?

4. Observe the structure of interaction between children and adults in a family or classroom setting. What sorts of rhetorical strategies do adults use to teach, praise, correct, and discipline children? How do children gain and retain adult attention? How do family strategies and classroom strategies compare?

5. Tape record casual conversation between peers. As you replay the tape, determine who talks most, who initiates conversation, who sets the topic, who interrupts, who ends the conversation. Do the speakers tend to give information in the form of descriptive analysis or as stories? Is the structure of conversation different for same-sex and cross-sex pairs?

6. Study the nonverbal component of interaction. Watch the head for such gestures as smiling, frowning, glancing, staring, looking down, covering the face, nodding. Watch the body for sitting and standing postures, use of hands, touching, and interpersonal distance. Notice particularly how these vary according to ethnicity and gender. What is the effect of intercultural differences?

APPALACHIAN ENGLISH

An Appalachian informant (Inf), a 67-year-old retired miner, speaks with a fieldworker (FW) who tape records the conversation:

FW: Did you read in the paper, a Huntington paper, where this couple had a young girl come in and babysit with their six-weeks-old daughter and while they were away, the parents were away, this girl had some friends in and they started taking pills, and she apparently went crazy or something and she put the baby in the oven, she thought that she was cooking a turkey.

INF: No, I didn't read that.

FW: That was in the news.

INF: But my aunt one time, she left the oven door down to put out a little more heat in the kitchen, it was in the wintertime, the old cat got up in 'ere to cool down to where he liked it and got in 'ere and set down and somebody come along, closed the oven door, so the next morning she gets up and builds a fire in the old coal range and baked the cat. She opened the door to put her bread in to bake it and there set the cat. Hide done busted off his skull and fell down and his meat just come off'n his bones.

FW: Oh, you're kidding!

Inf: It's a fact.

FW: Oh, isn't that awful?

Inf: Oh, I want to tell you one, maybe I shouldn't on this thing, but I'm a-gonna tell it anyway. My aunt was sick, and my uncle cooked breakfast. So, he washed his dishes up and everything and went out and harnessed up his horses to go plowing and run his hands in his pockets. Well, he hunted for the dishrag first, he couldn't find it. So he got him a new one, went out and harnessed his horses after while and went on to work and him, he chewed tobacco, you know, and reached his hand in his pocket to get him a chew of tobacco and found his dishrag. He'd stuck it in his pocket!

Inf: Do you remember any more interesting stories, Ike? Like, cooking the cat?

Inf: No, not right off hand, now, if it come to a bunch of jokes I could tell you enough to run that thing crazy.

FW: Well, have you heard any good jokes lately?

Inf: Well, they wouldn't be fit for that. Uh, I laughted at John Parker. Do you know John Parker over at Ashmeade?

FW: No.

Inf: Him and me and Jack Stern, we went to Bath County, Virginia, coon hunting. Went up to Leroy Buzzie's. And before I forgets I wanna tell you there's a Leroy Buzzie lived up there, and Al Crawley and Chuck McCoy, all of 'em lived in the same hollow 'ere.

FW: Buzzie. Where did you go, up in Bath County?

Inf: Bath County, Virginia. Up on Little Bath Creek.

FW: I think that's where Charley goes every year.

Inf: Yeah, I expect it is. Well, now they've got a cabin back down this side of that. Way down this side.

FW: They're mountain people, aren't they, Ike?

Inf: No, not really. No . . . They . . . he used to be an Army man, the old man Leroy Buzzie, see, he's dead now. He was a retired Army man, and, we went up 'ere and John supposedly had a sack to put the coon in if we caught one. We's gonna try to bring it back alive, so we tromped through the woods 'til along about six o'clock in the morning. The dogs treed up a big hollow chestnut oak, and we proceeded to cut the thing down. It's about three or four inches all the way around. About four foot through the stump. We tied the dogs and cut the thing down. Well, we cut it down and turned one dog loose, and he went down in that thing, way down in the old hollow of the tree and it forked, and we couldn't get up in there so he backed out and he tied 'im. And we's a-gonna chop the coon out if it was in there, I's kinda halfway thought maybe it just treed a possum or something. Well, I chopped in and lo and behold, right on top of the dang coon. Eighteen pounder, Jack Stern says, kitten coon. I run in with the axe handle down in behind him to keep him from getting out or backing down in the tree. He reached, fooled around and got him by the hind legs and pulled that thing out it looked big as a sheep to me. Turned 'im loose, he said "kitten, Hell." We had an old carbide light and he turned that over and the lights were . . . that's all the light we had. And, we had to hunt it then and the dogs took right after the coon right down the holler and the dogs caught it and Jack beat us all down there. Went down there and he's a-holding three dogs in one hand and the coon in the other hand. And they's all a-trying to bite the coon and the coon a-trying to bite Jack and the dogs, and Jack pulled out a sack and it wasn't a dang thing but an old pillow case that Maggie had used, his wife, it was about wore out. So we fumbled around 'ere and finally got that coon in that sack and he aimed to close the top of it and the coon just tore the thing in half, in two, and down the holler he went again. With that sack on him, half of it and we caught that thing, and you know, E.F. Wurst finally pulled off his coveralls and we put that thing down in one of the legs of his coveralls and tied that coon up. He's tearing up everything we could get, we couldn't hold him he's so stout. And I brought that thing home and kept 'im about a month, fed 'im apples and stuff to eat so we could eat 'im. Well, I did I killed him and tried eat that thing, I'd just soon eat a tom-cat or a polecat, I wouldn't make much difference. And, that's about the best coon hunt I believe I was on.*

PENNSYLVANIA GERMAN

A humorous story from Pennsylvania German folk literature:

Pᴇɴɴsʏʟᴠᴀɴɪᴀ Gᴇʀᴍᴀɴ Tᴇxᴛ

Diefe Gedonke

Ess wohr goot wedder fer fische. Der parre wohr am fische uf ee seidt fun die grick un eens fun seine eldischter wohr am fische uf die onner seidt. Iwwereweil hutt der parre en beis grickt, un er hutt en wunderbohrer scheener fisch g'heecheldt—eens fun denne oss mer nett lieye braych defun. Er hutt g'schpielt mitt den fisch, fer'n longi tzeit. Der eldischter hutt tzugeguckt.

Endlich iss der fisch miedt warre un hutt gerhucht owwe uf'm wasser.

*From Walt Wolfram and Donna Christian, *Appalachian Speech* (Arlington, Va.: Center for Applied Linguistics, 1976), pp. 180–81. Reprinted with permission of the publisher.

Der parre hutt der fisch geech sich getzoge un wie er der fisch schier gohr haldt hatte, hutt macht sich der fisch ee letschter tzuckt. Er hutt die ongel ferbruche un hutt sich ferschlupt unnich's wasser.

Der parre hutt datte g'huckt und hutt geguckt oss wonn der ferschondt hutt schtill schtee deet. Der eldischter hutt die gons g'schickt g'seehne. Er hutt so schpettlich iwwer's wasser niwwer gegrische, "Parre was bischt am denke?" "Well," sawgt der parre, "ich binn am denke wass du sawge deetscht."

ENGLISH TRANSLATION

Deep Thoughts

It was good weather for fishing. The preacher was fishing on one side of the creek and one of his elders was fishing on the other side. After a while the preacher got a bite, and he hooked a very beautiful fish—one that one need not lie about. He played with the fish, for a long time. The elder watched.

Finally the fish became tired and rested on the water. The preacher pulled the fish toward himself and as he had almost got hold of the fish, the fish made one last pull. He broke the hook and disappeared underneath the water.

The preacher sat there and looked out where it had disappeared and stood still. The elder had seen the whole story. He finally called across the water, "Preacher what are you thinking about?" "Well," said the preacher, "I am thinking about what you would say."

STANDARD GERMAN TRANSLATION

Tiefe Gedanken

Es war gutes Wetter für das Fischen. Der Pfarrer war beim Fischen auf einer Seite von dem Flüßchen und einer von seinen Älteren war auf der anderen Seite. In kurzer Zeit hatte der Pfarrer ein Anbeißen, und er hat einen wunderbaren, schönen Fisch gefangen—einen von dem man nicht lügen muß. Er hat mit dem Fisch eine lange Zeit gespielt. Der Ältester hat zugeguckt.

Endlich ist der Fisch müde geworden und hat sich oben auf dem Wasser gerastet. Der Pfarrer hat den Fisch gegen sich gezogen und als er den Fisch beinahe festgehalten hatte, hat sich der Fisch eine letzte Zuckung gemacht. Er hat die Angel gebrochen und hat sich unterhalb das Wasser verschlüpft.

Der Pfarrer hat da gehockt und hat hinausgeguckt, wo er verschwunden hatte und es still stand. Der Ältester hat die ganze Geschichte gesehen. Er hat endlich über das Wasser gegrüßt: "Pfarrer, was denkst du?" "Nun," sagte der Pfarrer, "ich denke nach, was du sagen würdest."

GULLAH

An elderly woman describes a severe food shortage on Edisto Island. In addition to the phonetic symbols represented in Tables A and B, this selection uses the following: /ɟ/ represents a voiced palatal stop (somewhere between English /g/ and /ǰ/); / ~ / over vowels indicates nasalization of the vowel; over n / ~ / represents /ny/, a nasal with palatal articulation (as in Spanish señor).

/ɔi sɛ: "dɛm bəkrə sɛn fid yɛ fə fid wi,
I say, "Them white people [the Red Cross] send feed here to feed we,
an dɛm ča əm ɟi dɪ
and them [the white people on Edisto Island] carry it [and] give [it to] the

ñɔŋ pipl wɔt də wək dɛ ɔn dɛm ples. de en də ɟi əm no
young people what were working there on them place. They ain't give it [to] no

wɪdo. dɛm də ča əm də ɟi əm dɪ pipl wɔt haw
widow. Them were carrying it [and] were giving it [to] the people what have

man n waɪf n čɪlən də wək fə dɛm."
man and wife and children working for them."

de ẽ ɟi wi nən. de lɔ sɛ wi tu ol. wi čã wək fə
They ain't give we none. They say [that] we too old. We can't work for

dɛm. yɛs mam! nɔu də fɔɪw ə wi ol pipl dɛ ẽ
them. Yes, Mam! Now there [are] five of we old people there [who] ain't

ɟit "taŋkɪ." si? fɔɪw! ẽ ɟit "taŋkɪ." si? dɛm dɛ
get [a] "thank you." See? Five! Ain't get [a] "thank you." See? Them there

də kəmplen. ɔɪ tɛl əm ɔɪ dõ kəmplen. ɔɪ lɛf ɔl
[the old people] complain. I tell them I don't complain. I leave all

tɪŋ in gɔd han. ɔɪ sɛ: "sistə ɟeni," ɔɪ sɛ, "gɔdz gɔɪn mɛk diz
thing in God hand. I say: "Sister Janie," I say, "God's going [to] make these

bəkrə ɟəmp əp ɔn ɛdɪsto." ɔɪ sɛ: "gɔdz gɔɪn in dɛm bɛd n
white people jump up on Edisto." I say, "God's going in them bed and

tək dɛm aʊt." ɔɪ tɛl əm so. de ẽ—nən əw əm—bɪn dɛ tɔk
take them out." I tell them so. They ain't—none of them—been there talk

lɔŋ tɔɪm. wɛn de si mi, de aks ples fə sɪt dɔʊŋ aftə unə gɔn.
[in a] long time. When they see me, they ask place to sit down after you gone.

. . . yu no wɔt dɛm pe fə bin? yu no wɔt dɛm pe fə
. . . You know what them pay for bean? You know what them pay for

bin? fɔɪw n wən sɛnt fə—wɛn yu pɪk əp dɛm bin—dat lɔɪmə
bean? Five and one cent for—when you pick up them bean—that lima

bin—yu ē nɛwə gɔt bət fɔɪw n wən sɛnt in tred. tu kret kəm
bean—you ain't never got but five and one cent in trade. Two crate come

tu—ē nəf fə bɔɪ mɔɪ bakə. dat dɪ dɛwəl we de də
to—ain't enough to buy my tobacco. That [is] the devil way they are

ɟi yu nɔʊ. dɛn yu nɔk ɔf wɛn sən hɔt. dɛn yu go bak in
giving you now. Then you knock off when sun hot. Then you go back in

fil. dɛn wɛn yu ho kɔn, de ɟi yu twɛlw sɛnt fə ho kɔn—
field. Then when you hoe corn, they give you twelve cent to hoe corn—

twɛlw sɛnt—twɛlw sɛnt—ɔl de. wɛn de kɔl bak fə go bak
twelve cent—twelve cent—all day. When they call [you] back to go back

yu go raɪt bak in dɪ sem sən. mi ē kəmɪn bak in dat bəkrə
you go right back in the same sun. Me ain't coming back in that white man

fil an du dat tɪŋ. nɔt mi! no! nɔt dɪšɛ dɔɪanə. dɔɪanə dən
field and do that thing. Not me! No! Not this here Diana. Diana done

bɪn tru so məč tɪŋ in rɛbəl tɔɪm: tɛk wɔtə, pɪɟɪn, n ɔl dɛm tɪŋ./
been through so much thing in slavery: take water, piggin, and all that thing.*

BLACK ENGLISH VERNACULAR

Larry, a fifteen-year-old core member of the Jets, a Harlem teenage hangout group, speaks with fieldworker John Lewis:

JL: What happens to you after you die? Do you know?

LARRY: Yeah, I know. (What?) After they put you in the ground, your body turns into—ah—bones, an' shit.

JL: What happens to your spirit?

LARRY: Your spirit—soon as you die, your spirit leaves you. (And where does the spirit go?) Well, it all depends . . . (On what?) You know, like some people say if you're good an' shit, your spirit goin' t'heaven . . . 'n' if you bad, your spirit goin' to hell. Well, bullshit! Your spirit goin' to hell anyway, good or bad.

JL: Why?

---

*Adapted from Lorenzo Dow Turner, *Africanisms in the Gullah Dialect* (Ann Arbor: University of Michigan Press, 1974), pp. 264–65. Used by permission of Lois Turner Williams.

LARRY: Why? I'll tell you why. 'Cause, you see, doesn' nobody really know that it's a God, y'know, 'cause I mean I have seen black gods, pink gods, white gods, all color gods, and don't nobody know it's really a God. An' when they be sayin' if you good, you goin' t'heaven, tha's bullshit, 'cause you ain't goin' to no heaven, 'cause it ain't no heaven for you to go to.

JL: Well, if there's no heaven, how could there be a hell?

LARRY: I mean—ye-eah. Well, let me tell you, it ain't no hell, 'cause this is hell right here, y'know! (This is hell?) Yeah, this is hell right here!

JL: . . . but, just say that there is a God, what color is he? White or black?

LARRY: Well, if it is a God . . . I wouldn' know what color, I couldn' say,—couldn' nobody say what color he is or really *would* be.

JL: But now, jus' suppose there was a God—

LARRY: Unless'n they say . . .

JL: No, I was jus' sayin' jus' suppose there is a God, would he be white or black?

LARRY: . . . He'd be white, man.

JL: Why?

LARRY: Why? I'll tell you why. 'Cause the average whitey out here got everything, you dig? And the nigger ain't got shit, y'know? Y'un-nerstan'? So—um—for—in order for *that* to happen, you know it ain't no black God that's doin' that bullshit.*

STUDENT ESSAY BY BLACK ENGLISH VERNACULAR SPEAKER

This essay was written by a black community college student after reading the first chapter of Norman Podhoretz's *Making It: The Brutal Bargain*, which describes Podhoretz's embarrassing experience in a "fancy" restaurant. This student rarely responded to class assignments with more than a sentence or two and dropped out of school the term after this essay was written.

[An Embarrassing Experience]

When I were in High school we had a football Banquite and I had not Ben to a fromer accesson Befor. and I also included a young Lady along.

I were like the young man in the story we read in class.

I came to the Banquite Proper dressed But I did not have no table Manner. Everyone Began to set down, I did not know I sirpose to assit the young lady with chair until she told me. after about 30 min the guss spoke Began to

---

*From William Labov, "The Logic of Nonstandard English," in *Georgetown Monograph in Languages and Linguistics No. 22* (Washington, D.C.: Georgetown University Press, 1970), pp. 12-13, 14, 15. Reprinted by permission of William Labov.

spake & I did not know when to Began to eat & after I saw all the other People eating I look around for my silverware, But I did not have any, than I tryed to get the water attanson. They finily Brage me my silverware. I though that were the lose embarrassment monet for tonight, But they had just Began. The main dish were chicken & it were fride cripe & when I Bit off it, it would make a loud nose and the other People would look aroung at me & my date would look the other way. From then on I promer myself I would learn good table manner.

HAWAIIAN CREOLE

Two Honolulu high school girls speak to each other in "Hawaii-kine-talk," a partially decreolized form of Hawaiian Creole popular with teenagers:

    A: We goin' ha[ve] one pa'ty—I like you come, eh?

    B: Fo' what?

    A: Mus' goin' be one jam session.

    B: Whe[re] da *kine* [it] goin' be dough?

    A: Puamana Day Ca[re] Cente[r].

    B: Wha' *kine* [kind of] food you folks goin' get?

    A: Ah—like *laulaus* [meat or vegetables steamed in ti or banana leaves], some drinks, an' cookies, ice cream, an' ah, all da *kine* can think of.

    B: Da *kine* records—what *kine* you folks goin' get?

    A: All rock an' roll.

    B: An' da gues[ts]—what *kine*?

    A: Ah, le's see. Ha'dly any *haoles* [white people] . . .

    B: Wha' time da pa'ty goin' be?

    A: Aroun'—le's see, I don' know. I tell you *bumbye* [later].

    B: *Bumbye*!

    A: I got tell my mode[r].

    B: What I goin' tell my mode[r]? My mode[r] tell, "What *kine* pa'ty dis goin' be? What time? No mo[re] time? [No time at all?]"*

*Adapted from *Da Kine Talk: From Pidgin to Standard English in Hawaii*, by Elizabeth Ball Carr. Copyright © 1972 by The University Press of Hawaii. Used by permission.

References

ADLER, SOL. 1979. *Poverty Children and Their Language: Implications for Teaching and Treating*. New York: Grune and Stratton.

ALATIS, JAMES E., ed. 1978. *International Dimensions of Bilingual Education. Georgetown University Round Table on Languages and Linguistics 1978*. Washington, D.C.: Georgetown University Press.

———, ed. 1980. *Current Issues in Bilingual Education. Georgetown University Round Table on Languages and Linguistics 1980*. Washington, D.C.: Georgetown University Press.

ALLEN, HAROLD B. 1973–5. *The Linguistic Atlas of the Upper Midwest*, 2 vols. Minneapolis: University of Minnesota Press.

———, and GARY N. UNDERWOOD, eds. 1971. *Readings in American Dialectology*. New York: Appleton-Century-Crofts.

ANDERSON, THEODORE, and MILDRED BOYER, eds. 1970. *Bilingual Schooling in the United States*, 2 vols. Washington, D.C.: U.S. Government Printing Office.

ATWOOD, E. BAGBY. 1950. "Grease and Greasy: A Study of Geographical Variation." *University of Texas Studies in English* 29:249–60.

———. 1962. *The Regional Vocabulary of Texas*. Austin: University of Texas Press.

BALL, ELIZABETH CARR. 1972. *Da Kine Talk*. Honolulu: The University Press of Hawaii.

BARBER, CARROLL G. 1973. "Trilingualism in an Arizona Yaqui Village." In *Bilingualism in the Southwest*, edited by Paul R. Turner, pp. 295–318. Tucson: University of Arizona Press.

BARKER, GEORGE C. 1975. "Pachuco: An American-Spanish Argot and Its Social Function in Tucson, Arizona." In Hernández-Chavez, Cohen, and Beltramo, pp. 183–201.

BAUMAN, RICHARD C. 1972. "An Ethnographic Framework for the Investigation of Communicative Behaviors." In *Language and Cultural Diversity in American Education*, edited by Roger D. Abrahams and Rudolph C. Troike, pp. 154–66. Englewood Cliffs, N.J.: Prentice-Hall.

BERTHOFF, ROWLAND TAPPAN. 1953. *British Immigrants in Industrial America: 1790–1950*. Cambridge, Mass.: Harvard University Press.

BOGGS, STEPHEN T. 1972. "The Meaning of Questions and Narratives to Hawaiian Children." In Cazden, John, and Hymes, pp. 299–327.

BOLINGER, DWIGHT. 1981. "Voice Imprints." *The New York Times Magazine* 26 July, pp. 7–8.

BOWEN, J. DONALD, and JACOB ORNSTEIN, eds. 1976. *Studies in Southwest Spanish*. Rowley, Mass.: Newbury House.

BRIGHT, ELIZABETH S. 1971. *A Word Geography of Colorado and Nevada*. Berkeley: University of California Press.

BURLING, ROBBINS. 1973. *English in Black and White*. New York: Holt, Rinehart and Winston.

BYERS, PAUL, and HAPPIE BYERS. 1972. "Nonverbal Communication and the Education of Children." In Cazden, John, and Hymes, pp. 3–31.

CÁRDENAS, DANIEL N. 1975. "Mexican Spanish." In Hernández-Chavez, Cohen, and Beltramo, pp. 1–5.

CASCAITO, JAMES, and DOUGLAS RADCLIFF-UMSTEAD. 1975. "An Italo-English Dialect." *American Speech* 50:5–17.

CAZDEN, COURTNEY B., ROBERT CARASSCO, ABDIL ABEL MALDONADO-GUZMAN, and FREDERICK ERIKSON. 1980. "The Contribution of Ethnographic Research to Bicultural Bilingual Education." In Alatis, pp. 64–80.

CAZDEN, COURTNEY B., and DAVID K. DICKINSON. 1981. "Language in Education: Standardization vs. Cultural Pluralism." In Ferguson and Heath, pp. 446–68.

CAZDEN, COURTNEY B., VERA P. JOHN, and DELL HYMES, eds. 1972. *Functions of Language in the Classroom*. New York: Teachers College Press.

CHALL, J. 1978. *Minimum Competency Testing. Harvard Graduate School of Education Association Bulletin* 22.

CHRISTIAN, DONNA. 1979. *Language Arts and Dialect Differences*. Arlington, Va.: Center for Applied Linguistics.

COHEN, ANDREW D. 1975. "Bilingual Schooling and Spanish Language Maintenance: An Experimental Analysis." *The Bilingual Review* 2, no. 1:3–12.

CONKLIN, NANCY FAIRES. 1978. "The Language of the Majority: Women and American English." In Lourie and Conklin, pp. 222–37.

COOK, STANLEY. 1969. *Language Change and the Emergence of an Urban Dialect in Utah*. Dissertation, University of Utah.

COOLEY, RALPH E. 1978a. "Delaware Language and Culture: A Case Study." Paper presented at Speech Communication Association Second Summer Conference on Intercultural Communication, Tampa, Fla.

———. 1978b. "An Investigation into How a Language Changes Late in Its Life." Paper presented at Top Three Program, Speech and Language Sciences Division, Speech Communication Association, Minneapolis, Minn.

———. 1979. "Spokes in a Wheel: A Linguistic and Rhetorical Analysis of Native American Public Discourse." In *Proceedings of the Fifth Annual Meeting*, pp. 552–58. Berkeley Linguistics Society.

———, and RAMONA BALLENGER. 1982. "Cultural Retention Programs and Their Impact on Native Americans." In St. Clair and Leap.

CRADDOCK, JERRY R. 1981. "New World Spanish." In Ferguson and Heath, pp. 196–211.

CUMMINS, JAMES. 1980. "The Construct of Language Proficiency in Bilingual Education." In Alatis, pp. 81–103.

CZARNECKI, GREG. 1973. "Detroit's Polish Community: A Matched-Guise Study." Mimeographed. Department of Linguistics, University of Michigan.

DECAMP, DAVID. 1971. "The Pronunciation of English in San Francisco." In Williamson and Burke, pp. 549–69.

DILLARD, J.L. 1972. *Black English: Its History and Usage in the United States*. New York: Random House.

DINNERSTEIN, LEONARD, ROGER L. NICHOLS, and DAVID M. REIMERS. 1979. *Natives and Strangers: Ethnic Groups and the Building of America*. New York: Oxford University Press.

DREYFUSS, GAIL RAIMI. 1978. "Pidgin and Creole Languages in the United States." In Lourie and Conklin, pp. 61–77.

DRIVER, HAROLD E., and WILLIAM C. MASSEY. 1957. *Comparative Studies of North American Indians. Transactions of the American Philosophical Society* n.s. 47, pt. 2.

DUBOIS, BETTY LOU, and ISABEL M. CROUCH, eds. 1978. *American Minority Women in Sociolinguistic Perspective. International Journal of the Sociology of Language* 17.

DUMONT, ROBERT V., JR., and MURRAY L. WAX. 1969. "Cherokee School Society and the Intercultural Classroom." *Human Organization* 28:217–26.

ECCLES, W.J. 1972. *France in America.* New York: Harper and Row.

ELÍAS-OLIVARES, LUCÍA. 1979. "Language Use in a Chicano Community: A Sociolinguistic Approach." In Pride, pp. 120–34.

EPSTEIN, NOEL. 1977. *Language, Ethnicity, and the Schools: Policy Alternatives for Bilingual–Bicultural Education.* Washington, D.C.: The George Washington University Institute for Educational Leadership.

ERVIN-TRIPP, SUSAN. 1968. "An Analysis of the Interaction of Language, Topic, and Listener." In Fishman, pp. 192–211.

———. 1978. "'What Do Women Sociolinguists Want?': Prospects for a Research Field." In DuBois and Crouch, pp. 17–28.

———. 1979. "Children's Sociolinguistic Competence and Dialect Diversity." In Pride, pp. 27–41.

ESPINOSA, AURELIA M. 1975. "Speech Mixture in New Mexico: The Influence of the English Language on New Mexican Spanish." In Hernández-Chavez, Cohen, and Beltramo, pp. 99–114.

FERGUSON, CHARLES A., and SHIRLEY BRICE HEATH, eds. 1981. *Language in the USA.* Cambridge: Cambridge University Press.

FERNANDEZ-FLOREZ, DARIO. 1971. *The Spanish Heritage in the United States,* 3rd ed. Madrid: Publicaciones Españolas.

FISCHER, JOHN L. 1958. "Social Influence in the Choice of a Linguistic Variant." *Word* 14:47–56.

FISHMAN, JOSHUA A. 1981. "The Need for Language Planning in the United States." In *Profession 81,* pp. 34–36. New York: Modern Language Association.

———, ed. 1968. *Readings in the Sociology of Language.* The Hague: Mouton.

———, et al. 1966. *Language Loyalty in the United States: The Maintenance and Perpetuation of Non-English Mother Tongues by American Ethnic and Religious Groups.* The Hague: Mouton.

FUCHS, ESTELLE, and ROBERT J. HAVIGHURST. 1972. *To Live on This Earth: American Indian Education.* Garden City, N.Y.: Doubleday.

GILBERT, GLENN G. 1972. *Linguistic Atlas of Texas German.* Austin: University of Texas Press.

———, ed. 1971. *The German Language in America.* Austin: University of Texas Press.

GILES, HOWARD, ed. 1977. *Language, Ethnicity, and Intergroup Relations.* New York: Academic Press.

GREELEY, ANDREW M., and WILLIAM C. MCCREADY. 1974. *Ethnicity in the United States: A Preliminary Reconnaissance.* New York: John Wiley and Sons.

GUMPERZ, JOHN J. 1977. "Sociocultural Knowledge in Conversational Inference." In Saville-Troike, pp. 191–211.

———, and EDUARDO HERNÁNDEZ-CHAVEZ. 1972. "Bilingualism, Bidialectalism, and Classroom Interaction." In Cazden, John, and Hymes, pp. 84–108.

———. 1975. "Cognitive Aspects of Bilingual Communication." In Hernández-Chavez, Cohen, and Beltramo, pp. 154–63.

GUMPERZ, JOHN J., and DELL HYMES, eds. 1964. *The Ethnography of Communication. American Anthropologist* 66, no. 6, pt. 2.

HANCOCK, IAN F. 1974. "Patterns of English Lexical Adoption in an American Dialect of Romanés." In *Southwest Languages and Linguistics in Educational Perspective (SWALLOW III)*, edited by Gina Cantoni Harvey and M.F. Heiser, pp. 83–108. San Diego: Institute for Cultural Pluralism, San Diego State University.

HASSELMO, NILS. 1974. *Amerikasvenska: En bok om språkutvecklingen in Svensk-Amerika*. Stockholm: Esselte Studium.

HAUGEN, EINAR. 1969. *The Norwegian Language in America: A Study in Bilingual Behavior*. Bloomington: Indiana University Press.

———. 1970. "The Analysis of Linguistic Borrowing." In *English Linguistics: An Introductory Reader*, edited by Harold Hungerford, Jay Robinson, and James Sledd, pp. 429–56. Glenview, Ill.: Scott, Foresman.

HENLEY, NANCY M. 1975. "Power, Sex, and Nonverbal Communication." In Thorne and Henley, pp. 184–203.

HERNÁNDEZ-CHAVEZ, EDUARDO, ANDREW D. COHEN, and ANTHONY F. BELTRAMO, eds. 1975. *El Lenguaje de los Chicanos: Regional and Social Characteristics of Language Used by Mexican Americans*. Arlington, Va.: Center for Applied Linguistics.

HIGHAM, JOHN. 1955. *Strangers in the Land: Patterns of American Nativism 1860–1925*. New Brunswick, N.J.: Rutgers University Press.

HUDSON, R.A. 1980. *Sociolinguistics*. Cambridge: Cambridge University Press.

HYMES, DELL, ed. 1971. *Pidginization and Creolization of Languages*. Cambridge: Cambridge University Press.

IORIZZO, LUCIANO J., and SALVATORE MONDELLO. 1971. *The Italian-Americans*. New York: Twayne Publishers.

"It's Your Turn in the Sun." 1978. *Time* 16 October, pp. 48–61.

JOHN, VERA P. 1972. "Styles of Learning/Styles of Teaching: Reflections on the Education of Navajo Children." In Cazden, John, and Hymes, pp. 331–43.

JONES, MALDWYN ALLEN. 1960. *American Immigration*. Chicago: University of Chicago Press.

JUTRONIĆ, DUNJA. 1974. "The Serbo-Croatian Language in Steelton, Pa." *General Linguistics* 14:15–34.

———. 1976. "Language Maintenance and Language Shift of the Serbo-Croatian Language in Steelton, Pennsylvania." *General Linguistics* 16:166–86.

KARTTUNEN, FRANCES. 1977. "Finnish in America: A Case Study in Monogenerational Language Change." In *Sociocultural Dimensions of Language Change*, edited by Ben G. Blount and Mary Sanches, pp. 173–84. New York: Academic Press.

KEENAN, ELINOR OCHS, BAMBI B. SCHIEFFELIN, and MARTHA PLATT. 1978. "Questions of Immediate Concern." In *Questions and Politeness: Strategies for Social Interaction,* edited by Esther N. Goody, pp. 44–55. Cambridge: Cambridge University Press.

KENNARD, EDWARD A. 1963. "Linguistic Acculturation in Hopi." *International Journal of American Linguistics* 29:36–41.

KESSLER, CAROLYN, and MARY ELLEN QUINN. 1980. "Positive Effects of Bilingualism on Science Problem-Solving Abilities." In Alatis, pp. 295–308.

KLOSS, HEINZ. 1966. "German-American Language Maintenance Efforts." In Fishman et al., pp. 206–52.

———. 1977. *The American Bilingual Tradition*. Rowley, Mass.: Newbury House.

KOCHMAN, THOMAS. 1972a. "Toward an Ethnography of Black American Speech Behavior." In Kochman 1972b, pp. 241–64.

———, ed. 1972b. *Rappin' and Stylin' Out: Communication in Urban Black America*. Urbana: University of Illinois Press.

KURATH, HANS. 1939. *Handbook of the Linguistic Geography of New England*. Providence, R.I.: Brown University Press.

———. 1949. *A Word Geography of the Eastern United States*. Ann Arbor: University of Michigan Press.

———, and RAVEN I. MCDAVID, JR. 1961. *The Pronunciation of English in the Atlantic States*. Ann Arbor: University of Michigan Press.

LABOV, WILLIAM. 1966. *The Social Stratification of English in New York City*. Washington, D.C.: Center for Applied Linguistics.

———. 1970. *The Study of Non-Standard English*. Urbana: The National Council of Teachers of English.

———. 1972a. *Language in the Inner City: Studies in the Black English Vernacular*. Philadelphia: University of Pennsylvania Press.

———. 1972b. *Sociolinguistic Patterns*. Philadelphia: University of Pennsylvania Press.

LAFERRIERE, MARTHA. 1979. "Ethnicity in Phonological Variation and Change." *Language* 55:603–17.

LAKOFF, ROBIN. 1975. *Language and Woman's Place*. New York: Harper and Row.

LANCE, DONALD M. 1977. "Determining Dialect Boundaries in the United States by Means of Automatic Cartography." *Germanistische Linguistik* 3-4:289-303.

LEARSI, RUFUS. 1972. *The Jews in America: A History*, new ed. New York: KTAV Publishing House.

LEVINE, LEWIS, and HARRY J. CROCKETT, JR. 1966. "Speech Variation in a Piedmont Community: Postvocalic *r*." In Lieberson, pp. 204-36.

LIEBERSON, STANLEY. 1981a. "The Causes of Bilingualism Differ from the Causes of Mother-Tongue Shift." In *Language Diversity and Language Contact*, edited by Anwar S. Dil, pp. 126-30. Stanford, Cal.: Stanford University Press.

———. 1981b. "Language Shift in the United States: Some Demographic Clues." In *Language Diversity and Language Contact,* edited by Anwar S. Dil, pp. 158-72. Stanford, Cal.: Stanford University Press.

———, ed. 1966. *Explorations in Sociolinguistics. Sociological Inquiry* 36, no. 2.

LOPATA, HELENA ZNANIECKI. 1976. *Polish Americans: Status Competition in an Ethnic Community*. Englewood Cliffs, N.J.: Prentice-Hall.

LOURIE, MARGARET A., and NANCY FAIRES CONKLIN, eds. 1978. *A Pluralistic Nation: The Language Issue in the United States*. Rowley, Mass.: Newbury House.

LYMAN, STANFORD M. 1974. *Chinese Americans*. New York: Random House.

MANN, ARTHUR. 1979. *The One and the Many: Reflections on the American Identity*. Chicago: University of Chicago Press.

MARCKWARDT, ALBERT H. 1958. *American English*. New York: Oxford University Press.

MCCLURE, ERICA. 1977. "Aspects of Code-Switching in the Discourse of Bilingual Mexican-American Children." In Saville-Troike, pp. 93-115.

MCDAVID, RAVEN I., JR. 1958. "The Dialects of American English." In *The Structure of American English*, by W. Nelson Francis, pp. 480-543. New York: The Ronald Press.

———. 1980. *Varieties of American English*, edited by Anwar S. Dil. Stanford, Cal.: Stanford University Press.

MEIER, MATT S., and FELICIANO RIVERA. 1972. *The Chicanos: A History of Mexican Americans*. New York: Hill and Wang.

MELENDY, H. BRETT. 1977. *Asians in America: Filipinos, Koreans, and East Indians*. Boston: Twayne Publishers.

MENCKEN, H.L. 1977. *The American Language*. With annotations and new material by Raven I. McDavid, Jr., with the assistance of David W. Maurer. New York: Alfred A. Knopf.

MERCER, J.R., and W.C. BROWN. 1973. "Racial Differences in I.Q.: Fact or Artifact." In *The Fallacy of I.Q.,* edited by Carl Senna, pp. 56–113. New York: Third Press.

MICHAELS, SARAH, and JENNY COOK-GUMPERZ. 1979. "A Study of Sharing Time with First Grade Students: Discourse Narratives in the Classroom." In *Proceedings of the Fifth Annual Meeting,* pp. 647–60. Berkeley Linguistics Society.

MITCHELL-KERNAN, CLAUDIA. 1972. "Signifying, Loud-Talking, and Marking." In Kochman, pp. 315–35.

MORRILL, RICHARD L., and O. FRED DONALDSON. 1972. "Geographical Perspectives on the History of Black America." *Economic Geography* 48:1–23.

NICHOLS, PATRICIA C. 1978. "Black Women in the Rural South: Conservative and Innovative." In DuBois and Crouch, pp. 45–54.

———. 1981. "Creoles in the USA." In Ferguson and Heath, pp. 69–91.

NUNBERG, GEOFFREY. 1980. "The Speech of the New York City Upper Class." In Shopen and Williams, pp. 150–73.

ONG, WALTER. 1979. *Literacy and Orality in Our Time. Profession 79.* New York: Modern Language Association.

ORNSTEIN, JACOB. 1975. "The Archaic and the Modern in the Spanish of New Mexico." In Hernández-Chavez, Cohen, and Beltramo, pp. 6–12.

PATERNOST, JOSEPH. 1976. "Slovenian Language on Minnesota's Iron Range: Some Sociolinguistic Aspects of Language Maintenance and Language Shift." *General Linguistics* 16:95–150.

PEÑALOSA, FERNANDO. 1980. *Chicano Sociolinguistics: A Brief Introduction.* Rowley, Mass.: Newbury House.

PHILIPS, SUSAN U. 1972. "Participant Structures and Communicative Competence: Warm Springs Children in Community and Classroom." In Cazden, John, and Hymes, pp. 370–94.

PHILIPSEN, GERRY. 1975. "Speaking 'Like a Man' in Teamsterville: Culture Patterns of Role Enactment in an Urban Neighborhood." *The Quarterly Journal of Speech* 61:13–22.

PHILLIPS, ROBERT N., JR. 1975. "Variation in Los Angeles Spanish Phonology." In Hernández-Chavez, Cohen, and Beltramo, pp. 77–98.

PITT, LEONARD. 1966. *The Decline of the Californios: A Social History of the Spanish-Speaking Californians, 1846–1890.* Berkeley: University of California Press.

PRIDE, J.B., ed. 1979. *Sociolinguistic Aspects of Language Learning and Teaching.* Oxford: Oxford University Press.

PULTE, WILLIAM. 1979. "Cherokee: A Flourishing or Obsolescing Language?" In *Language and Society: Anthropological Issues,* edited by William C. McCormack and Steven A. Wurm, pp. 423–32. The Hague: Mouton.

REDLINGER, WENDY. 1978. "Mothers' Speech to Children in Bilingual Mexican-American Homes." In DuBois and Crouch, pp. 73–82.

REED, CARROLL E. 1977. *Dialects of American English*, rev. ed. Amherst: University of Massachusetts Press.

REINECKE, JOHN E. 1969. *Language and Dialect in Hawaii: A Sociolinguistic History to 1935,* edited by Stanley M. Tsuzaki. Honolulu: University of Hawaii Press.

REYES, ROGELIO. 1981. "Independent Convergence in Chicano and New York City Puerto Rican Bilingualism." In *Latino Language and Communicative Behavior*, edited by Richard P. Durán, pp. 39–48. Norwood, N.J.: Ablex.

RICKFORD, JOHN R. 1974. "The Insights of the Mesolect." In *Pidgins and Creoles: Current Trends and Prospects*, edited by David DeCamp and Ian F. Hancock, pp. 92–117. Washington, D.C.: Georgetown University Press.

———. 1977. "The Question of Prior Creolization in Black English." In *Pidgin and Creole Linguistics*, edited by Albert Valdman, pp. 190–221. Bloomington: Indiana University Press.

RYAN, E. BOUCHARD, and M.A. CARRANZA. 1977. "Ingroup and Outgroup Reactions to Mexican American Language Varieties." In Giles, pp. 59–82.

SALOUTOS, THEODORE. 1964. *The Greeks in the United States*. Cambridge, Mass.: Harvard University Press.

SAVILLE-TROIKE, MURIEL, ed. 1977. *Linguistics and Anthropology. Georgetown University Round Table on Languages and Linguistics 1977.* Washington, D.C.: Georgetown University Press.

SAWYER, JANET B. 1975. "Spanish-English Bilingualism in San Antonio, Texas." In Hernández-Chavez, Cohen, and Beltramo, pp. 77–98.

SEAMAN, P. DAVID. 1972. *Modern Greek and American English in Contact.* The Hague: Mouton.

SELLER, MAXINE. 1977. *To Seek America: A History of Ethnic Life in the United States.* New York: Jerome S. Ozer.

SHOPEN, TIMOTHY, and JOSEPH M. WILLIAMS, eds. 1980. *Standards and Dialects in English.* Cambridge, Mass.: Winthrop Publishers.

SHORES, DAVID L., and CAROL P. HINES, eds. 1977. *Papers in Language Variation.* University, Ala.: University of Alabama Press.

SHUY, ROGER W., WALTER A. WOLFRAM, and WILLIAM K. RILEY. 1967. *Linguistic Correlates of Social Stratification in Detroit Speech.* Washington, D.C.: U.S. Office of Education, Cooperative Research Project no. 6-1347.

———. 1968. *Field Techniques in an Urban Language Study.* Washington, D.C.: Center for Applied Linguistics.

SIMMONS, R.C. 1976. *The American Colonies: From Settlement to Independence.* New York: David McKay.

SIMON, JOHN. 1980. *Paradigms Lost: Reflections on Literacy and Its Decline.* New York: Clarkson N. Potter.

SMITH, RILEY B., and DONALD M. LANCE. 1979. "Standard and Disparate Varieties of English in the United States: Educational and Sociopolitical Implications." *International Journal of the Sociology of Language* 21:127–40.

SMITH-THIBODEAUX, JOHN. 1977. *Les Francophones de Louisiane.* Paris: Editions Entente.

SPOLSKY, BERNARD. 1978. "American Indian Bilingual Education." In *Case Studies in Bilingual Education*, edited by Bernard Spolsky and Robert L. Cooper, pp. 332–61. Rowley, Mass.: Newbury House.

ST. CLAIR, ROBERT, and WILLIAM LEAP, eds. 1982. *Language Renewal among American Indians.* Rosslyn, Va.: National Clearinghouse for Bilingual Education.

SWAIN, MERRILL. 1978. "Bilingual Education for the English-Speaking Canadian." In Alatis, pp. 141–54.

TANNEN, DEBORAH. 1980. "Implications of the Oral/Literate Continuum for Cross-Cultural Communication." In Alatis, pp. 326–47.

——. 1982. "Oral and Literate Strategies in Spoken and Written Narratives." *Language* 58:1–21.

TAYLOR, ALLAN R. 1981. "Indian Lingua Francas." In Ferguson and Heath, pp. 175–95.

TAYLOR, PHILIP. 1971. *The Distant Magnet: European Emigration to the U.S.A.* London: Eyre and Spottiswoode.

TEMPLIN, REBECCA. 1980. "Rock Point Community School: A Model for Bilingual Education." *Linguistic Reporter* 22, no. 9 (June):4, 11.

THORNE, BARRIE, and NANCY HENLEY, eds. 1975. *Language and Sex: Difference and Dominance.* Rowley, Mass.: Newbury House.

TRAUGOTT, ELIZABETH CLOSS. 1976. "Pidgins, Creoles, and the Origins of Vernacular Black English." In *Black English: A Seminar*, edited by Deborah Sears Harrison and Tom Trabasso, pp. 57–93. Hillsdale, N.J.: Lawrence Erlbaum Associates.

TRUDGILL, PETER. 1974. *Sociolinguistics: An Introduction.* Baltimore: Penguin Books.

TSUZAKI, STANLEY. 1971. "Coexistent Systems in Language Variation." In Hymes, pp. 327–39.

TURNER, LORENZO DOW. 1974. *Africanisms in the Gullah Dialect.* Ann Arbor: University of Michigan Press. Originally published 1949.

U.S. DEPARTMENT OF COMMERCE BUREAU OF CENSUS. 1982. *Provisional*

Estimates of Social, Economic, and Housing Characteristics. Washington, D.C.: U.S. Government Printing Office.

WAGGONER, DOROTHY. 1978. "Non-English Language Background Persons: Three U.S. Surveys." *TESOL Quarterly* 12:247-62.

WALKER, WILLARD. 1981. "Native American Writing Systems." In Ferguson and Heath, pp. 145-74.

WARD, CHARLES C. 1976. "The Serbian and Croatian Communities in Milwaukee." *General Linguistics* 16:151-65.

WARD, MARTHA COONFIELD. 1970. *An Ethnography of Linguistic Socialization: A Functional Approach.* Dissertation, Tulane University.

WATSON-GEGEO, KAREN ANN, and STEPHEN T. BOGGS. 1977. "From Verbal Play to Talk Story: The Role of Routines in Speech Events among Hawaiian Children." In *Child Discourse*, edited by Susan Ervin-Tripp and Claudia Mitchell-Kernan, pp. 67-90. New York: Academic Press.

WEAVER, GLENN. 1970. "Benjamin Franklin and the Pennsylvania Germans." In *The Aliens: A History of Ethnic Minorities in America*, edited by Leonard Dinnerstein and Frederic Cople Jaher, pp. 47-64. New York: Appleton-Century-Crofts.

WEINREICH, URIEL. 1974. *Languages in Contact: Findings and Problems.* The Hague: Mouton. Originally published 1953.

WESLAGER, C.A. 1972. *The Delaware Indians: A History.* New Brunswick, N.J.: Rutgers University Press.

WHATLEY, ELIZABETH M. 1980. "Black English: Implications of the Ann Arbor Decision for the Classroom." In Whiteman, pp. 61-76.

WHITEMAN, MARCIA FARR, ed. 1980. *Reactions to Ann Arbor: Vernacular Black English and Education.* Arlington, Va.: Center for Applied Linguistics.

WILLIAMSON, JUANITA V., and VIRGINIA M. BURKE, eds. 1971. *A Various Language: Perspectives on American Dialects.* New York: Holt, Rinehart and Winston.

WOLFRAM, WALTER A. 1969. *A Sociolinguistic Description of Detroit Negro Speech.* Washington, D.C.: Center for Applied Linguistics.

———. 1973. "Objective and Subjective Parameters of Language Assimilation among Second-Generation Puerto Ricans in East Harlem." In *Language Attitudes: Current Trends and Prospects*, edited by Roger W. Shuy and Ralph W. Fasold, pp. 148-73. Washington, D.C.: Georgetown University Press.

———. 1980. "Beyond Black English: Implications of the Ann Arbor Decision for Other Non-Mainstream Varieties." In Whiteman, pp. 10-23.

———, and DONNA CHRISTIAN. 1976. *Appalachian Speech.* Arlington, Va.: Center for Applied Linguistics.

———, and RALPH W. FASOLD. 1974. *The Study of Social Dialects in American English.* Englewood Cliffs, N.J.: Prentice-Hall.

———, LANCE POTTER, NANCY M. YANOFSKY, and ROGER W. SHUY. 1979. *Reading and Dialect Differences*. Arlington, Va.: Center for Applied Linguistics.

WOLFORTH, SANDRA. 1978. *The Portuguese in America*. San Francisco: R & E Research Associates.

WOOD, GORDON R. 1972. *Vocabulary Change: A Study of Variation in Regional Words in Eight Southern States*. Carbondale: Southern Illinois University Press.

ZENTELLA, ANA CELIA. 1981. "Language Variety among Puerto Ricans." In Ferguson and Heath, pp. 218–38.

ZIMMERMAN, DON H., and CANDACE WEST. 1975. "Sex Roles, Interruptions, and Silences in Conversation." In Thorne and Henley, pp. 105–29.

Index

Index